Making Music That Matters

This book presents a transformative vision for musicians seeking meaningful careers while revitalising community wellbeing. In an era of unprecedented social disconnection, this groundbreaking book weaves together positive and social psychology, leadership studies, and interpersonal neurobiology to illuminate powerful pathways for musicians to engage in rewarding work with profound social impact.

Through evidence-based frameworks and compelling case studies, this book provides practical strategies for musicians to harness their strengths, foster belonging within diverse groups, and articulate their work's value as a public health resource. Organised in three parts—focused on leading self, leading others, and understanding context—the chapters include frameworks for identifying strengths, creating energising relationships, building group identities, and developing systems thinking, alongside reflective exercises and real-world applications. Readers will discover how to create transformative musical experiences that build personal fulfilment and strengthen community connections.

This accessible book speaks to musicians seeking to diversify their career portfolios, educators developing future music leaders, and health professionals interested in harnessing music's connective power through innovative social programs. It reveals how approaching musicianship as positive leadership creates dual impact—enriching both musicians' careers and the social health of the communities they serve.

Melissa Forbes is Associate Professor of Contemporary Singing at the University of Southern Queensland and a leading advocate for the transformative power of music, particularly singing. Her music career spans performance, higher music education, research, and community engagement. Melissa's work bridges academic research with practical community music leadership, demonstrating music's role in supporting social health and quality of life.

"This book stands as a testimony to so many outstanding transformational creative leaders, and I've been fortunate to experience their 'magic' personally! Congratulations on this paradigm-expanding piece of work that will be referenced for years to come."

Marianne Wobcke, *Indigenous artist, curator, story-teller, midwife, and nurse*

"*Making Music That Matters* is a wonderfully engaging and accessible resource— an essential read for emerging music leaders to help make sense of the complex and exciting traditions of socially transformational music making."

Dr. Dave Camlin, *Lecturer in Music Education, Trinity Laban, UK*

"A clarion call for social change inviting us to re-examine our values as music educators and performers. Extensively researched, theories of positive psychology and leadership are interwoven with reports from singing and music leaders. For any musician looking to make a difference for themselves and their communities."

Dr Gillyanne Kayes, *VocalProcess*

"This inspiring book interweaves theoretical ideas and existing evidence with narratives from community and participatory music leaders to tell a compelling story about how to support musical engagement. Well-researched and theoretically-grounded, it explores the less well-studied worlds of those who lead and facilitate democratic participatory music making."

Professor Alexandra Lamont, *University of Queensland*

"This book provides a powerful case for positive music leadership to improve social health. While complex, the author has presented information in a reader-friendly way so practical uptake is easy. I highly recommend this book to musicians, leaders, and all who work with community or in social health."

Professor Georgina Barton, *University of Southern Queensland, University of Wyoming (adjunct)*

Making Music That Matters
Positive Music Leadership for Social Health

Melissa Forbes

Routledge
Taylor & Francis Group

LONDON AND NEW YORK

Designed cover image: vitranc

First published 2026
by Routledge
4 Park Square, Milton Park, Abingdon, Oxon OX14 4RN

and by Routledge
605 Third Avenue, New York, NY 10158

Routledge is an imprint of the Taylor & Francis Group, an informa business

© 2026 Melissa Forbes

Declaration of AI use: The author used Claude 3.5 and 3.7 Sonnet as detailed in the acknowledgments, under human oversight. The author ensured compliance with ethical standards including data privacy and bias minimisation. All conclusions and interpretations are strictly those of the author. Any AI usage beyond common grammar correction tools has been acknowledged.

British Library Cataloguing-in-Publication Data
A catalogue record for this book is available from the British Library

Library of Congress Cataloging-in-Publication Data
Names: Forbes, Melissa (Singer) author
Title: Making music that matters : positive music leadership for social health / Melissa Forbes.
Description: [1.]. | Abingdon, Oxon ; New York : Routledge, 2026. | Includes bibliographical references and index. |
Summary: 'This book presents a transformative vision for musicians seeking meaningful careers while revitalising community wellbeing. In an era of unprecedented social disconnection, this groundbreaking book weaves together positive and social psychology, leadership studies, and interpersonal neurobiology to illuminate powerful pathways for musicians to engage in rewarding work with profound social impact. Through evidence-based frameworks and compelling case studies, this book provides practical strategies for musicians to harness their strengths, foster belonging within diverse groups, and articulate their work's value as a public health resource. Organised in three parts-leading self, leading others, and understanding context-the chapters include frameworks for identifying strengths, creating energising relationships, building group identities, and developing systems thinking, alongside reflective exercises and real-world applications. Readers will discover how to create transformative musical experiences that build personal fulfilment and strengthen community connections. This accessible book speaks to musicians seeking to diversify their career portfolios, educators developing future music leaders, and health professionals interested in harnessing music's connective power through innovative social programs. It reveals how approaching musicianship as positive leadership creates dual impact-enriching both musicians' careers and the social health of communities they serve"-- Provided by publisher.
Identifiers: LCCN 2025031408 (print) | LCCN 2025031409 (ebook) |
ISBN 9781032730660 hardback | ISBN 9781032724157 paperback |
ISBN 9781003426509 ebook
Subjects: LCSH: Music--Social aspects | Music--Instruction and study--Social aspects | Community music--Social aspects | Community leadership | Music--Vocational guidance | Public health
Classification: LCC ML3916 .F65 2025 (print) | LCC ML3916 (ebook) |
DDC 306.4/842--dc23/eng/20250718
LC record available at https://lccn.loc.gov/2025031408
LC ebook record available at https://lccn.loc.gov/2025031409

ISBN: 978-1-032-73066-0 (hbk)
ISBN: 978-1-032-72415-7 (pbk)
ISBN: 978-1-003-42650-9 (ebk)

DOI: 10.4324/9781003426509

Typeset in Galliard
by Taylor & Francis Books

To Jim and Vivi—you are everything, and everything is you

Contents

Figures

Tables

Boxes

Interviewees

Emma Dean (Australia) is a musician, performer, and recording artist who founded the Cheep Trill community choir in 2014. Emma's career includes touring shows around Australia and internationally, with performances off-Broadway and at Edinburgh Fringe. Emma was a featured soloist in The Commonwealth Games opening ceremony and has written arrangements for John Farnham, Katie Noonan, Kate Ceberano and Glenn Shorrock. Her recent work includes writing and arranging music for the Emmy Award-winning show *Bluey* and serving as music director, songwriter and voice artist for all-girl puppet kid's band, Rainbow Bop! Emma conducts the Absolutely Everybody choir (Upbeat Arts), working with marginalised communities to promote social inclusion, positive mental health and overall wellbeing.

Kym Alexandra Dillon (Australia) is a Melbourne-based composer, pianist, and conductor who leads two choirs for Creativity Australia's "With One Voice" program. Kym holds a master's degree in composition from the University of Melbourne and has had works commissioned by organisations including the Melbourne Symphony Orchestra, Astra Chamber Music Society, and Musica Viva. Kym regularly presents pre-concert talks for the Australian Chamber Orchestra and Melbourne Symphony Orchestra, and her performances as a pianist span classical and jazz contexts.

Emily Foulkes (UK) is the director of Music for Good, a music for wellbeing charity in Cornwall, and the founder of the Singing for Health Network, a membership network for anyone interested in singing for health research and practice. With more than 20 years of experience in music education and wellbeing, Emily has developed pioneering Singing for Health programs that have secured NHS and Social Prescribing funding. Her work spans practitioner, researcher, and strategic roles, including previous work with the National Foundation for Youth Music where she established national programs and networks. Emily holds a master's degree in voice pedagogy, specialising in singing for health, trauma-informed practice, and pain management, and was a senior lecturer at the Voice Study Centre. She has published research and articles on her work in a range of journals. Emily regularly presents her research at conferences across the UK and internationally and provides training in singing for health.

Allison Girvan (Canada) is an internationally respected singer who has been a featured soloist with ensembles ranging from jazz trios to full orchestra, and is a studio vocalist for TV and feature film. Allison is known for her living sound installations, innovative choral direction, and cross-disciplinary collaborative projects. Allison's exploration spans genre, style, and language, and is recognised for its unique approach to co-creativity and community building across cultural groups. Allison's performances and human soundscapes promote collective voicing to nurture connection in a time of increasing ideological division while exploring themes central to our shared human experience of climate emergency. Allison lives in Nelson, British Columbia, where she continues to create, perform, record, and teach.

Gillian Howell (Australia) is a musician, researcher, and community arts practitioner whose creative practice and applied research explore the contributions of music making in settings of social, political, and environmental rupture. Gillian has worked in complex social settings worldwide including with remote Indigenous communities, and people impacted by war and displacement in Balkans, the Caucasus, Australia, and Asia. She has transformed community engagement programs for symphony orchestras and new music ensembles and has won multiple Australian Art Music Awards for programs under her creative direction. Her research advances understanding about the arts in peacebuilding, language revitalisation, community dialogue, and place-based community arts collaborations. She holds a PhD from Griffith University and has taught at several institutions including the University of Melbourne, Australian National Academy of Music, Melbourne Polytechnic, and Boston University, and as a visiting scholar in Norway. Through her teaching, she aims to nurture and train musicians and community artists for socially engaged, participatory arts practice.

Nsamu Moonga (South Africa) is a Zambian-born music therapist, psychotherapist, and educator who bridges Indigenous musical arts with health and wellbeing. Nsamu holds degrees in psychology and music therapy and has served on multiple international boards including the World Federation of Music Therapy and the International Association for Music and Medicine. Currently a doctor of music candidate at the University of Pretoria, where he also lectures alongside teaching at the University of Johannesburg, Nsamu's research explores how people with cancer can use Indigenous musical arts to manage anxiety and distress. Nsamu's work emphasises anti-oppressive and non-interventionist practices across health, spirituality, and psychosocial support.

Graham Sattler CF (New Zealand) is CEO of the Christchurch Symphony Orchestra and a Churchill Fellow. Graham's career has evolved from orchestral trombonist to opera singer to conductor, artistic director and researcher. Graham has performed as both trombonist and singer with the Australian Opera, served as executive director of regional conservatoriums and contributed to music education course design and delivery with Central Queensland, Charles Sturt, and Canterbury (New Zealand) Universities. As a 2019 Churchill

Fellow, Graham investigated best-practice musical inclusion and community music leadership training programs in the United States, Canada, England, Ireland, Scotland, Norway, Portugal, and Armenia. He holds a diploma of operatic art and music theatre, master of performance (conducting), a PhD in music education, and a graduate certificate in the psychology of risk.

James Sills (UK) is a musician, author, and speaker who founded the Sofa Singers online community and Wrexham One Love Choir, Wales's first homeless choir. James facilitates singing at events worldwide and works with corporate and government organisations including Olympus, Saatchi and Saatchi, and the National Health Service. In 2019, James authored *Do Sing: Reclaim Your Voice—Find Your Singing Tribe* and received a Points of Light Award for his online singing work during the pandemic. James performs with the Spooky Men's Chorale and writes a monthly column for *Psychologies* magazine titled "Sing For Your Life". James is choral director for the BBC project "Bantom of the Opera" which will see Bradford City football fans transform from singing in the stadium terraces to singing opera.

Naomi Sunderland (Australia) is director of the Creative Arts Research Institute at Griffith University and an interdisciplinary arts-health researcher, singer-songwriter, and community music facilitator. She is a proud descendant of the Wiradjuri First Nations People of Australia alongside her mixed European heritage. Naomi has an expansive research and publishing record in arts-health, wellbeing, and First Nations social justice, with a particular focus on creative, anti-oppressive, and trauma-informed research approaches. Naomi has led significant research initiatives including an Australian Research Council Fellowship studying First Nations' music as a determinant of health (2021–2024) and a Fulbright Senior Scholar award to develop collective music making for healing at the University of New Mexico (2024). Her work spans international collaborations across Australia, Asia, and the Pacific, with particular focus on collaborative community-led research with Central Australian First Nations communities. She holds a PhD in applied ethics and human rights from the Queensland University of Technology.

Jane York (Australia) is a singing leader, musician, program manager, and facilitator working in community arts, development and engagement. Jane has experience founding and developing community music groups, projects and performances, alongside creating educational and strategic programs. Her background includes work in small business, hospitality, and urban strategy, with Jane's practice centred on social and ecological justice, equity, and access. Jane lives and works on the unceded lands of the Wurundjeri, Boonwurrung, Dja Dja Wurrung, Taungurung, and Wathaurung of the Kulin Nations and pays respect to elders past and present.

Prologue

Nestled in the verdant snow-capped peaks of the Selkirk Mountains in Canada's remote Southwest, the small city of Nelson (pop. 10,664) sits on the traditional lands of the Sinixt Nation. This place is a long way from anywhere—Vancouver is eight hours away in one direction; eight hours in the other direction takes you to Calgary. During wintertime, it can be difficult to get in and out of Nelson by air, let alone by vehicle—driving the treacherous mountain roads is not for the faint of heart.

Due to its isolation, Nelson has developed a kind of artistic self-sufficiency and has a history of drawing some very liberal-minded people. Over the last few decades, the townsfolk have been busy transitioning the local economy from felling and milling trees to making art. When the forestry industry collapsed in the 1980s, some locals saw an opportunity to transform the town from one of extraction to a thriving cultural hub of generativity.

These days, in addition to traditional forms of commerce, Nelson is a magnet for writers, artists, musicians, and artisans. Historic Baker Street's heritage facades and public artworks are a tourist drawcard. But Nelson isn't all amiable arts and crafts. With a blue-collar heritage, the population is quite diverse, and with that diversity comes differences of opinion and people who don't always see eye to eye.

Community music practitioner Allison Girvan has been living in Nelson for almost three decades. Her practice seeks to "find the common threads" of the diverse people living in her community. Allison leads large-scale community singing events with the Fireworks Choir, bringing together hundreds of locals for one-day massed choral events. The first such gathering drew an incredible 420 participants. Allison has also established several community choirs in Nelson for singers of various ages.

Standing in the middle of a semi-circle of singers, Allison moves her body to the music, her elegant gestures communicating the musical cues ever so subtly. For Allison, music is a means of expression but also a metaphor for building community. As one of her participants says, "[The singing] is so woven with community. I don't think that you can really pull community out of music" (participant quoted in Community Music in Canada, 2024).

Allison's community music practice is deeply aligned with a sense of purpose—to build community and a sense of belonging for those she works with. Allison describes her work as like that of a conductor, but not in the traditional, baton-waving, "sage on the stage" sense:

> The role of conductor is oftentimes perceived, I think, as you making the music. Rather I think the word "conductor" needs to be thought of as an electricity, that it's moving through you. So, the idea of conducting something is you're taking the energy and allowing it to pass through you so it becomes a very easy and selfless way to stand in front of a group with a bit of a checked ego. To think that your role is to allow things to pass through you and reflect back.
>
> (Allison quoted in Community Music in Canada, 2024)

While Allison is conducting the music and the musicians, she is also doing something even more profound—she is conducting "connection". Like electrical conductivity, which requires charged particles to move freely, positive music leadership creates conditions where energy can flow naturally between people. The way Allison leads, the conductor becomes a vessel through which the group's musical energy (in the form of sound waves—this is physics, after all!) flows freely. Conducting connection is about music leaders creating the conditions for moments to spark between people making music together.

For Allison, community music is the practice of using the voice and music as tools to bridge divides between people. Allison sees her role as a community music practitioner who creates opportunities for human beings to find common ground through shared musical experiences, even—and especially—when they might otherwise feel very different to each other.

Allison's inclusive, positive approach to music leadership has implications far beyond the rehearsal room or community hall. It offers a model for how we might rediscover the common threads of our humanity in an increasingly fractured and fragmented world.

Reference

Community Music in Canada. (2024, 30 April). Allison Girvan: Music is the vehicle for community building [Video]. YouTube. www.youtube.com/watch?v=_9HuLzg6ACY.

Preface

> The growing good of the world is partly dependent on unhistoric acts; and that
> things are not so ill with you and me as they might have been, is half owing to the
> number who lived faithfully a hidden life, and rest in unvisited tombs.
> —George Eliot, *Middlemarch*

Across the globe, music leaders are promoting social health using the power of participatory music making. It might be through leading a singing group for people with dementia, a community band for the homeless, or a songwriting session for people facing mental health challenges. The leaders of these groups are not household names. Their achievements are "unhistoric acts"; quiet but remarkable feats that otherwise go unnoticed. These musicians are *positive music leaders* working within our communities to repair our social fabric during unprecedented change, upheaval, and disconnection.

This book is not about world-famous musicians who make us feel good when we listen to their music or attend their concerts. Arguably, this is the view most people have of musicians—the rich and famous megastars who represent a tiny percentage of musicians worldwide. Many of us also have a similarly narrow view of leaders, perhaps believing that leaders are those in the news headlines or the well-known names and faces of politicians, authority figures, and corporate giants.

But sometimes the most inspiring musicians and leaders are found in the most unlikely places. In an unassuming community hall in the town where I live, music leaders volunteer each week to lead a singing group for people with Parkinson's, an incurable neurological disease. The enthusiasm and joy these leaders display is palpable. They dress up for themed sessions, lead sing-alongs of music of all types, play various instruments to accompany the singing, and do it all without a shred of ego. The Parkinson's singers and the people who care for them leave the hall feeling just a little—and sometimes a lot—better than when they arrived. My journey to writing this book was inspired by the Parkinson's singers and the musicians who lead them.

Since 2017, I've worked with this group, first as a researcher and then as a leader. Many of our singers have conveyed in that time how much the group means to them, often remarking that singing is one activity worth leaving the house for. Equally, the leaders comment on the group's importance *to them*. It is a source of highly rewarding work where the benefits of music making are evident in every session—Carol's uproarious laugh when we bust out the kazoos in the chorus of "Tequila" or the sparkle in Ray's eyes when we sing a song about Glen Miller (Ray used to play in a dance band in his younger years).

Parkinson's can be incredibly isolating for both the person with Parkinson's and their carers. Singing together helps our group members better cope with the burden of an incurable disease, and it helps carers feel supported—it's a place of belonging for all. The social connections that form through music making are fortified by the group leaders and by the music itself.

Singing and making music together are good for our social health. Social health is an important pillar of overall health, just like physical and mental health. In fact, social health is *so* fundamental to our quality of life that poor social health adversely impacts *both* mental *and* physical health. Music making therefore creates something of great value—human connection, belonging, and healing.

This book illuminates a path for musicians to become influential positive music leaders through an innovative blend of positive and social psychology, leadership theory, and interpersonal neurobiology. Using these frameworks, musicians can intentionally cultivate their leadership skills to revitalise the social health of their communities and develop the language to champion positive music leadership as an indispensable public health resource.

While music leaders' acts may be "unhistoric" in the eyes of the world, their ripple effects transform lives, strengthen our communities, and can help mend our thread-bare social fabric. This is the paradox of positive music leadership—through small, local acts of connection, we contribute to something far greater than ourselves.

Throughout, we will explore what it means to make music that truly matters—both to musicians seeking meaningful career paths beyond traditional roles in education and industry, and to the communities whose social health and wellbeing can be transformed through participatory music experiences. Throughout these pages, we'll discover how positive music leadership creates this dual impact, enriching the lives of both leaders and participants.

If you're a musician, how might your musical gifts become a force for connection, belonging, and healing in your community? If you're a health professional or community worker, how might you help champion this powerful resource for social health and wellbeing?

As you turn these pages, I invite you to imagine your own role in this quiet revolution.

Acknowledgments

I sincerely thank the music leaders who agreed to be interviewed for this book. Your insight, energy, and compassion have helped bring the ideas in this book to life.

To my wonderful colleagues and friends who provided feedback on drafts, I deeply appreciate your time, interest, and contributions to improving this work.

I am deeply grateful to Kate Cantrell, whose enthusiasm for this book, combined with her editorial finesse and attention to detail, elevated the manuscript in ways I could not have accomplished alone.

Thank you to the University of Southern Queensland for supporting the research for this book through the Academic Professional Development Program.

This book was written on the traditional lands of the Jagera, Giabal, and Jarowair peoples of the Toowoomba region. I acknowledge the cultural diversity of all Aboriginal and Torres Strait Islander peoples and pay respect to Elders past, present and future. I acknowledge the important contributions Aboriginal and Torres Strait Islander people have and continue to make to Australian society and culture.

This book's refrains and tables were developed with assistance from Claude 3.5 and 3.7 Sonnet, a large language model created by Anthropic. The author edited initial drafts of these elements to ensure continuity of the author's voice and views, and this model provided constructive feedback on drafts.

Overture
Introducing positive music leadership

Introduction

When we sing, play music, or write songs together, we become something greater than the sum of our parts. We create magic, and this magic is beneficial for our social health because it fulfils one of our basic human needs—the need to belong and to connect with others.

One of the key catalysts for this magical sense of connection is positive music leadership. (Spoiler alert—later in the book, we'll explore how to strike a balance between appreciating the "magic" of music making and obtaining robust evidence of its positive impacts.) Musician Emma Dean describes her journey to discovering this magic by establishing "Cheep Trill", a community choir based in Brisbane, Australia:

> In my late 20s, I moved to New York to get my original music out to a broader audience. I was working night and day. I was burnt out. I realised that all of the things that I valued I just couldn't achieve in that lifestyle. My spark for music had totally dried up.
>
> I decided to move back to my hometown in Australia and start a singing group—just something low-key in my parents' loungeroom. I put a call out on social media and was completely inundated with messages. I started the singing group on a friend's verandah—two nights a week with about 20 people each night.
>
> My spark for music completely returned.
>
> I thought to myself, "Oh my God, *what is this magic?* What is *happening* to me?" People were saying how energised they felt ... everyone with their own amazing stories coming onto this verandah to sing. We were just healing together. We eventually had to move off the verandah because I was actually afraid that we'd fall through!
>
> That was almost 10 years ago, and we now have 200 people in the groups with a waiting list. All these people just wanting to be part of this amazing thing, just singing together.

Emma Dean's story is a striking example of becoming a positive music leader. Through a process of discovering what she valued musically, professionally, and personally, Emma found a way to use her musical strengths and leadership skills in

DOI: 10.4324/9781003426509-1

service of others. Like Canadian community music practitioner Allison Girvan, who was featured in the Prologue, Emma is "conducting connection" through her work with the Cheep Trill community choir. She is making music that matters, both to her, and to her choir members.

This metaphor of electrical energy and connection appears repeatedly in positive music leaders' descriptions of their practice. For example, Kym Dillon, another music leader for social inclusion choirs who was interviewed for this book, describes a similar phenomenon:

> As a jazz pianist, I love leading my group from the piano. My accompanying creates a bedrock that empowers singers to join in, knowing they have strong musical support. When it's live accompaniment rather than a backing track, we create something in that space … a spark of electricity. And while I have no formal singing training, that means in one very important respect, I am just like everyone else in the group—I love singing and the joy it brings to others.

Here, Kym illuminates one of the beautiful paradoxes of positive music leadership—while her musical expertise as a pianist provides the foundational structure that supports and empowers the group, her position as a fellow amateur singer places her shoulder-to-shoulder with participants. This dual role—being both expert guide and fellow traveller—exemplifies how positive music leadership works best when technical mastery serves to illuminate pathways to connection rather than to demonstrate superiority.

By building connection, positive leaders support social health. Social health, an often-undervalued aspect of wellbeing, encompasses the quality of our relationships, our sense of belonging, and our feelings of support and connection within our communities and personal networks (Killam, 2024). We will explore the relationship between social health and positive music leadership in Part II.

To bring the concept of positive music leadership alive for this book, I interviewed ten music leaders including Emma, Allison, and Kym. As you hear from them, you may wish to consult their biographies at the front of the book. Their practices span four continents and diverse forms of music making, from collaborative songwriting to group singing to peace-building and large-scale community performances. These leaders were interviewed due to their extensive practice working with diverse communities and their shared desire to positively impact others (see Appendix 1 for more information about how this research was conducted). Throughout the book, text boxes titled RESONANCE showcase the voices and experiences of these positive music leaders. Each RESONANCE feature presents insights from music leaders that exemplify and amplify key theoretical concepts.

Setting the scene

This book spotlights musicians who are working in *community* leading *participatory* music making activities. Where music performance (at least in Western societies) is arguably focused on aesthetic outcomes, participatory music's main concern is fostering positive relationships and social connection (Camlin, 2023; Small, 1998).

Briefly, *community music* is defined as "participatory music-making by, for and/or with a community" (Bartleet, 2023, p. 36). *Participatory music* activities are led by musicians who balance active music making with pursuing broader social aims such as fostering dialogue between cultures, strengthening community bonds, and supporting marginalised individuals and groups (van Zijl & De bisschop, 2023). In Australia, the Creative Change (2024) project has mapped community music activities and classified them under six categories: wellbeing, social connection, community cohesion, inclusion and accessibility, visibility and opportunity, and cultural and environmental sustainability. *Community music* and *participatory music* are key terms which are discussed in more detail in Appendix 2. These two terms are used interchangeably throughout the book.

Who is this book for?

If, like Emma, you're a musician who is already leading a community group, you know within your soul that making music with others in a safe, non-judgmental space connects us like few other activities can. The strategies explored in this book are designed to give you fresh ways to look at your work and deepen your practice.

For performing musicians, this book offers insights into diversifying your work portfolio and using your skills to support social health.

Music students will find guidance on career options that make meaningful contributions to their communities. As community musician, music educator, and researcher Dave Camlin writes:

> Although it may not be even on the radar of young people embarking on a career in music, developing a modest musical practice which is woven into the heart of a community's social life can be a deeply rewarding profession.
>
> (Camlin, 2023, p. 194)

Health professionals can gain understanding of how music leaders support clients' social health, while music educators will discover frameworks for developing future music leaders.

Regardless of your background, interests, or expertise, this book aims to empower you to either become a positive music leader, deepen your existing practice, or champion positive music leadership as a valuable health resource. Like Emma, Kym, and Allison, you too can discover the magic that happens when we use our musical strengths to foster connection and belonging. You will also be equipped with theoretical tools to convey this "magic" in ways that are robust and convincing for diverse stakeholders, from participants through to policy-makers and funding bodies.

What this book is not

This book focuses on developing musicians as people and leaders, not on practical music skills or technical development. And while I acknowledge ongoing debates in music research and community music, I don't dwell on these academic discussions. Instead, the focus is on practically empowering musicians to view and develop themselves as positive leaders and to champion the value of this work for social health. As such, the strategies presented here are not intended as strict pre-scriptions, but as flexible tools to help you understand and enhance your practice. You are encouraged to adapt these ideas to fit your unique context and musical and personal style.

The book's structure

The book's three-part structure mirrors the "triple focus" of Daniel Goleman's framework for leaders (Goleman, 2013; Goleman & Senge, 2014; see also Gaunt et al., 2021 who use this framework for their concept of "musicians as makers in society"). Goleman says that effective leaders pay attention to themselves, to their relationships with others, and to the broader context or systems within which they work.

Like the leader's triple focus, this book is arranged in three parts:

- Part I—"Solo": by focusing on self-leadership, you develop self-awareness, self-management, and a clearer understanding of what you are drawn to and what matters to you; this fosters intrinsic motivation in your work as a music leader.
- Part II—"Ensemble": by focusing on your leadership of others, you develop empathy and compassion and the ability to positively influence those you make music with, building health-enhancing positive relationships and social identities, which in turn can create social connection and belonging.
- Part III—"Tutti": by developing contextual awareness, you can be more intentional as a music leader and better understand how your work is shaped by the world around you. This will empower you to convincingly champion the value of positive music leadership as a public health resource that supports social connection.

Why "positive" music leadership?

The "positive" in positive music leadership draws from the field of positive psy-chology, which is dedicated to helping human beings flourish (Rashid et al., 2024; Seligman, 2011). I have applied theories from positive psychology and positive leadership in my previous research and writing to explore what happens when we make music together to support connection (e.g. Forbes & Bartlett, 2020b; Forbes, 2025).

Over the past two decades, research has demonstrated the benefits of music making on health and wellbeing. While these benefits are wide-ranging, a common thread across most research is the positive impact of music making on social con-nection and belonging. As vocal leader James Sills has observed based on his many years of practice as a musician, "You can talk about all the different benefits of singing, but it always comes back to connection. In particular, for me, it's about human connection to each other". Music making in groups has been shown to increase participants' psychological resources (our inner reserves), including social support and a sense of belonging (e.g. Dingle et al., 2013; Forbes, 2021).

Positive music leadership uses evidence-based practices from positive and social psychology, positive leadership, and interpersonal neurobiology to amplify social connection and belonging for community music group participants, and for leaders as well. (Don't worry if you don't know what terms like "interpersonal neurobiology" mean. We will explore them in detail as we move through the book.)

Some of you may cringe at the word "positive", associating it with the "toxic positivity" that demands we maintain a sunny outlook despite genuine challenges. This is not the way the term positivity is invoked in this book. Life is far more complex than trite solutions like "grin and bear it". The word "positive" is a reminder that we have an innate negativity bias (Baumeister et al., 2001), which is something we must consciously acknowledge and balance. Positive approaches— to psychology and leadership—in no way ignore the complex reality of being human. Rather, they are offered in a spirit of countering or balancing the dominance of negativity.

Simply put, by framing music leadership positively, I hope to cast the terms "musician" and "leader" in an expansive, generative, and constructive light. This approach reflects the many impactful ways that music leadership is already being practised in communities worldwide, characterised as it is by compassion, inclusivity, and respect for human dignity and diversity.

Understanding "transformation" in positive music leadership

Like positive psychology's focus on helping people flourish, community or participatory music making is concerned with personal transformation, as well as social transformation. Social transformation takes the form of challenging systemic inequalities and social stigmas, and personal transformation results from changes in confidence, identity, and capability (Humphrey, 2025). While both forms of transformation remain important, personal transformation has become increasingly emphasised in recent decades, particularly in response to neo-liberal funding and policy priorities (Humphrey, 2025).

Positive music leadership acknowledges that personal and social transformation are possible, but focuses primarily on personal transformation through building connection and belonging—that is, by nurturing better social health among individuals. This aligns with positive psychology's emphasis on helping individuals reach their full potential. When people experience personal transformation through music making—developing their confidence, shifting their self-perception, gaining a sense of agency, connecting with themselves and others, and feeling they belong—they are better positioned to maintain positive relationships, thrive, and contribute to their communities.

An important caveat is that any argument about participatory music making as a vehicle for transformation must also acknowledge music's ambiguity (Kertz-Welzel, 2025). Music can play positive and negative roles in society—on a personal level, it can support new relationships and build new identities, but it can also divide nations and be a medium for propaganda. The relationship between music and society is complex (Born, 2012; Kertz-Welzel, 2025). In other words, promoting a model such as positive music leadership, which seeks to help people thrive and flourish through music making, should not be presented uncritically, and the values which inform such a model—the desire to see each person reach their potential—must be laid bare for scrutiny.

Finally, just like the tendency to describe this work as "magic", we must be mindful that transformation too can be difficult to measure, and as such, we should avoid using transformation simply as a buzzword (Humphrey, 2025). Instead, we should strive to understand and articulate specific ways that positive music leadership supports meaningful change for individuals. Later in this book (Chapter 9), we will explore Bartleet's (2023) multidimensional framework to help us understand how transformation can occur across several different levels—from the individual level through to macro or structural changes—and how these levels interact. Bartleet's framework provides a robust way to conceptualise and communicate the transformative potential of positive music leadership while at the same time acknowledging its complexity.

Music and leadership: A powerful duet

In writing this book, I have drawn on the synergies between the psychology and leadership literature, and my personal experience as a music leader and practitioner–researcher. When I first encountered the fields of positive leadership (Chapter 5), identity leadership (Chapter 6), and interpersonal neurobiology (Chapter 8), I immediately felt resonances with music leadership in community contexts. The philosophy, characteristics, and practices of these approaches closely align with the work of various music leaders I've known, admired, and researched (e.g. Forbes & Bartlett, 2020a, 2020b).

Vocal leader James Sills also recognises these same synergies:

> I learn as much from outside my practice as I do from inside it. I would describe myself as a vocal leader because I'm interested in voice on every level, not just the singing voice but voices in terms of empowerment and amplifying voices, particularly those that have been disempowered. I'm also interested in leadership. I don't shy away from the fact that, even though I'm holding space and consider myself an encourager, I am also a leader. That's fine, and I embrace that. I also think about it carefully and the responsibilities that come with that.

In these reflections, James connects musicianship with leadership because he seeks to positively impact others, empowering them to find their voice, literally and figuratively.

Positive leadership, which is rooted in positive psychology, aims to bring out the best in people and help them flourish. It encompasses various leadership theories including authentic, charismatic, servant, and transformational leadership (Avolio & Gardner, 2005). Positive leaders create psychologically safe environments, build on strengths, foster flourishing, manage negativity while promoting positivity, practice optimism and hope, find meaning in their work, and prioritise healthy relationships and connections (Cameron, 2018, 2021; Lucey & Burke, 2022).

Identity leadership and the social cure approach (discussed in Chapter 6) provide powerful lenses for understanding and enhancing the practice of music leaders in community settings. These approaches highlight how group memberships and shared social identities can act as psychological resources, supporting wellbeing and fostering a sense of belonging (Haslam et al., 2018; Haslam et al., 2020).

Moreover, the interpersonal neurobiology framework (explored in Chapter 8) helps us appreciate the complexity involved in building social connection through music making, while also providing concrete and actionable strategies.

While these frameworks are all theoretical and may sound abstract, as the old saying goes, "there is nothing as practical as a good theory" (Bedeian, 2016)! These frameworks will help to illuminate your practice in ways that are impactful for you and your music making participants.

Applying these frameworks and strategies offers a comprehensive approach to music leadership. The approach aligns with emerging trends in music education that emphasise musicians' emotional intelligence, social responsibility, and civic engagement (Gaunt et al., 2021; Grant, 2019; Westerlund & Karttunen, 2024).

RESONANCE—"Leader" as a contested term

The term "facilitator" rather than "leader" is often also used within the fields of arts in health and community music. Some musicians hesitate to call themselves "leaders". Musical inclusion advocate Graham Sattler reflects on the debate surrounding the term "leader" in participatory or community music contexts:

> While some practitioners avoid the term "leader" due to its connotations of power imbalance, my research across multiple case studies of participatory/community music making has revealed that "leadership" is a prominent theme. Based on extensive research with hundreds of participants, I've observed a clear desire for informed guidance and problem-solving—functions that align with leadership, albeit of a benevolent and facilitative nature. While remaining sensitive to concerns about power dynamics, particularly in post-colonial contexts, I maintain that "leadership" most accurately describes this multifaceted role, though I remain open to alternative terminology that can effectively encompass all these elements.

"Positive music leadership" is a positive reframing of the term leadership within the context of participatory music making. It incorporates aspects of "facilitation" (which effectively means, "to make easy"), but as Graham points out, it encompasses more than that. It is a strengths-based style of leadership which supports others to thrive and flourish through positive relationships and social connections.

The book's argument

We are living through a public health crisis of social connection, where the very fabric of our societies has become threadbare (Ending Loneliness Together, 2022; Way et al., 2018). Our news media abounds with reports of the "loneliness epidemic" and the perils of social isolation for our health and wellbeing. We need to empower more musicians to be positive leaders because we are living in socially challenging times. Positive music leadership greatly benefits music leaders themselves, as well as the communities they work with. Through positive music leadership, we can revitalise our social connections and improve our social health.

Why do we need more positive music leadership in the world?

First, many musicians are searching for meaning in their careers, and frankly, post-COVID-19, it's never been tougher for musicians. We need more musicians to take up positive music leadership in our communities because music leaders can and do find this work meaningful (Forbes & Bartlett, 2020b). Many musicians, however, are not yet aware of the opportunities for working in the community or that this work can be personally rewarding and gratifying.

This book challenges musicians to expand their perceptions of who they are and what they do. This is the process of "self-leadership"—leading yourself to greater awareness of your strengths and values and aligning these with your work. Self-leadership also includes self-care to build resilience and wellbeing, so that you have a strong foundation of self, which is required to lead others. When musicians become aware of their signature strengths and personal values they are better placed to do "good work"—"work that is of *excellent technical quality*, work that is *ethically pursued and socially responsible*, and work that is *engaging, enjoyable, and feels good*" (Gardner, 2007, p. 5; emphasis in original). Fundamentally, "good work" is socially engaged work that is valued by the musician themselves and by society more broadly (see also Grant, 2019).

The second reason for needing more positive music leadership in the world is one that touches us all. Recently, the World Health Organization (2023) and the US Surgeon General (Murthy, 2023) acknowledged that our world is more socially disconnected than ever before. This disconnection seriously impacts our mental and physical health and wellbeing. Across the world, the prevalence of social isolation in older adults is one in four; 15% of adolescents are lonely (World Health Organization, 2023). In modern, technology-driven, capitalist societies, our social health is suffering.

Positive music leaders are perfectly placed to revitalise our social health. Humans have a biological need to belong, which is fundamental to our health and happiness.

Belonging is the subjective experience of the unconditional positive regard of others (Allen, 2021). When we feel we belong, we feel valued and accepted and become integrated within a social group. Belonging has an evolutionary basis (Baumeister & Leary, 1995). According to the highly influential psychologist Carl Rogers, we feel we belong when we experience the unconditional positive regard of others—no judgement, no strings attached. We feel we belong when we are loved for who we are. When we belong, our dignity—our inherent value and worth as human beings—is recognised (Hicks, 2021). When we belong, we feel "seen" and "heard"; we feel "felt" (Camlin et al., 2020; Siegel & Drulis, 2023). When we belong, we are healthier and happier people (Allen, 2021; Hotz, 2024; Killam, 2024).

Social connection is a quality or feeling within a person that represents their lasting sense of being close and connected with others (Lee et al., 2001). When we are socially connected, we feel consistently and meaningfully linked to others and to society more broadly.

The terms *belonging* and *social connection* are discussed more fully in Appendix 2.

Finally, for positive music leaders to be valued in a time when our social health is suffering, we need the language, evidence, and contextual understanding to champion music leadership as a highly valuable public health resource. We need to convince politicians, policy-makers, and communities of the value of positive music leadership, so that everyone can benefit.

How music making is good for us

There has been a veritable explosion of research over the last two decades about the ways participatory music making supports health and wellbeing; many reviews of the literature are now available if you want to explore this evidence in detail (e.g. Daykin et al., 2018; Dingle et al., 2021; Fancourt & Finn, 2019). Participatory music making has been shown to have positive impacts on the health and wellbeing of clinical and non-clinical populations (clinical meaning those with a diagnosed health condition). Music has been used to provide emotional and psychological support to people with depression, cancer, and dementia, as well as those suffering with social isolation and loneliness. Music has also been used to improve physical health conditions such as Parkinson's, stroke, long COVID, and chronic obstructive pulmonary disease (COPD), to name a few.

Indeed, there are many ways music making is good for us. In their study of musical activity and wellbeing, Krause et al. (2018) found 562 benefits of musical participation! Another study conducted at the intersection of leisure and health identified over 600 "mechanisms of action" or different ways in which leisure activities like participatory music making affect our health and wellbeing (Fancourt et al., 2021). These mechanisms can be classified into psychological, biological, behavioural, and social processes, and can operate at the individual, group, or societal levels (Fancourt et al., 2021). This book focuses on participatory music making and the associated psychological and social benefits at the individual and group levels, while acknowledging that every individual and group exists as part of a much more complex environment.

There are many studies that demonstrate the health, psychological, and social benefits of participatory music making for individuals. For example, health and wellbeing singing groups have been shown to increase individual singers' psychological resources such as social support and belonging through group singing (e.g. Dingle et al., 2013; Forbes, 2021). Indeed, social connection and belonging are common positive outcomes of participatory music making. Group singing can be beneficial for individuals' cognitive and mental health, for those with lung disease or suffering from stroke, and for people with dementia (see the review by Dingle et al., 2021).

The study of leisure activities mentioned above identifies over 600 individual mechanisms of action, but in doing so, the authors acknowledge that the health effects cannot be understood as a simple "sum of the parts" (Fancourt et al., 2021, p. 333). The health effects, including the social benefits of collective music making, are increasingly understood as the emergent property of a complex system with many different mechanisms dynamically interacting at multiple levels (Fancourt et al., 2021). In other words, when we make music together, the experience is something greater than the sum of its parts. We experience this "emergent property" as the "magic moments" of music making (Camlin, et al., 2020; Camlin, 2023; Pavlicevic, 2013). We will explore these issues in more detail in Part III.

Perhaps one of the best things about participatory music making is that it is "low stakes, high connection". As singing leader Jane York observes, group singing creates an intimacy with others, without the social pressures of conversation. This "low stakes, high connection" dynamic makes participatory music making particularly valuable for those who find traditional social settings challenging, including people experiencing anxiety, burnout, or social isolation. The structured yet expressive nature of group music making allows connection to develop organically, without the performance demands of everyday social interaction. As Jane reflects, this lack of social pressure is "something that is really, really special about making music regularly ... surrounded by the warmth of that community to take care of you".

Despite the many studies which lay claim to music's positive impact on our health and overall wellbeing including promoting social connection, strong scientific evidence is still limited (McArton & Mantie, 2023). Much of the evidence base for music's benefits is drawn from scoping reviews, and this approach has been criticised for its lack of rigour (see, for example, Clift et al., 2021). While we may experience the "magic" of making music together, we do need to exercise some caution in overstating these benefits.

Elsewhere, I have written about singing's ability to help us connect with each other, arguing that "from an experiential perspective, regular singers do not need evidence from randomized controlled trials to convince them that singing builds belonging and connection" (Forbes, 2025, p. 55). In Part III, I argue that to champion the value of positive music leadership for social connection, we need *both* robust evidence *and* stories of lived experience to honour the "magic moments" of connecting through music. However, there may ultimately be aspects of this experience which are simply not reducible to measurable, quantifiable components.

Perhaps most importantly, we can't assume that all musical activities lead to positive outcomes for all participants (Camlin, 2023). We need to develop an "ethic of care" as the foundation for building welcoming, inclusive, and accessible musical communities based on principles of social justice and equity (Camlin & Schei, 2024, p. 2).

RESONANCE—An Indigenous perspective on leadership

Nsamu Moonga is a music therapist, psychotherapist and educator who bridges Indigenous musical arts with health and wellbeing. Nsamu reflects on both the role and meaning of "leader" within the Batonga cultural tradition from southern Zambia. He explains how leadership is exercised within a particular position in the community (e.g. spiritual leader or ritual presider) but clarifies that one's leadership doesn't transfer to other contexts:

> These hierarchies of leadership would come up for lots of questions in the Batonga consciousness, for example, because historically the Batonga have always been decentralised. So, leadership is very democratic in that sense, when we think about leadership from the human element and the human social perspective. So, in the exercise of that leadership, those are some of the values that we're speaking about, that leadership is not entirely deposited in one individual for the rest of their lives, or in all aspects of human life. So, in the exercise of it, in the exercise of leadership, everything is shared within those relational spaces. That's where those values come in, and they become really important. But in my exercise of leadership, however it is functioned and provided for, I'm accountable to the community and the community of beings.

The call to leadership in a particular role identifies that person as a representative of the community. Nsamu explains that the call comes with

> responsibility to sit outside of the circle and know that I'm a steward. I'm not a steward to myself, I'm a steward of the interests of this particular group, and I'm accountable to them, and I'm accountable with them, and I will respect them. I will hold them with dignity.

Nsamu contrasts this view of leadership with "the megalomaniac leadership of the world", which is characterised by a sense of importance of the individual leader:

> [Batonga leadership] is very different. This is why leadership in Indigenous cultures comes with a descent, not a rise, and that's why people refuse it. For a long time, people refused. They refused to take on leadership because it comes with a lot of pain and suffering and the descent. You descend—you become really humble. So, even these rituals of appointment or enthronement, they speak about how you've been called to be the poorest of the community. For years, people resisted these calls. Then eventually it lands because [they've] run everywhere. [They've] run everywhere, and [they] still have failed to run away.

Nsamu describes leadership in his cultural context as a descent into humility rather than an ascent to power, which comes with a great responsibility to the community. The concepts of humility in leadership and community responsibility resonate with positive music leadership.

How to read this book

Because of the reciprocal relationship between research and practice, the book has a mix of theoretical/contextual chapters, and chapters which focus on practical application. If you are interested in argument, context, and theory, see Chapters 1, 4, and 7. For those who prefer the practical stuff, see Chapters 2, 3, 5, 6, 8, and 9. Every chapter ends with a brief summary—"Refrain"—and provides reflective questions—"Call and response"—for you to think about how the ideas presented might apply to your circumstances.

Throughout this book you will be invited to reflect on a range of important issues and to consider how these issues might be relevant to your leadership practice. It's important to be clear on what is meant by reflection, and to acknowledge that sometimes reflection can venture into less helpful territory and become rumination (Schultz, 2017; see Table 0.1). Engaging in self-reflection can help us gain valuable insights and make positive changes, while rumination can perpetuate negative thought patterns that detract from productivity and wellbeing.

Reflection is central to learning and can take many forms. In this book, we are mostly focused on self-reflection—that is, thinking deeply about who we are and how we align this with the type of work we want to do. We need to deliberately take time out for self-reflection (as you are being encouraged to do in this book!) rather than only reflecting spontaneously. Practising self-reflection is an important leadership quality because it contributes to deeper self-awareness, self-development, and resilience.

On the other hand, rumination tends to be more passive, unconscious, and repetitive. When we ruminate, we focus on things we can't control which means it is difficult to formulate concrete strategies or actions. Rumination can be involuntary and unproductive because it often focuses on negative aspects of ourselves or our situation.

Table 0.1 Differences between reflection and rumination.

Reflection	Rumination
active	passive
constructive	critical
planned	spontaneous
voluntary	involuntary
purposeful	purposeless
structured	repetitive
empowering	disempowering

As you engage in self-reflection throughout this book, be sure to monitor your thinking for any signs of rumination rather than reflection.

Refrain

You have now been introduced to the transformative potential of positive music leadership. This approach combines the power of music with positive and social psychology and leadership principles to create meaningful experiences that support social health in our communities. Positive music leadership is about aligning your musical and personal strengths and values with impactful community work. Whether you are a seasoned musician, a student, or a health professional, this book offers you practical tools to develop as a positive music leader. As you venture forward, keep in mind the urgent need for this work in our increasingly disconnected world. Your role as a positive music leader can be pivotal in revitalising social connections and improving social health.

In the next chapter, we will present an expanded view of musicians' work, empowering you to embrace positive music leadership as an integral part of your practice and career portfolio. We will explore how understanding and harnessing your musical and personal strengths and talents can create positive change in your community.

Call and response

Take five to ten minutes to reflect on the main ideas presented in this introduction.

1 How might the concept of positive music leadership expand your understanding of what it means to be a musician or a leader in your community?
2 Have you experienced positive music leadership, either as a leader yourself or as a community music group participant? How did it make you feel?
3 If you are already working as a music leader, have you ever taken the time to reflect on your values, strengths, and vision for your work? If no, why not?
4 How aware are you of the importance of social health?

References

Allen, K.-A. (2021). *The psychology of belonging*. Routledge.
Avolio, B. J., & Gardner, W. L. (2005). Authentic leadership development: Getting to the root of positive forms of leadership. *The Leadership Quarterly*, *16*(3), 315–338. doi:10.1016/j.leaqua.2005.03.001.
Baumeister, R. F., Bratslavsky, E., Finkenauer, C., & Vohs, K. D. (2001). Bad is stronger than good. *Review of General Psychology*, *5*(4), 323–370. doi:10.1037/1089-2680.5.4.323.
Baumeister, R. F., & Leary, M. R. (1995). The need to belong: Desire for interpersonal attachments as a fundamental human motivation. *Psychological Bulletin*, *117*(3), 497–529. doi:10.1037/0033-2909.117.3.497.

Bartleet, B.-L. (2023). A conceptual framework for understanding and articulating the social impact of community music. *International Journal of Community Music, 16*(1), 31–49. doi:10.1386/ijcm_00074_1.

Bedeian, A. G. (2016). A note on the aphorism "there is nothing as practical as a good theory." *Journal of Management History, 22*(2), 236–242. doi:10.1108/JMH-01-2016-0004.

Born, G. (2012). Music and the social. In M. Clayton (ed.), *The cultural study of music* (pp. 261–274). Routledge.

Cameron, K. S. (2018). *Positive leadership: Strategies for extraordinary performance* (2nd ed.). Berrett-Koehler.

Cameron, K. S. (2021). *Positively energizing leadership: Virtuous actions and relationships that create high performance* (1st ed.). Berrett-Koehler Publishers.

Camlin, D. A. (2023). *Music making and civic imagination*. Intellect Books.

Camlin, D. A., Daffern, H., & Zeserson, K. (2020). Group singing as a resource for the development of a healthy public: A study of adult group singing. *Humanities and Social Sciences Communications, 7*(1), article 1. doi:10.1057/s41599-020-00549-0.

Camlin, D. A., & Schei, T. B. (2024). Reaping the harvest of joy: Practitioner enquiry into intercultural group singing. *Australian Voice, 25*, 1–15. doi:10.56307/DLAZ9779.

Clift, S., Phillips, K., & Pritchard, S. (2021). The need for robust critique of research on social and health impacts of the arts. *Cultural Trends, 30*(5), 442–459. doi:10.1080/09548963.2021.1910492.

Creative Change. (2024). Community music and social impact map. https://creativecha nge.org.au/mapping.

Daykin, N., Mansfield, L., Meads, C., Julier, G., Tomlinson, A., Payne, A., Grigsby Duffy, L., Lane, J., D'Innocenzo, G., Burnett, A., Kay, T., Dolan, P., Testoni, S., & Victor, C. (2018). What works for wellbeing? A systematic review of wellbeing outcomes for music and singing in adults. *Perspectives in Public Health, 138*(1), 39–46. doi:10.1177/1757913917740391.

Dingle, G. A., Brander, C., Ballantyne, J., & Baker, F. (2013). "To be heard": The social and mental health benefits of choir singing for disadvantaged adults. *Psychology of Music, 41*(4), 405–421.

Dingle, G. A., Sharman, L. S., Bauer, Z., Beckman, E., Broughton, M., Bunzli, E., Davidson, R., Draper, G., Fairley, S., Farrell, C., Flynn, L. M., Gomersall, S., Hong, M., Larwood, J., Lee, C., Lee, J., Nitschinsk, L., Peluso, N., Reedman, S. E., … Wright, O. R. L. (2021). How do music activities affect health and well-being? A scoping review of studies examining psychosocial mechanisms. *Frontiers in Psychology, 12*, 3689. doi:10.3389/fpsyg.2021.713818.

Ending Loneliness Together. (2022). Strengthening social connection to accelerate social recovery: A white paper. https://endingloneliness.com.au/ending-loneliness-together-white-pap er-social-connection-to-accelerate-social-recovery.

Fancourt, D., Aughterson, H., Finn, S., Walker, E., & Steptoe, A. (2021). How leisure activities affect health: A narrative review and multi-level theoretical framework of mechanisms of action. *The Lancet Psychiatry, 8*(4), 329–339. doi:10.1016/S2215-0366 (20)30384-9.

Fancourt, D., & Finn, S. (2019). *What is the evidence on the role of the arts in improving health and well-being? A scoping review*. World Health Organization. www.euro.who. int/en/publications/abstracts/what-is-the-evidence-on-the-role-of-the-arts-in-improvin g-health-and-well-being-a-scoping-review-2019.

Forbes, M. (2021). "We're pushing back": Group singing, social identity, and caring for a spouse with Parkinson's. *Psychology of Music, 49*(5), 1199–1214.

Forbes, M. (2025). Addressing the global crisis of social connection: Singers as positively energizing leaders who create belonging in our communities. *Voice and Speech Review*, *19*(1), 44–60. doi:10.1080/23268263.2024.2368961.

Forbes, M., & Bartlett, I. (2020a). "It's much harder than I thought": Facilitating a singing group for people with Parkinson's disease. *International Journal of Community Music*, *13*(1), 29–47. doi:10.1386/ijcm_00009_1.

Forbes, M., & Bartlett, I. (2020b). "This circle of joy": Meaningful musicians' work and the benefits of facilitating singing groups. *Music Education Research*, *22*(5), 555–568. doi:10.1080/14613808.2020.1841131.

Forbes, M., Dingle, G. A, Aitcheson, N., & Powell, C. (2025). Music from performance to prescription: A guide for musicians and health professionals. *Music & Science*, online ahead of print. doi:10.1177/20592043251338013.

Gardner, H. (ed.). (2007). *Responsibility at work*. Jossey-Bass.

Gaunt, H., Duffy, C., Coric, A., González Delgado, I. R., Messas, L., Pryimenko, O., & Sveidahl, H. (2021). Musicians as "makers in society": A conceptual foundation for contemporary professional higher music education. *Frontiers in Psychology*, *12*, article 713648. doi:10.3389/fpsyg.2021.713648.

Goleman, D. (2013). *What makes a leader a leader: Why emotional intelligence matters*. More Than Sound.

Goleman, D., & Senge, P. (2014). *The triple focus: A new approach to education*. More Than Sound.

Grant, C. (2019). What does it mean for a musician to be socially engaged? How undergraduate music students perceive their possible social roles as musicians. *Music Education Research*, *21*(4), 387–398. doi:10.1080/14613808.2019.1626360.

Haslam, C., Jetten, J., Cruwys, T., Dingle, G. A., & Haslam, S. A. (2018). *The new psychology of health: Unlocking the social cure*. Routledge.

Haslam, S. A., Reicher, S., & Platow, M. J. (2020). *The new psychology of leadership: Identity, influence and power*. Routledge.

Hicks, D. (2021). *Dignity: Its essential role in resolving conflict* (10th anniversary edition). Yale University Press.

Hotz, J. (2024). *The connection cure: The prescriptive power of movement, nature, art, service and belonging*. Headline.

Humphrey, R. (2025). Unpacking transformation in community music discourse. *Arts and the Market*, online ahead of print. doi:10.1108/AAM-07-2024-0038.

Kertz-Welzel, A. (2025). What we should consider before proposing music education for social change. In *Zukunft: Musikpädagogische Perspektiven auf soziale und kulturelle Transformationsprozesse* (pp. 36–43). Hochschule für Musik Franz Liszt Weimarr. doi:10.25656/01:32533.

Killam, K. (2024). What is social health? The little-known idea that could make all the difference. *The Guardian*, 14 June. www.theguardian.com/wellness/article/2024/jun/14/what-is-social-health.

Krause, A. E., Davidson, J. W., & North, A. C. (2018). Musical activity and well-being: A new quantitative measurement instrument. *Music Perception: An Interdisciplinary Journal*, *35*(4), 454–474.

Lee, R. M., Draper, M., & Lee, S. (2001). Social connectedness, dysfunctional interpersonal behaviors, and psychological distress: Testing a mediator model. *Journal of Counselling Psychology*, *48*(3), 310–318.

Lucey, C., & Burke, J. (2022). *Positive leadership in practice: A model for our future* (1st edition). Routledge.

McArton, L., & Mantie, R. (2023). Music, health and well-being in IJCM articles: An integrative review. *International Journal of Community Music*, *16*(1), 51–81. doi:10.1386/ijcm_00075_1.

Murthy, V. H. (2023). Our epidemic of loneliness and isolation: The US Surgeon General's advisory on the healing effects of social connection and community. www.hhs.gov/sites/default/files/surgeon-general-social-connection-advisory.pdf.

Pavlicevic, M. (2013). Between beats: Group music therapy transforming people and places. In R. MacDonald, G. Kreutz, & L. Mitchell (eds), *Music Health and Wellbeing* (pp. 196–212). Oxford University Press.

Rashid, T., Summers, R. F., & Seligman, M. E. P. (2024). Positive psychology model of mental function and behavior. In A. Tasman, M. B. Riba, R. D. Alarcón, C. A. Alfonso, S. Kanba, D. Lecic-Tosevski, D. M. Ndetei, C. H. Ng, & T. G. Schulze (eds), *Tasman's psychiatry* (pp. 1055–1078). Springer International Publishing. doi:10.1007/978-3-030-51366-5_28.

Sattler, G. (2023). *Community music and facilitative leadership: Relationship, relevance and respect* [Fellowship Report]. Winston Churchill Trust.

Schultz, M. (2017). Reflection or rumination? MSU Extension, Michigan State University, 17 February. www.canr.msu.edu/news/reflection_or_rumination.

Seligman, M. E. P. (2011). *Flourish: A visionary new understanding of happiness and well-being*. Simon & Schuster.

Siegel, D. J., & Drulis, C. (2023). An interpersonal neurobiology perspective on the mind and mental health: Personal, public, and planetary well-being. *Annals of General Psychiatry*, *22*(1), article 5. doi:10.1186/s12991-023-00434-5.

Small, C. (1998). *Musicking: The meanings of performing and listening*. Wesleyan University Press.

van Zijl, A. G. W., & De bisschop, A. (2023). Layers and dynamics of social impact: Musicians' perspectives on participatory music activities. *Musicae Scientiae*, *28*(2), 348–364. doi:10.1177/10298649231205553.

Way, N., Ali, A., Gilligan, C., & Noguera, P. (eds). (2018). *The crisis of connection: Roots, consequences, and solutions*. NYU Press.

Westerlund, H., & Karttunen, S. (2024). The protean music career as a sociopolitical orientation: The mutually integrated, non-hierarchical work values of socially engaged musicians. *Musicae Scientiae*, *28*(3), 502–519.

World Health Organization. (2023). WHO commission on social connection. www.who.int/groups/commission-on-social-connection.

Part I
Solo

1 Positive music leadership for meaningful careers

Introduction

This book seeks to inspire musicians to harness their unique strengths to create vibrant, connected communities through the power of music. In Part I, we'll explore how you can transform your approach to working in music, setting you on a trajectory to becoming a vital force for promoting social health in your community. By embracing a strengths-based approach to self-leadership, you can forge a career path that is both personally rewarding and profoundly impactful.

Many musicians have yet to discover the transformative power of participatory music making for social connection, or perhaps see this as the work of music therapists or community volunteers. However, working in community is a largely untapped frontier for any musician seeking to make a positive impact. As we move through Part I, you'll see how your musical talents and personal strengths can be leveraged to create positive change in exciting new ways.

Stepping into the realm of community music for social connection may feel like a leap into the unknown. How can you determine if this is the right path for you? The answer lies in positive self-leadership—a powerful practice that will open your eyes to new possibilities for yourself as a musician and help align your work with your aspirations, strengths, and values. As Daniel Goleman notes, "a primary task of leadership is to direct attention" (Goleman, 2013, location 1681). It's time to direct your attention towards yourself to examine your fundamental assumptions about what musicians do.

By dedicating time to self-reflection and to understanding the broader context of your practice—who you are, what drives you, what society needs, and how your work can address these needs—you can ensure that your precious attention and energy are invested in meaningful activities.

And if you decide after all this reflection that you really do want to be the next Taylor Swift, that is fine too! As long as the decisions you make are fully informed and aligned with *your* vision. None of this is meant to disparage the incredible contribution music performers, creatives, and educators make to our communities. On the contrary, we need to celebrate these contributions, just as we need to celebrate our positive music leaders.

The message here is that community work can be a powerful way to *diversify* your music career portfolio. Positive music leadership for social connection is

DOI: 10.4324/9781003426509-3

presented *in addition to*, rather than as a replacement for, musicians' work as performers and educators. Indeed, the philosophy of positive music leadership—to harness the power of music making for social health and connection—can be applied to performance and education, as well as in the community contexts we explore throughout this book.

As mentioned in the Overture, this book is structured in three parts, each of which aligns with the "triple focus" of effective leaders—leaders need to simultaneously focus on themselves, others, and the context in which they are working (Goleman, 2013; Goleman & Senge, 2014). In Part I, we'll develop self-leadership to uncover the work that resonates with your core values and strengths. This journey of self-discovery will fuel your intrinsic motivation, driving you to engage in activities not only for external rewards, but for the sheer satisfaction, enjoyment, and challenge they provide. Later, in Parts II and III, we'll expand our focus to leading others to promote their social health and the broader context of positive music leadership, equipping you with the tools to become a transformative force in your community.

From performance to participation

When you think of a musician, who comes to mind? A world-famous concert pianist, perhaps, or the latest K-pop sensation? Musician and community choir leader Emma Dean says, "When the general public thinks about music and what a successful musician looks like, generally they're going to picture someone like Lady Gaga. The soloist." Singing leader Jane York encounters similar stereotypes when she describes her work: "I work in community music. Because when you say you're a musician, people go, oh, great, what kind of stuff do you play? I say, no, no, not *that* kind of musician!"

Zambian-born music therapist, psychotherapist, and educator Nsamu Moonga offers a different perspective on who a musician is, reflecting that in Indigenous cultures, "you're raised musically". As Nsamu explains:

> You show up at these musical events that are integrated arts, that include the costumes, the dances, the songs, the drums, and all kinds of instrumentations that happen in that particular space. There's a place for everyone, even if it's somebody who's just an observer, a witness, or somebody who's clapping or singing or dancing or laughing. Some of the performances are just meant for sheer entertainment. Others are meant for problem solving.

Nsamu describes a broad range of uses or applications of music in his culture and how everyone and everything has a role, even the elements of human nature and the cycle of nature itself:

> There are performances that are meant for healing, right? They are rituals. There are multiple expressions of this musicality, which in itself is informed by the elements. It's informed by the elemental nature of people's existence. People dance when they're perplexed. People dance when they're delighted.

People dance when they're amused or bemused. That's part of a lot of the Indigenous cycle. Indigenous daily cycles include some form of musical performance, either at the end of the day or when the moon sets or around the fire as people are telling stories, the musical story songs. So, [musical performance] is always something that captures the people's imagination.

Nsamu vividly portrays the role of "musician" as one that is fully integrated into the daily rhythms and fabric of society, fulfilling a wide range of vital functions in culture.

In stark contrast, according to the music psychology literature, a musician is conceived in more quantifiable terms, as someone who has at least six years of musical expertise (Zhang et al., 2020). Within music education, the word "musician" has become practically synonymous with "professional [performing] musician" (Kratus, 2019). Musician Gillian Howell's experience of her music training supports this idea. When Gillian reflects on her study as an undergraduate music student in Australia, she says that "it felt like you weren't really allowed to move around [from performance] as much as, of course, you are. But I think that was a sense that I had as a young performer, partly perhaps because it was such a lot of work." Gillian goes on to say that the recognised pathways during her study were progressing "upwards" to a performance or composing career ("although, probably not as a woman") or you might "progress downwards" to teaching.

But the idea of music being the exclusive domain of the trained professional performer is a historical glitch. As community musician and researcher Dave Camlin writes:

> In western societies, we have grown accustomed to the idea that music is something performed by talented (and often highly trained) musicians for others to listen/dance to, whereas a more holistic view of music recognizes that it is something that people *do*—and that *all* humans have always done— throughout our species' 230,000-year history.
> (Camlin, 2023, p. 4, emphasis in original)

In Western, educated, industrialised, rich, and democratic (WEIRD) societies, our understanding of music and musicians arguably limits our perception of music's true potential (Camlin, 2023). Within WEIRD societies, the label "musician" carries connotations of autonomous music making (Proctor & DeNora, 2022) that is presentational rather than participatory (Shilton et al., 2023; Turino, 2008). This limited view can lead to an undervaluation of music in community settings, where success is measured not by artistic innovation, technical virtuosity, or commercial success, but rather by music's ability to support social, health, and developmental needs (see Elliott & Silverman, 2012; Turino, 2008 as discussed in Spiro et al., 2023).

This emphasis on presentation or performance over direct experience is evidenced in many ways, for example, by the separation of musicians and audiences at concerts, by the act of listening to music alone, through the maintenance of hierarchical structures such as conductor and orchestra, and even in the student–

teacher relationship within music education. In each of these examples, musicians (as the experts) do the presenting, while others occupy a relatively passive role, as audience members, listeners, or, in the case of music students, receivers of wisdom. According to Shilton et al. (2023), societies with pronounced hierarchies and inequalities are more likely to prioritise individual, presentation-focused musical performances. In contrast, smaller-scale or more equitable societies tend to place greater emphasis on collective participation and group singing activities. When music is primarily presentational, the right to present or perform music for others is reserved for those who are trained, skilled, or otherwise ordained as being qualified and sufficiently expert to do so. According to the presentational view of music, musicians are primarily performers who present or create music for the passive consumption of others. It's interesting to contrast this with Nsamu's reflections on the deeply embedded and integrated role of music making within Batonga culture!

Modern society's view of musicians as performers is an example of recency bias, meaning that music was not always predominantly presentational or performative. Certainly, human beings have been intuitively called to make music and sing together for millennia (Fancourt, 2017; Norton, 2016) as part of cultural and religious practices which are thought to have promoted social bonding (Shilton et al., 2023). In these practices, the arts, health, and healing have long intermingled (Fancourt, 2017). Indeed, examination of extensive audio and ethnographic texts has shown that music making is in fact, a predominantly participatory activity (Shilton et al., 2023). For example, group singing is far more common than solo singing in 70–73% of societies (Shilton et al., 2023). While those in WEIRD societies may exclude themselves from musical participation on the grounds they are not "good enough", this way of thinking is not necessarily universal.

Music can and should be understood as a participatory practice *for everyone*, not just those designated as "musicians" (see, for example, Camlin, 2022a, 2023). Engaging in participatory music can also be a transformative experience for performing musicians, who may be used to working within an "aesthetic tradition" (Camlin, 2022b). Through participatory music, musicians discover a complex, unfamiliar, and often exciting world of "performing relationships" through music (Camlin, 2022a, 2022b; see also Camlin et al., 2020; Forbes & Bartlett, 2020b). The aesthetic mode of music making emphasises individual talent, technical perfection, and the creation of beautiful musical artefacts for appreciation by a cultivated audience. This approach tends to foster competition, reinforce hierarchal structures, and privilege individual achievement. In contrast, within participatory music practice, the "quality" of the music is tied to the social context of participation, and the emphasis is on creating a shared meaningful experience among participants. The act of making music together initiates relationships between sounds, people, and the wider world, and the meaning of the music lies in these relationships, not in the final aesthetic product (Camlin, 2022a, 2022b, 2023).

While anyone can participate in music, and while participation itself does not necessarily require expertise or skill, those who choose music *as a career* require a certain level of expertise if they are to *lead* participatory activities. But the type of expertise required needs to be considered in the context of the different roles musicians undertake (Forbes et al., 2025). Gillian Howell has worked in contexts as diverse as post-war peacebuilding and facilitating in remote Indigenous communities. She observes that the reality is that most musicians wear multiple hats, and each musician will have their own quality criteria:

> Musicians ... may perform ... arrange ... organise events. They may lead groups. They may teach. They'll talk about music with others. They may advocate, but they also investigate or enquire. They'll lead creative processes as creative thinkers and makers and doers.

Certainly, concepts of excellence and expertise are relevant when we discuss musicians' training further below, which, at the post-school level, has tended to focus on artistic or performance excellence (Gaunt et al., 2021; Harmes et al., 2024). As will hopefully become clear as this chapter progresses, musicians working in community contexts for social connection can still strive for excellence. However, it is important to understand that excellence is always context-dependent (Renshaw, 2013; Gaunt et al., 2021).

Moreover, positive music leaders do not need to sacrifice musical goals for social ones. James Sills, vocal leader, reflects: "In my work, I wanted to marry two things together: work that is accessible and inclusive with high social impact, while also having strong musical impact and integrity. Integrity is one of my key values." James, like other positive music leaders, understands that excellence takes different forms in different contexts—what defines excellence in a concert hall may be quite different from what constitutes excellence in a local park. This difference does not imply a hierarchy of quality; rather, it simply acknowledges that excellence in participatory music making can manifest in ways that may be unfamiliar to those steeped in traditional performance contexts. Ultimately, traditional dichotomies of access and inclusion versus excellence not only shut down critical reflection on practice but fail to acknowledge the broad array of practices that are possible within participatory music making (Camlin, 2015).

Positive music leadership as socially engaged practice

Positive music leadership calls musicians to consider how they can incorporate more participatory ways of music making into their music practice. In this respect, positive music leadership can be understood as a socially engaged arts initiative in which creative artists work together to achieve positive social impact and change (Bartleet & Howell, 2020). Socially engaged, participatory music making has been identified as a "growing if still somewhat niche pursuit" for musicians, and as a way for the music profession to respond to the complexity of modern life (Westerlund & Karttunen, 2024, p. 2).

Community music encompasses a wide range of participatory musical activities that are created "by, for, and/or with community members" (Bartleet, 2023, p.

36; Creative Change, 2024). At its core, community music is about fostering inclusive, grassroots musical experiences that are deeply situated in local contexts (Bartleet, 2023). Community music is uniquely shaped by the culture, participants, and environments in which it takes place (Bartleet, 2023). Community music, as approach to participatory music making, prioritises community empowerment and typically champions socio-relational values such as inclusivity, accessibility, fairness, social justice, and community self-determination (Bartleet, 2023).

Community musician and researcher Lee Higgins (2012) outlines three strands of community music: the music of a particular ethno-cultural community, communal music making, and community interventions led by skilled musicians. The participatory music activities which are the subject of this book largely fall into the last category of "interventions". These interventions have evolved in response to the increasing commercialisation and commodification of music practices, where society has become divided into "performers" and "audiences" (Howell et al., 2017; Turino, 2008). In these interventions, skilled facilitators or leaders "consciously engage with people to find pathways through which music making opportunities might allow them to personally flourish with full and engaged participation" (Howell et al., 2017, p. 605). These interventions take place across diverse settings, from schools and educational institutions to community spaces, medical and residential facilities, and rural locations (Howell et al., 2017).

Many of these interventions intersect with the field of music for health and wellbeing, but they are not "music therapy". Music therapists are registered health professionals who are trained to work with individuals with acute illnesses or with those who may be in crisis or rehabilitation (O'Grady & McFerran, 2007). In contrast, musicians delivering community music interventions generally do not work with individuals at the acute/crisis end of the health continuum. Rather, community musicians (including those supporting social prescribing—more on this in Chapter 4) tend to work with those who would benefit from improved social connection and wellbeing (Forbes et al., 2025).

This blurring of roles has the potential to lead to ethical issues or the overstepping of professional boundaries. Understanding professional boundaries and ethical practice is crucial for positive music leaders, both for their own protection and wellbeing, and for that of the people they work with. Just as a singing teacher might refer a student who frequently confides in them to a psychologist or counsellor, musicians working in community contexts must be aware of the limits of their professional roles and responsibilities. For music leaders in community, participating in aligned networks or mentoring can help to navigate the nuances and complexities of professional boundaries. It is also important to undertake training which equips leaders with the skills to anticipate issues. For example, in Australia, Mental Health First Aid trains participants to provide initial support to someone experiencing mental health distress. Music leaders should be proactive in seeking out these opportunities.

In summary, the work of musicians promoting social connection within their communities can be understood as a form of socially engaged, participatory arts practice which intersects with the field of music for health and wellbeing but is distinct from the clinical work of accredited music therapists. By clearly articulating the role and boundaries of positive music leaders to support social health, we can better support their efforts to foster social change and improve the lives of individuals and communities through participatory music making.

Music leaders' attributes, skills, and values

Music leaders require a unique blend of musical and interpersonal expertise (Howell et al., 2017; Irons et al., 2024; Forbes & Bartlett, 2020a). In 2024, a systematic review of "group singing facilitators" found that important characteristics were adaptability and flexibility, the ability to create a relaxed and inclusive environment, a "democratic" leadership style, empathy and genuine interest in group members, and effective coaching and communication skills (Irons et al., 2024). My research with colleague Irene Bartlett on Parkinson's singing group facilitators found that facilitation required a unique blend of pedagogical, musical, creative, technological, and leadership skills; important facilitator attributes were confidence and the ability to enthuse others; and facilitators needed a working understanding of Parkinson's as an incurable neurological disease to work effectively with their groups (Forbes & Bartlett, 2020a). In another study of facilitators working with a range of health and wellbeing singing groups, Irene and I found that facilitators experienced their work as highly meaningful, and very much in alignment with their personal values of service and their strengths as musicians (Forbes & Bartlett, 2020b). In their discussion of the broad range of skills and values required of facilitators, Howell and colleagues noted that effective facilitators maintain a positive, calming presence while remaining flexible enough to adapt to unpredictable situations (Howell et al., 2017). This adaptability extends to their teaching approach in that they recognise learning flows in multiple directions, and they remain open to learning alongside their participants.

In addition, music facilitators hold certain core values (Howell, et al., 2017). For example, they fundamentally believe that everyone has the capacity to engage meaningfully with music. This belief drives their commitment to creating inclusive, accessible musical experiences. They understand that success means achieving both musical and social outcomes, always working towards participant empowerment rather than leader-centred authority (Higgins & Willingham, 2017). Jane York discusses how access and inclusion are central to her philosophy as a community musician and singing leader:

> I think everyone should have access to music making. I think there should be an equity to it, in some form in their lives, if they want, but everyone should have access to it somewhere, whether it's in the education setting, whether it's within their community. For some people, it might be at their church. [Music] is a really healthy part of a community. I am constantly trying to work with organisations to expand those opportunities for people. It's really

difficult to make those opportunities for those who are possibly least able to access it on their own.

Similarly, musician Kym Dillon says that while she had never sung in choirs growing up, when the opportunity to lead a social inclusion choir arose, with a focus "not so much on the musical side, but on the sort of caring, pastoral, social inclusion side", those values resonated with her. Like Jane, Kym believes that "everyone deserves access to meaningful musical experiences, regardless of their background or context". For vocal leader James Sills, who leads numerous "open access singing groups", it is important that singing is "accessible and inclusive", but also that singing has "musical impact and integrity".

In essence, effective music leaders artfully balance musical excellence with social purpose, and technical skill with human connection, working to ensure everyone feels welcomed, safe, and valued. In later chapters, we will look in more depth at the process of enacting these skills within a positive leadership framework.

Diversifying your career portfolio

The call for positive music leadership encourages musicians to consider diversifying their career portfolios to include leading participatory music making for social connection. Since the late 2000s, the "portfolio career" has emerged as a viable model for musicians, acknowledging the need to balance various roles and income streams (Bennett, 2009; Teague & Smith, 2015). This approach allows musicians to spread risk, much like an investment portfolio, using stable part-time work to support riskier ventures. Echoing Gillian Howell's comments above about musicians wearing multiple hats, a portfolio career acknowledges that, at any one time, musicians may work across a range of different contexts to craft a career, rather than focusing on one role.

However, the work landscape for musicians continues to evolve rapidly. In any discussion of musicians' careers, it is impossible to ignore the devastating impact of the COVID-19 pandemic on musicians' livelihoods and their health and wellbeing (Crosby & McKenzie, 2022; Spiro et al., 2021). Nicole Canham, a musician, researcher, and careers counsellor, argues for a shift to a "post-portfolio careers paradigm" in response to the pandemic-induced "career shock" (Canham, 2022, 2023). This shift reflects a growing desire for meaningful, purposeful work among musicians and workers more broadly (Spurk & Straub, 2020). Specifically, it calls for:

1 a more holistic understanding of music's complexity and musicians' societal roles (Canham, 2023);
2 development of a wide range of entrepreneurial, generic, and musical skills (Camlin, 2023);
3 the dismantling of traditional hierarchies within professional music practice (Westerlund & Karttunen, 2024); and
4 a greater emphasis on compassion and a reduced focus on competition in career narratives (Canham, 2022).

As the music world grapples with these changes, a new career orientation is emerging—the protean career. Driven by personal values and passion, rather than external rewards, the protean career aligns closely with socially engaged music practice. Westerlund and Karttunen's (2024) study of Finnish musicians revealed a shift towards intrinsic and social-relational values, forming a holistic foundation for practice. Specifically, Westerlund and Karttunen (2024) found that individuals who are drawn towards a protean career value their own autonomy, development, and self-determination over the extrinsic motivators that tend to drive a traditional or portfolio careerist. This approach resonates with the "call to serve" that characterises much community music work (Willingham & Carruthers, 2018; Forbes & Bartlett, 2020b).

But again, there is a caveat here; as always, we need to acknowledge music's "ambiguity" (Kertz-Welzel, 2025). For example, while many university music students see the value in socially engaged music careers, some feel strongly that musicians should *not* be involved in social causes (Grant, 2019). In Grant's (2019) study of undergraduates' perceptions of their possible social role as musicians, three young men felt very strongly that it was "irrelevant or even immoral for musicians to be socially engaged" (p. 395). While Grant argues that this finding supports the value of educating music undergraduates of the potential for musicians to play a vital role in society, it also underscores a crucial point—there is no one-size-fits-all approach to crafting a music career. This book argues that the key is alignment with an *individual's* aspirations, strengths, and values.

As we navigate this new terrain, then, how can we balance meaningful work with financial stability? The reality is that socially engaged practice, while fulfilling, is unlikely to be lucrative and could even threaten a musician's credibility in some professional circles (Westerlund & Karttunen, 2024). This undeniable reality presents a key challenge—as a society, we must recognise and support musicians working to build social health as a valuable public health resource. It is only through this recognition that positive music leaders working in community will be supported financially to do this work. We will return to the critical issue of career sustainability in Part III.

The changing nature of musicians' careers is characterised by a shift towards a more holistic, values-driven approach. For those whose strengths and values align with socially engaged, participatory music making, a career that is part portfolio, part protean, yet also accounting for precarity, may be the way forward.

The question, then, is how can music education and the broader music industry adapt to prepare and support musicians for this complex, ever-changing world?

The evolving role of higher music education institutions

The training of professional musicians—in WEIRD societies, at least—has traditionally focused on developing performance skills and technique, either for solo or ensemble performance, and often at the expense of supporting individual aspirations, strengths, and values (Howell et al., 2017). Musician and community choir leader Emma Dean's experience reflects this: "A lot of my training was geared towards the soloist outcome. For several years, I felt like I had failed because I wasn't famous or anything like that. That training didn't really help me when it came to community choir work." Musician Kym Dillon, who leads several community choirs for social inclusion, also believes that her university training as a musician was highly valuable in a musical sense, but that it did not prepare her for working in community—Kym says this "wasn't part of my university training at all … it was very much a learning on the job kind of thing".

As values and priorities change, the role and purpose of higher music education institutions (HMEIs) in Western societies is increasingly being scrutinised and reimagined from multiple perspectives (Gaunt et al., 2021). Historically, these HMEIs have adopted the master–apprentice model to professional musicians which dates to the establishment of the Paris Conservatoire in the eighteenth century. Based on a one-to-one relationship between expert performer/educator and student, and with a strong focus on developing technique and performance skills, the master-apprentice approach has dominated Western music education. The centrality of this model reinforces the centrality of performance skills as the primary outcome of much music education. Despite some broadening of music styles and skills taught in HMEIs, performance units still comprise most music education offerings, with 55% of all music units in Australian HMEIs focusing on performance (Harmes et al., 2024).

RESONANCE—A new approach to inspiring excellence and growth through music education

Music inclusion advocate Graham Sattler reflects on how traditional Western music training, despite its emphasis on technical and performance excellence, can instil a damaging belief that musicians are never "good enough":

> I've been reflecting lately on a fundamental weakness in traditional performer training—the embedded belief that one is never "good enough". While striving for improvement is valuable, the traditional Western European master–apprentice model often instils a perpetual sense of inadequacy. This goes beyond healthy ambition and can be genuinely damaging.
>
> Although my own non-linear career path has benefited from varied experiences, I frequently encounter performers who are psychologically injured by this "never good enough" mindset. The irony is that while music itself naturally creates cohesive communities, the traditional training model can produce troubled individuals who struggle to contribute to that community spirit.
>
> The challenge lies in finding ways to inspire excellence and growth without undermining a performer's sense of worth. We need to question whether the conventional approach to music education, despite its long history, truly serves our goals in music education and community building.

As Graham suggests in the RESONANCE box above, today's HMEIs face complex challenges in balancing artistic craft with social engagement, in preparing musicians for diverse career paths, and in addressing issues of equity, diversity, and inclusion. From the perspective of those working within conservatoires, Gaunt et al. (2021) propose a paradigm shift towards viewing the "musician as a maker in society". This approach emphasises the development of musicians' vision for their craft and their societal engagement and recognises the interdependence of the artistic and social dimensions of music making. Gaunt and colleagues argue for moving beyond either/or thinking, such as choosing between international reputation or local impact, towards a "partnering of values". Their conceptual foundation brings together the musician's vision and identity, artistic craft and expertise, and engagement with society. This approach retains the central value of craftsmanship while highlighting the importance of creative emergence and social orientation in music practice.

From the community music perspective, Camlin (2023) critiques the traditional approach of training musicians for specific roles within performing traditions. Instead, Camlin argues for an education that empowers students to take on active musical roles in a broad range of practices uniquely situated within their communities. Camlin emphasises a humanistic and dialogic approach to educating musicians, focusing on the relational nature of music and the pluralistic ways in which music making occurs in different situations with different groups of people.

Despite their different vantage points, both perspectives—one from the conservatoire and the other from the world of community music—converge on the need for a more holistic, socially engaged approach to music education. This shift aligns well with the concept of positive music leadership because it moves beyond the traditional single-minded focus on performance excellence to a broader view of musicianship that includes community engagement and social impact (Shaughnessy et al., 2024).

By embracing this broader vision, HMEIs can better prepare musicians to navigate the contemporary landscape of work precarity and social need, fostering not just technical excellence but also the ability to create meaningful social connections through music. This evolution in music education is crucial for developing the next generation of positive music leaders who can effectively support and enhance social health in their communities.

RESONANCE—Where do community musicians learn their craft?

Within the field of community music, there is debate about whether training for music leaders should be formalised or not. Some argue that the roots of community music are within political activism and that institutionalising the practice runs counter to these foundations. Nonetheless, there are HMEIs across the world who are offering formal qualifications in community music and leadership.

Graham Sattler, chief executive officer at Christchurch Symphony Orchestra and musical inclusion advocate, travelled the world during a

Churchill Fellowship to learn more about formal training opportunities for music leaders. He found that community music leadership requires a specific set of skills and capabilities, including skills in group pedagogy, entrepreneurship, artistic capability, communication, advocacy, confidence, insight, and of course, leadership. According to Graham's project report (Sattler, 2023), these skills are best developed through formal education and training, and by combining theoretical knowledge with practical experience. Graham advocates for music leadership to be a valued outcome in music education, calling for micro-credentials through to postgraduate degrees.

Crafting your musical identity: Aligning passion with purpose

Before turning to Chapter 2 and the practice of positive self-leadership, it's crucial to consider: who are you as a musician? Are you a performer who strives for artistic mastery and excellence? Are you someone who teaches others to be their best? Or are you drawn to using your musical abilities to share the joy of music with others, perhaps with specific groups like children with autism or elderly people in care? Maybe you're still exploring and eager to discover your path. Whatever your aspirations, they will only feel realistic if they align with your authentic self and your identity as a musician. This book in large part seeks to bring to life the unique "identity" of the role of a music leader.

Many musicians may feel pressure to prioritise prestigious performance venues over community spaces, seeing the former as "legitimate" or "superior". However, positive music leaders move fluidly between these worlds, recognising the inherent value in all forms of music making. Kym Dillon, a highly trained jazz pianist and composer who also leads community singing groups, communicates this perspective:

> I've reflected deeply on what drives my community work, and I keep coming back to my fundamental love of music and my desire to share that joy with others. I believe everyone deserves access to meaningful musical experiences, regardless of their background or context. Recently, while I performed as a jazz pianist at a prestigious concert hall one day, my community choir sang at a local hardware store the next. I love that there's no real difference in worth between these audiences; you can create musical magic anywhere when you're fully engaged and passionate about what you're doing.

This ability to see equal value in both concert hall and hardware store performances exemplifies how positive music leaders are redefining excellence. Rather than measuring success solely through traditional metrics of technical perfection or venue prestige, positive music leaders understand that excellence can also mean creating meaningful connections and joyful musical experiences in any setting. This more contextualised understanding of excellence aligns with the broader goals of positive music leadership—to use musical expertise in service of connection rather than status.

However, changing the way we practise music, especially after years of dedication to a particular tradition or goal, can be deeply challenging to a musician's sense of identity. As Westerlund and Karttunen note:

> although musicians may combine performing and teaching in their careers without any conflict of interests or hierarchy ... it may make considerable demands on them to reconcile their traditional performance-related work with socially engaged practice, since the latter fundamentally blurs boundaries between established and novel performance practices.
>
> (Westerlund & Karttunen, 2024, p. 14)

This shift may require musicians to reconsider what success looks like. Within the classical tradition, for instance, success might be measured by international reputation, prestigious performance venues, and critical acclaim. However, these markers don't apply when working to build social connections and improve social health in local communities. For some, this shift might initially feel like an admission of failure or a dilution of standards, but it's important to understand that our identities can evolve, and we have the power to craft our own identity stories and definitions of success.

RESONANCE—Positive identity shifts

Musical inclusion advocate Graham Sattler reflects on how his identity as a musician transformed when he expanded his work beyond traditional performance:

> Though I was a capable musician from childhood, I initially defined my identity narrowly through traditional performance. Paradoxically, it was only when I moved beyond exclusively performing—into research, presenting, and community engagement—that I discovered a broader understanding of what it means to be a performer. I realised that the same "flow" I experienced in musical performance was present in other aspects of my work, from staff meetings to community project development. This shift coincided with discovering a passion for learning at age 25, leading to further studies and eventually a PhD.

For Graham, finding this expanded identity has been a privilege, allowing him to integrate performance, research, and community engagement in ways he never imagined.

In a recently published study, classical musicians who played via Zoom for patients in a maternity ward during the COVID-19 pandemic also experienced shifts in both identity and values (Shaughnessy et al., 2024). For these musicians, excellence was not simply about technical perfection but included creating personal, impactful musical experiences for patients. This research demonstrates that classical musicians are adaptive artists who can blend their craft with social engagement to create meaningful experiences for themselves and for others in unexpected settings. In doing so, these musicians are helping to redefine what success and excellence look like for other highly trained classical musicians (Shaughnessy et al., 2024). In fact, the authors of this study emphasise "the imperative for higher music education to prepare and train musicians for this type of work" (Shaughnessy et al., 2024, p. 58).

Another study of Danish student musicians' experiences of playing music to patients in an intensive care unit (ICU) also found this practice expanded students' musical identities (Bro et al., 2024). The researchers discovered that performing in an ICU setting fundamentally transformed musicians' relationship with their craft by removing the usual pressures of traditional concert performances. Instead of focusing on technical perfection, audience approval, or external validation, musicians discovered a more authentic and purposeful approach to music making. The tangible impact of their music on patients' stress levels provided a different kind of validation than audience applause, leading to increased empathy and self-awareness. This experience helped these student musicians to develop a deeper understanding of their musical identity and enhanced their ability to communicate through music, with some participants noting that these insights also positively influenced their approach to traditional concert performances (Bro et al., 2024).

While these examples of musicians playing in healthcare settings may not be strictly examples of participatory music making, they help to illustrate the point that musicians can accommodate different contexts for their practice into their professional identities in ways that enhance, rather than detract from, their sense of self and the quality of their musicianship.

As we move into the next chapter on self-leadership, we'll explore how developing deep self-awareness of your strengths, values, and aspirations can help you navigate these identity shifts. By understanding yourself better, you'll be better equipped to shape your musical identity in a way that feels authentic and fulfilling, whether that involves traditional performance, community engagement, teaching, or a blend of different musical practices. The journey of self-discovery and identity formation is ongoing, and the tools of positive self-leadership can guide this process.

RESONANCE—Love as a unifying force

Kym Dillon, whose career spans classical composition, jazz performance, and community choir leadership, demonstrates how musicians can find unity across seemingly disparate musical identities. Certainly, the breadth of Kym's musical roles could potentially create a fragmented professional identity. Yet when asked to describe her work in one word, Kym doesn't hesitate: "love".

"I use the word love to tie it all together", Kym explains. She says:

> I love music; that's what gives me energy in what I'm doing. I love people. Doing this kind of work feels like showing love by wanting to share this experience with others and by making them feel included. It's about seeing someone and saying, "It's important to me that you feel included in this". And that feels like a loving act.

Placing love at the heart of Kym's practice bridges the seemingly distant worlds of performance and community music making. For Kym, love is the force that drives both her musical passion and her connection with others. When leading her choir, for example, Kym describes how her love of music creates an energy and joy that naturally flows to participants. This is the same joy she shares when performing as a jazz artist.

Refrain

It's both a challenging and exciting time to be a musician. Within Western societies, musicians' identities are expanding beyond the traditional boundaries of performance and formal education to encompass roles as social change agents, healthcare contributors, and adaptable professionals capable of meeting diverse societal needs. The first step in expanding who *you* could be as a musician is to develop your self-awareness and your capability to lead yourself in new directions which align with your aspirations, strengths, and values. The following chapter provides a clear framework for taking this exciting step towards making music that matters by crafting impactful, fulfilling, and meaningful work.

Call and response

1   Reflect on your own musical identity. How do you see yourself? In what ways does this direct or limit your music practice?
2   Consider the concept of "excellence" in music. How might excellence be redefined or reimagined when applied to participatory, community-based, socially engaged musical practices? How does this compare to traditional notions of musical excellence?
3   This chapter has focused on the narrow role of musicians in WEIRD societies. Reflect on the ways Nsamu Moonga's experiences of music making and musicians' roles differ from the narrow Western concept of musician.

References

Bartleet, B.-L. (2023). A conceptual framework for understanding and articulating the social impact of community music. *International Journal of Community Music, 16*(1), 31–49. doi:10.1386/ijcm_00074_1.

Bartleet, B.-L., & Howell, G. (2020). A typology of social change agendas in Australian arts organizations and NGOs. *Journal of Arts & Communities, 12*(1), 23–40. doi:10.1386/jaac_00021_1.

Bennett, D. (2009). Academy and the real world: Developing realistic notions of career in the performing arts. *Arts and Humanities in Higher Education, 8*(3), 309–327. doi:10.1177/1474022209339953.

Bro, M. L., Smilde, R., Thorn, L., Fischer, S., Hosbond, K., Larsen, C. S., & Dreyer, P. (2024). Live music in the ICU: A qualitative study of music students' perspectives. *Musicae Scientiae, 29*(2). doi:10.1177/10298649241300440.

Camlin, D. A. (2015). "This is my truth, now tell me yours": Emphasizing dialogue within participatory music. *International Journal of Community Music, 8*(3), 233–257. doi:10.1386/ijcm.8.3.233_1.

Camlin, D. A., Daffern, H., & Zeserson, K. (2020). Group singing as a resource for the development of a healthy public: A study of adult group singing. *Humanities and Social Sciences Communications, 7*(1), article 1. doi:10.1057/s41599-020-00549-0.

Camlin, D. A. (2022a). Encounters with participatory music. In M. Doğantan-Dack (ed.), *The chamber musician in the twenty-first century* (pp. 43–71). MDPI.

Camlin, D. A. (2022b). Empowering the portfolio musician: Innovative chamber music pedagogy for the 21-century artist. In M. Doğantan-Dack (ed.), *The chamber musician in the twenty-first century* (pp. 103–129). MDPI.

Camlin, D. A. (2023). *Music making and civic imagination.* Intellect Books.

Canham, N. (2022). *Preparing musicians for precarious work: Transformational approaches to music careers education* (1st ed.). Routledge.

Canham, N. (2023). Living with liminality: Reconceptualising music careers education and research. *Research Studies in Music Education, 45*(1), 3–19. doi:10.1177/1321103X221144583.

Creative Change. (2024). What is the creative change project?https://creativechange.org.au/.

Crosby, P., & McKenzie, J. (2022). Survey evidence on the impact of COVID-19 on Australian musicians and implications for policy. *International Journal of Cultural Policy, 28*(2), 166–186. doi:10.1080/10286632.2021.1916004.

Elliott, D. J., & Silverman, M. (2012). Why music matters: Philosophical and cultural foundations. In R. MacDonald, G. Kreutz, & L. Mitchell (eds), *Music, health, and wellbeing* (pp. 25–39). Oxford University Press.

Fancourt, D. (2017). *Arts in health: Designing and researching interventions.* Oxford University Press.

Forbes, M., & Bartlett, I. (2020a). "It's much harder than I thought": Facilitating a singing group for people with Parkinson's disease. *International Journal of Community Music, 13*(1), 29–47. doi:10.1386/ijcm_00009_1.

Forbes, M., & Bartlett, I. (2020b). "This circle of joy": Meaningful musicians' work and the benefits of facilitating singing groups. *Music Education Research, 22*(5), 555–568. doi:10.1080/14613808.2020.1841131.

Forbes, M., Dingle, G., Aitcheson, N., & Powell, C. (2025). Music from performance to prescription: A guide for musicians and health professionals. *Music & Science*, online ahead of print. doi:10.1177/20592043251338013.

Gaunt, H., Duffy, C., Coric, A., González Delgado, I. R., Messas, L., Pryimenko, O., & Sveidahl, H. (2021). Musicians as "makers in society": A conceptual foundation for contemporary professional higher music education. *Frontiers in Psychology, 12.* doi:10.3389/fpsyg.2021.713648.

Goleman, D. (2013). *What makes a leader a leader: Why emotional intelligence matters.* More Than Sound.

Goleman, D., & Senge, P. (2014). *The triple focus: A new approach to education.* More Than Sound.

Grant, C. (2019). What does it mean for a musician to be socially engaged? How undergraduate music students perceive their possible social roles as musicians. *Music Education Research, 21*(4), 387–398. doi:10.1080/14613808.2019.1626360.

Harmes, M., Hogan, O., & Charles, M. B. (2024). The beat goes on? The current presence of music education in Australian public universities. *Arts Education Policy Review,* 1–16. doi:10.1080/10632913.2024.2351971.

Higgins, L. (2012). *Community music: In theory and in practice.* Oxford University Press.

Higgins, L., & Willingham, L. (2017). *Engaging in community music: An introduction.* Routledge.

Howell, G., Higgins, L., & Bartleet, B.-L. (2017). Community music practice: Intervention through facilitation. In R. Mantie & G. D. Smith (eds), *The Oxford handbook of music making and leisure* (pp. 601–618). Oxford University Press. doi:10.1093/oxfordhb/9780190244705.013.26.

Irons, J. Y., Bonshor, M., Tip, L., Boyd, S., Wydenbach, N., & Sheffield, D. (2024). What are the skills, attributes and knowledge for group singing facilitators? A systematic review. *International Journal of Community Music, 17*(2), 129–160. doi:10.1386/ijcm_00101_1.

Kertz-Welzel, A. (2025). What we should consider before proposing music education for social change. In *Zukunft: Musikpädagogische Perspektiven auf soziale und kulturelle Transformationsprozesse* (pp. 36–43). Hochschule für Musik Franz Liszt Weimarr. doi:10.25656/01:32533.

Kratus, J. (2019). A return to amateurism in music education. *Music Educators Journal, 106*(1), 31–37. doi:10.1177/0027432119856870.

Norton, K. (2016). *Singing and wellbeing: Ancient wisdom, modern proof.* Routledge.

O'Grady, L., & McFerran, K. (2007). Community music therapy and its relationship to community music: Where does it end? *Nordic Journal of Music Therapy, 16*(1), 14–26. doi:10.1080/08098130709478170.

Proctor, S., & DeNora, T. (2022). Musical care in adulthood: Sounding our way through the landscape. In N. Spiro & K. R. Sanfilippo (eds), *Collaborative insights: Interdisciplinary perspectives on musical care throughout the life course* (pp. 86–101). Oxford University Press.

Renshaw, P. (2013). Being in-tune: A provocation paper. https://static1.squarespace.com/static/5525556ae4b0256f7f48c6ab/t/574ee8eb555986bd012e5b53/1464789229569/Renshaw%2C+Being+in+Tune%2C+ch.+4%2C+synergy+between+social+and+artisticgoals.pdf.

Sattler, G. (2023). Community music and facilitative leadership: Relationship, relevance and respect. www.churchilltrust.com.au/project/to-evaluate-international-best-practice-musical-inclusion-models-for-application-in-australia/.

Shaughnessy, C., Hall, A., & Perkins, R. (2024). Becoming the right musician for the job: Versatility, connectedness, and professional identities during personalized, online music-making in hospital maternity wards. *Musicae Scientiae, 28*(1), 58–75. doi:10.1177/10298649231165028.

Shilton, D., Passmore, S., & Savage, P. E. (2023). Group singing is globally dominant and associated with social context. *Royal Society Open Science, 10*(9), article 230562. doi:10.1098/rsos.230562.

Spiro, N., Perkins, R., Kaye, S., Tymoszuk, U., Mason-Bertrand, A., Cossette, I., Glasser, S., & Williamon, A. (2021). The effects of COVID-19 lockdown 1.0 on working patterns, income, and wellbeing among performing arts professionals in the United Kingdom (April–June 2020). *Frontiers in Psychology, 11.* www.frontiersin.org/articles/10.3389/fpsyg.2020.594086.

Spiro, N., et al. (2023). Perspectives on musical care throughout the life course: Introducing the musical care international network. *Music & Science, 6.* doi:10.1177/20592043231200553.

Spurk, D., & Straub, C. (2020). Flexible employment relationships and careers in times of the COVID-19 pandemic. *Journal of Vocational Behavior, 119,* article 103435. doi:10.1016/j.jvb.2020.103435.

Teague, A., & Smith, G. D. (2015). Portfolio careers and work-life balance among musicians: An initial study into implications for higher music education. *British Journal of Music Education, 32*(2), 177–193. doi:10.1017/S0265051715000121.

Turino, T. (2008). *Music as social life: The politics of participation.* University of Chicago Press.

Westerlund, H., & Karttunen, S. (2024). The protean music career as a sociopolitical orientation: The mutually integrated, non-hierarchical work values of socially engaged musicians. *Musicae Scientiae, 28*(3), 502–519. doi:10.1177/10298649231222548.

Willingham, L., & Carruthers, G. (2018). Community music in higher education. In B.-L. Bartleet & L. Higgins (eds), *The Oxford handbook of community music* (pp. 595–616). Oxford University Press.

Zhang, J. D., Susino, M., McPherson, G. E., & Schubert, E. (2020). The definition of a musician in music psychology: A literature review and the six-year rule. *Psychology of Music, 48*(3), 389–409. doi:10.1177/0305735618804038.

2 Finding your forte

A positive leadership capability framework for musicians

Introduction

Kym, a highly trained and skilled jazz pianist and composer, sits at the piano. Her eyes are closed, and her body moves effortlessly, rising and falling subtly with the phrasing of the music. She is completely immersed in the sound, sometimes so much so, that she loses track of time.

But Kym is not in a dimly lit jazz club. She's in a community hall, surrounded by a diverse group of singers. This is no ordinary choir; it's a social inclusion choir, where people from all walks of life come together to find connection through music. As Kym's fingers dance across the keys, playing an arrangement she's crafted just for this group, she notices the singers start to "create something in that space ... a spark of electricity". Kym loves to lead her group from the piano. She has no singing training, but that's ok, because that means in one very important respect, she is just like everyone else in the group. Kym simply loves singing and the joy it brings to others.

Kym Dillon is an inspiring positive music leader who has taken her jazz training and compositional skills and applied them in an entirely new context, creating a unique approach to music leadership. As we saw at the end of the last chapter, Kym is motivated to do her community work because she "loves music". As Kym says, "That's what's at the heart of the magic of these sessions".

Kym's story shows that the very skills that make her an outstanding jazz musician—adaptability, creativity, and the ability to connect with an audience—are the same skills that make her an exceptional music leader.

Kym is a great example of self-leadership because she has a strong self-awareness of what matters to her, and how she can apply her strengths in different contexts to share her love of connecting through music with others. Self-leadership is about knowing yourself inside out and taking charge of your life to reach your goals, both in music and beyond. When viewed through the lens of positive psychology, self-leadership means "the capacity to identify and apply one's signature strengths to initiate, maintain, or sustain self-influencing behaviors" (Du Plessis, 2019, p. 445).

DOI: 10.4324/9781003426509-4

This chapter challenges you to cultivate your self-leadership beyond the discipline of the practice room and apply it to other aspects of your personal and professional life. While traditional music education excels at honing your technical skills, it often overlooks this crucial aspect of personal development. The ideas and exercises that follow will push you to think differently about your skills and how you can apply them in new, potentially challenging ways.

Self-leadership requires a high degree of self-awareness. A self-aware person deeply understands their emotions, drives, goals, needs, strengths, values, and weaknesses (Goleman, 2013). Self-leadership is an ongoing process of continuous monitoring and reflection to gain control over how we think and feel and then aligning this with what we do in our work (Gambill & Carbonara, 2021).

For musicians wanting to harness the power of music for social connection, developing this keen sense of self-awareness is crucial. It forms the foundation for doing "good work", by which we mean work that is excellent, engaging, and ethical (Gardner et al., 2001; Gardner, 2007). Self-leadership empowers us to take responsibility for our own work roles and to optimise our potential by aligning our signature strengths, personal values, and motivations for purposeful and meaningful living (Du Plessis, 2019).

When we change ourselves for the better through self-leadership, others inevitably benefit (Friedman, 2008). Our increased fulfilment and positive energy can inspire those around us, creating a ripple effect of positive change (Cameron, 2018, 2021).

In the following sections, we'll explore both the theoretical foundations of self-leadership and its practical applications, providing you with the tools to navigate change, expand your impact, and find greater fulfilment in your music practice.

The roots of self-leadership

While self-leadership began as a workplace practice, it has evolved into a powerful tool for personal development (Imru-Mathieu, 2018) and is particularly relevant for musicians navigating the complexity of their careers. Self-leadership has its roots in transformational leadership, an approach that focuses on inspiring and motivating others to achieve higher levels of performance and personal growth. Transformational leadership challenges traditional hierarchical models, viewing leadership as a collaborative process rather than an exercise of power over others (Haslam et al., 2020). For musicians, this shift in perspective can be transformative, encouraging a more collaborative and empowering approach to music making and leadership.

At the core of self-leadership is the development of self-awareness, a critical skill for musicians seeking to enhance their artistry, expand their impact, and thoughtfully navigate their careers. By understanding and applying these self-leadership principles, musicians can take greater control of their professional development, creative processes, and career trajectories.

RESONANCE—Self-awareness

Musician and community choir leader Emma Dean shares how her self-awareness has grown and evolved over time. When reflecting on her practice, Emma recognises the importance of having the language to express the values that inform our work as musicians and music leaders:

> When I was younger, I listened a lot to the "should". Like, "You should do this because you're really good at that". That message was the loudest for me. If you're not in the spotlight, then you're not doing well enough or you've failed. There was always that sense of comparison; that I'm not doing enough, or I'm not doing well enough, or I'm not good enough. I didn't stop to think about my values. I was just following the path that I thought I should follow to be a successful musician.
>
> I think the lightbulb moment was being in New York and realising I missed community. I couldn't connect in the way that I wanted to. I definitely redefined what "making it" meant. I think that naturally links into what my values are. They've remained pretty constant since. My personal values are community and connection, creativity, health of all types, kindness, and sustainability.

A positive framework for self-leadership

Now that we've considered the roots of self-leadership, let's explore a framework that can help musicians harness its power. We'll use the positive self-leadership capability framework developed by Marieta Du Plessis (2019), which combines positive psychology with self-leadership principles. Before we go into the specifics of the framework, let's engage in a brief self-reflection exercise to begin building your self-awareness.

The following exercise is adapted from *Getting it Right When it Matters Most: Self-Leadership for Work and Life* (2021) by Tony Gambill and Scott Carbonara. To begin, consider the following statements:

1   I can easily articulate my goals and ambitions.
2   I can describe the environment that brings out my Best Self.
3   I can describe the environment that brings out my Worst Self.
4   I understand my strengths and how to use them to achieve my goals.
5   I understand my weaknesses and how they can get in the way of achieving my goals.
6   I can name the personal values I believe in most.
7   I consider these personal values when taking action.
8   I prioritise self-care to address my most basic needs.
9   I am aware of when my most fundamental needs are not being met.

How easy (or difficult) were these prompts? Did you struggle to articulate your position? Were some questions easier to answer to than others?

If you struggled to respond to some of these prompts, don't worry! The framework which follows will help you gain a clearer understanding of yourself, so that you can lead yourself in a direction which is fulfilling, meaningful and impactful.

Unlike traditional leadership models that focus on formal roles and addressing weaknesses, Du Plessis's positive self-leadership framework (Du Plessis, 2019) emphasises identifying and developing your individual strengths. This approach can enhance your adaptability and versatility, and help you anticipate and overcome challenges. It can also help you align your strengths with good work, which ultimately supports your wellbeing. This framework is all about positioning you as an effective leader of others, using self-leadership as the foundation of your practice.

Du Plessis's framework is based on Stander and van Zyl's (2019) strengths capability framework. Du Plessis's framework consists of four dynamically related core capabilities, each of which is aligned with different competencies (Table 2.1).

While a *capability* refers to the potential ability to perform, a *competency* refers to a demonstrated ability. A capability is more abstract in nature, while competency is concrete and observable. For example, character strengths are a capability in that we have the potential to use our strengths at any given time, whereas strengths-based decision-making is the observable behaviour of using our strengths to inform our decisions.

Character strengths

The first core capability in Du Plessis's positive self-leadership framework is identifying and drawing on your "character strengths" (Du Plessis, 2019). Character strengths are positive traits that are fulfilling and morally valued, and which enable individuals to thrive (Boniwell & Tunariu, 2019). For musicians, understanding and leveraging these strengths can significantly enhance both performance and wellbeing.

Table 2.1 Positive self-leadership capability model.

Core capabilities	Aligned competencies
Character strengths	Strengths-based decision-making
	Strengths-based recovery
Interests and aspirations	Purposeful vision
	Authentic engagement
Abilities and talents	Psychological capital
	Job crafting
	Mindfulness
Environmental strengths	High-quality connections

Source: adapted from Du Plessis (2019)

In their book *Positive Psychology for Musicians: Character Strengths*, Raina Murnak and Nancy Kirsner emphasise the value of recognising your character strengths:

> Learning your character strengths will give you a lens and language of positivity that will shift your mindset from wrong to strong. In other words, they will facilitate moving you into a growth/open mindset. This helps you become a better, more resilient, and more confident version of yourself.
>
> (Murnak & Kirsner, 2023, p. 1)

The most widely recognised assessment tool is the Values in Action (VIA) survey of character strengths, which identifies 24 character strengths, classified into six core virtues (Peterson & Seligman, 2004). Your top five are considered your "signature strengths" (Table 2.2).

The evidence for the benefits of recognising and using your character strengths is extensive. Murnak and Kirsner (2023) summarise research showing that leveraging your strengths enhances overall wellbeing by fostering positive emotions, work engagement, relationship building, and a sense of meaningful contribution. Using your strengths can help you make better progress towards your goals, leading to greater fulfilment and life satisfaction (Linley et al., 2012). For musicians, this approach offers a powerful way to boost performance, amplify creativity, and enhance satisfaction in practice.

To identify and leverage your character strengths:

1 Take the free VIA survey at www.viacharacter.org.
2 Reflect on how your top strengths have manifested in your musical journey.
3 Build "strengths fluency" by spotting strengths in yourself and others.

Murnak and Kirsner (2023) stress that nothing is too small to notice when identifying your strengths in action. As the pair suggest, "Give yourself the gift of spending time to learn and spot your own character strengths. This will develop 'strengths fluency'. This secret superpower will light up your life and the lives of others you share it with" (Murnak & Kirsner, 2023, p. 10).

Table 2.2 Virtues and character strengths in positive psychology.

Virtues	Character strengths
Wisdom and Knowledge	creativity, curiosity, love of learning, open-mindedness, perspective
Humanity	kindness, love, social intelligence
Justice	fairness, leadership, teamwork
Courage	bravery, enthusiasm, integrity, perseverance
Temperance	forgiveness, humility, prudence, self-control
Transcendence	appreciation of beauty and excellence, gratitude, humour, optimism, purpose

Source: Peterson and Seligman (2004)

RESONANCE—Strengths fluency in action

Jane York's approach to music leadership demonstrates "strengths fluency" in action, illustrating how character strengths can become powerful leadership tools within the community music setting. While traditional musical leadership often emphasises projecting expertise and establishing authority, Jane identifies love, learning, and humour as three crucial strengths for singing leaders. As Jane explains, "I'm not afraid to make a mistake publicly". In fact, Jane will say to her singing group, "We're going to have a go at it; make a loud mistake please!" Jane says her willingness to make mistakes and to actively encourage mistake making demonstrates the reality of "the learning process", which always involves "trying, trying, trying" and "getting a little bit better through that act". Jane is not afraid to appear silly in front of her group. Quite the contrary, Jane actively embraces silliness as a way to lower the stakes for her singers, and to encourage their genuine engagement with learning.

Without a doubt, Jane's approach outlined in the RESONANCE box challenges conventional notions of musical expertise. Rather than positioning herself as an infallible expert, Jane models vulnerability through public risk-taking, demonstrating a true love of learning and perseverance. Jane says that when the leader demonstrates comfort with imperfection and a willingness to "try again", participants feel safer taking risks themselves. Jane pairs this perseverance with humour—another one of the 24 VIA character strengths—to further enhance group learning. Humour serves multiple functions here: it diffuses tension around making mistakes, builds connection between group members, and maintains a sense of fun even when facing the challenges of learning new skills. This combination of perseverance and humour creates an environment where participants can authentically engage with learning without fear of failure or judgment.

However, Jane goes on to explain that leaders need to balance vulnerability with bravery. While embracing vulnerability, leaders must also project confidence in handling uncertainty. Jane explains that "If our leader's nervous or unsure, is skittish, *we* start to get nervous. There needs to be confidence and bravery to be okay with [the uncertainty of the learning] process". This combination of vulnerability and bravery creates what Jane calls "the space of play" where genuine transformation can occur. She notes that while serious issues may arise during sessions, ultimately "when we make music together, it's an act of play". Holding this space requires the confidence to know that "whatever happens is going to be fine" while maintaining the flexibility to respond in the moment. For Jane, music leaders, who often have to adapt to wildly different contexts, need to be "incredibly open to figuring it out as [they] go". In character strength terms, Jane is identifying curiosity and open-mindedness as keys to her style of music leadership.

Jane's practice demonstrates how positive music leaders can leverage their strengths—such as curiosity, bravery, love of learning, and humour—to help others flourish. Jane acknowledges that she too is always learning: "every session is a learning opportunity as a leader". By being genuine about both the challenges and joys of learning, she creates conditions where group members feel supported to grow at their own pace. Jane's strengths-based leadership fosters an environment of collective learning and mutual support.

Competencies—Strengths-based decision-making and recovery

Understanding your strengths can support better decision-making and recovery from setbacks. For example, understanding that one of your signature strengths is teamwork will help you decide whether an opportunity to work completely independently is going to be right for you. Understanding strengths can help us make informed choices which leads to greater satisfaction in the long term. Importantly, understanding our strengths can help us build resilience when faced with challenges. It provides a foundation of positive self-worth which can counterbalance negative thoughts or help us to take on feedback constructively; we are better able to reframe setbacks as opportunities for growth. Taking a strengths-based approach to both decision-making and setbacks makes us more adaptable, flexible, and resilient.

QUESTIONS FOR REFLECTION

1 What are your top five strengths—your signature strengths? How do they align with the work you currently do in music? Could the alignment be stronger?
2 How do you see awareness of your strengths helping you to confront challenges in your work?
3 What is the key motivator for you in your current work? Is that motivation in alignment with your signature strengths?

Aspirations, interests, and values

The second core capability in Du Plessis's positive self-leadership framework is identifying your aspirations, interests, and values (Du Plessis, 2019). When we are interested in something, we feel more motivated to pursue related longer-term goals and aspirations. Similarly, our values are important drivers of our actions, and because they can be shaped unconsciously by culture and society, values require our conscious attention to ensure they truly align with our most cherished beliefs. For example, capitalist societies encourage the valuing of things over people. When we are born into such a society, it may be some time before we realise that we hold the belief that material possessions and wealth are very important to our happiness. However, when we truly reflect on this belief, we may realise it runs counter to our values of fairness, freedom, or adventure. When we act in accordance with the values of others rather than our own, we feel out of alignment and dissatisfied. Sometimes acting outside of our values can have serious consequences for our mental health.

RESONANCE—Balancing values and challenges

Musician Kym Dillon, who leads choirs for people who are socially isolated, has a strong sense of the core values that drive her work: love of music and a belief in the importance of inclusion. It is important to Kym that she creates a "safe space" in her singing groups where everyone feels included, even though this can present its own challenges. For instance, when a participant has a particularly powerful voice that overwhelms others, Kym must balance her value of inclusion with the group's collective experience. Rather than asking someone to "sing better" or stop singing altogether, she adopts a strengths-based approach:

> I'll have a chat with the person and tell them they have a really powerful, strong sound, which not everyone else has. Then, I explain that part of choir is about managing that power so all voices can form a whole together.

This careful framing acknowledges the singer's strength while gently guiding them toward more balanced participation. Kym's approach demonstrates how positive music leaders can uphold their values even when faced with practical challenges, finding ways to honour both individual expression and group cohesion.

Kym's practice shows that having a purposeful vision for our work drives motivation and aligns with the eudaimonic view of wellbeing, which emphasises finding significance through realising one's potential, and engaging in pursuits that extend beyond personal interests (Du Plessis, 2019; Ryff & Singer, 2008).

Competencies—Purposeful vision and authentic engagement

When we undertake tasks based on our strengths, values, and interests, we are much more likely to become fully engaged and enter a state of flow. Flow is a state of "optimal experience" where we lose track of time, feel present in the moment, and become completely absorbed in the task at hand; we have focused concentration; we feel playful and that our task is effortless (Csikszentmihalyi, 2002).

The following quotes from a study by Forbes and Bartlett (2020) offer some examples of how music leaders describe the experience of flow. In this study, music leaders of various community singing groups for health and wellbeing reported how it feels to engage in work which aligns with their strengths and personal mission to serve others:

- "I feel intensely proud of their [the participants'] work."
- "That's priceless to me—that I've actually made a wee bit of difference, just because I've been singing."

- "I've made a good choice here [about the work]."
- "I feel really well suited to [the work]."
- "I'm the most creative and the best musician I can be."
- "Choir leading aligns [all my interests]."
- "[The work] makes sense of the skills I have."
- "[I'm] using the gifts I have and it's to the advantage of these people."
- "At this phase of my life, at my age, with my skill base, I don't think there's anything that would suit me better."
- "I'm finally here and this is working, and I'm really good at it and it's really cool."

From these music leaders' descriptions, when aspirations, interests, and values align, work becomes highly engaging and meaningful. Finding opportunities to experience flow can also play a role in musicians' self-care, as we will see in Chapter 3.

Another study, this time involving Finnish musicians working in socially engaged contexts, revealed how they found participatory music rewarding. Their work in participatory music was artistically liberating and not driven by traditional extrinsic values of status and economic gain. Instead of separating musical and social values, these musicians saw social values as integral to what makes music meaningful. As one musician, Liisa, reflected, "I've started to think a lot about the question of value, what we really value and why ... when in a way something different can also sound pretty good ... what is the motive behind the making?" (Westerlund & Karttunen, 2024, p. 8). Many participants in the study saw their role within socially engaged practice as one of righting the wrongs of music education. For example, one participant, Susanna, explained, "There are many people in this country who may have a somewhat traumatised relationship with their own music making, having been told that you're the one who can't sing" (Westerlund & Karttunen, 2024, p. 9). By blurring the lines between aesthetic and social values, these musicians created work that was both "artistically and personally rewarding" (Westerlund & Karttunen, 2024, p. 1).

As Graham's story in the box below demonstrates, increasing self-awareness of your genuine interests, sense of direction in life, and core values is an important competency for positive self-leadership.

RESONANCE—Striving for connection

In both studies mentioned above, music leaders had a purposeful vision that aligned with their aspirations, interests, and values. Musical inclusion advocate Graham Sattler, who is the CEO of the Christchurch Symphony Orchestra, describes how throughout his career, he has been drawn to working in contexts where he receives immediate, direct feedback from others. He's delivered community programs in regional areas in response to community interest and received direct feedback on how meaningful the programs were:

I'm getting direct feedback about the meaning that participatory music making has, and it's not just from conservatorium students with a sense of a pathway. It's not just musicians who feed off this wonderful experience, but doctors, builders, whoever … members of the community keep telling me how meaningful it is … It's the striving for absolutely direct connection [with others] so that I can communicate what I am 100 per cent convinced about, which is the value and values of musical participation.

Receiving direct feedback about the power of community music has spurred Graham to pursue his life's work and charged him with a purposeful mission—to serve others through music.

QUESTIONS FOR REFLECTION

1   What aspects of your music practice interest you the most?
2   What aspects of your music practice interest you the least?
3   Where do you want your music career to take you? What is your long-term career vision?
4   Do you seek financial security? Recognition and reward? Do you wish to be of service to others?
5   Are your interests and aspirations currently being nurtured by the work you do?
6   Find a list of values online and choose your top five. How do these values align with your work? Your personal life?
7   When it comes to making music, what do you value most?
8   Is your current work in music allowing you to live according to your values? Do you experience authentic engagement or flow? If the answer is no, what other work contexts would be more aligned with your values?

Abilities and talents

The third core capability in Du Plessis's positive self-leadership framework is identifying and exploiting your unique abilities and talents (Du Plessis, 2019). For musicians, one's abilities and talents are typically conceived as the skills acquired through training and practice. Many professional musicians dedicate years to mastering their craft and in the process commit to lifelong learning. The topic of developing musical abilities and talents is beyond the scope of this book, so in this section we will focus on the related competencies of job crafting and building psychological capital (Du Plessis, 2019).

Competencies—Job crafting and psychological capital

Job crafting is a concept from management literature that refers to the process of employees—or in this case, musicians—redesigning aspects of their jobs to better align with their abilities and talents (Wrzesniewski & Dutton, 2001). By modifying tasks, relationships, and perceptions of their work, musicians can find greater meaning, engagement, and satisfaction.

Closely related to job crafting is the concept of psychological capital (PsyCap) (Luthans et al., 2007a, 2007b). PsyCap is defined as a positive state of psychological development characterised by:

1   Confidence (self-efficacy) to succeed at challenging tasks.
2   Positive attribution (optimism) about succeeding now and in the future.
3   Perseverance toward goals (hope).
4   Resilience in the face of adversity.

Research has shown that PsyCap is related to various positive work outcomes, such as increased engagement at work and improved job satisfaction and performance (Luthans et al., 2007a).

Many musicians don't work within organisations, but this doesn't mean they can't actively engage in job crafting to build their PsyCap. Whereas many employees may be actively supported within an organisation to enact these types of principles to purposefully shape their work, musicians (especially those working as sole-traders or contractors) must undertake these activities independently, as a form of self-leadership. However, this doesn't mean you need to undertake this work in isolation. Consider how you might collaborate with a trusted friend or mentor to work through these approaches to align your abilities and talents with your work portfolio.

QUESTIONS FOR REFLECTION

1   What are your top abilities and talents as a musician? What are your top abilities and talents as a leader?
2   How could you reshape your current musical roles to better align with your abilities and talents, aspirations, interests, strengths, and values? (Job crafting)
3   As a musician, what aspects of your work bring you the most satisfaction? How can you build more satisfaction? (Job crafting)
4   Think of a challenging situation in your music career. How confident were you in your ability to overcome it? How could you build this confidence for future challenges? (PsyCap—Self-efficacy)
5   How do you maintain optimism about your music career, especially during setbacks? (PsyCap—Optimism)
6   What are your long-term goals as a musician? How do you break these down into achievable steps? What systems do you have in place to move towards these goals? (PsyCap—Hope)
7   Recall a time when you faced a significant obstacle in your music career. How did you bounce back? What did you learn from this experience? (PsyCap—Resilience)
8   How can you use your unique abilities and talents to create new opportunities for yourself as a music leader?

RESONANCE—Crafting musical opportunities

Australian musician Gillian Howell actively shaped her career by strategically pitching her unique skill to potential funders and employers. After studying in the UK and working in post-war Bosnia, she returned to Australia with a clear vision:

> I pitched myself at orchestras ... because I'd seen that's where the opportunities were in the UK. I'd also had this extraordinary experience working in Bosnia after the war. I was really interested in music as a space of storytelling, gentleness, laughter, and playfulness, particularly when those opportunities had been completely disrupted in children's lives.

Gillian went on to work extensively in English language schools, creating music projects that supported children in transition. Using improvisation and collaborative composition, Gillian developed processes that brought together musicians of different abilities. Rather than waiting for opportunities to arise, she consciously crafted a career that aligned her diverse experiences and skills with organisational needs. As Gillian explains, "I didn't fall into [the work]. I saw it as a very specific set of training that I'd had, opportunities that I wanted to create for other musicians."

Gillian's experience shows how musicians can proactively shape their careers by leveraging unique experiences, identifying market opportunities, and creating innovative roles that serve community needs.

Gillian also demonstrates self-awareness of her strengths:

> I've got a pretty high threshold for ambiguity and for sitting in an ambiguous space for a long period of time, trusting in process and knowing that, if we keep working in a certain way then we're going to get somewhere ... I don't have a strong need to control the creative direction or the creative process. Processes are very important to me. I trust in the process to take us to an outcome that is going to be exactly what it needs to be and exactly right if we followed a good process, a process with integrity.

Environmental strengths

The fourth capability in Du Plessis's positive self-leadership framework is the ability to draw on external resources (Du Plessis, 2019). This capability echoes the broadest level of the leader's triple focus (leading self, others, and contextual awareness), namely the ability to keep the bigger picture in mind while also focusing on yourself and those you lead (Goleman, 2013; Goleman & Senge, 2014). Many musicians work in isolation, with no formal requirements for ongoing professional development or network engagement. For musicians, establishing these crucial professional relationships requires proactive self-leadership.

This might involve connecting to professional associations or networks, establishing mentoring relationships with experienced practitioners, engaging with existing services and organisations that are aligned with one's interests and values, or conducting ongoing "environmental scanning" to identify growth opportunities. For instance, a musician aspiring to work with people with disabilities might approach other creative artists or community workers to establish mentoring relationships. As Du Plessis (2019) points out, these "high quality connections" can be with others within your field, or beyond. For positive music leaders, reaching out to allied health professionals who are supportive of the arts' role in health could be a source of valuable connection.

Competency—High-quality connections

Professional networks play a vital role in building high-quality connections. The Singing for Health Network is a professional organisation based in the UK that connects people involved or interested in health-focused singing programs. Its membership includes singing leaders, researchers, and healthcare professionals from both the UK and internationally. The network bridges research and practical application, allowing members to share their experiences and discover new opportunities for learning and collaboration.

One important role of the network is research translation for practitioners. This means that singing for health practitioners can have access to the latest research on effective practice and continuously evolve and improve their practice. One of the most important features of the network is the partnership between practitioners, researchers, and those who straddle both worlds.

You can learn more about the Singing for Health Network at www.singing forhealthnetwork.co.uk.

QUESTIONS FOR REFLECTION

1   What professional networks or associations are relevant to your musical interests? How could you engage more actively with them to form "high-quality connections"?
2   Who do you admire in and beyond your field? How might you approach them for mentorship or guidance?
3   What community organisations align with your musical aspirations? How could you initiate partnerships with them?
4   How do you stay informed about new opportunities in your field?
5   What external resources have you not yet tapped into that could enhance your musical career and build new opportunities for working in community?

Putting self-leadership into practice

To recap, the key capabilities of the positive self-leadership framework are identifying your abilities and talents, character strengths, interests, aspirations and values, and understanding the strengths in your environments. Implementing the positive self-leadership capability framework involves three phases:

1 Building (self) awareness of each capability.
2 Developing competence and increasing confidence in each self-leadership capability.
3 Sustaining the self-leadership competencies over the long term (Du Plessis, 2019).

As you can see, there is much to consider when it comes to positive self-leadership! Ongoing reflection and commitment is needed to put positive self-leadership into practice. This is not a "one and done" process! It is important to:

- Regularly reflect on your abilities and talents, character strengths, and values, as well as the environmental resources available to you.
- Look for opportunities to apply your strengths in new ways within your music practice.
- Seek feedback from mentors or peers to gain different perspectives on your strengths and to identify potential blind spots.
- Continuously update your self-leadership strategies as you grow, and as your circumstances change.

Remember, developing self-leadership is an ongoing journey, not a destination. By consistently applying the capability framework in this chapter, you can craft a more fulfilling and impactful musical practice that aligns with your unique profile.

RESONANCE—Finding your path

Self-leadership is an intentional practice, and not without challenges. However, finding the path that is aligned with your aspirations, values, and strengths is vitally important to our longer-term wellbeing as musicians (and as humans!). Musician Emma Dean reflects:

> Get rid of the noise and what everyone tells you you should be doing. Figure out, or feel into, what brings you the most joy. Go with your curiosity and what lights you up. That's really hard, I think. It sounds so easy, but it is really hard. Because sometimes, what makes you happy is not the most glamourous path. Sometimes it's not the one where your name's in lights. But it's what makes you happy and that's what I find myself getting closer to.

Singing for health practitioner-researcher Emily Foulkes reflects on the alignment of her work with her values, and the impact that synergy has on her personally:

I think ultimately it's about helping people and supporting people. I really believe that everybody should have the opportunity to explore their creativity and to be able to progress and discover that they can do things that they never thought they could do. I think that for me, just that passion of seeing the transformation, and helping people, and facilitating that journey, is just incredible. It's an incredible honour. That's what drives me.

Heartfulness as character strengths in action

The 24 character strengths have been described as a "language of the heart" and a motivating force "to improve, connect, to assist, and to be good" (Niemiec, 2017, p. 124). Thus, an over-arching framework for putting character strengths into action is "heartfulness" (Niemiec, 2017), which means to "take meaningful action with our character strengths to promote common goodness" (Niemiec, 2017, p. 124). As Niemiec explains:

Heartfulness involves the meaningful application of character strengths to bring benefit to the world. Mindfulness catalyzes heartfulness. When we are mindful, we are present to ourselves and others. When we are heartful, we are expressing our best strengths within ourselves or directly to others. Mindfulness and heartfulness create the ultimate virtuous circle that synergizes good within us and around us.

(Niemiec, 2017, p. 128)

There is a clear connection here between heartfulness—using your character strengths to benefit the world—and the idea of "good work", which was first mentioned in the "Overture" chapter. You may recall that "good work" is "work that is of *excellent technical quality,* work that is *ethically pursued and socially responsible,* and work that is *engaging, enjoyable, and feels good*" (Gardner, 2007, p. 5; emphasis in original; see also Gardner et al., 2001). Taking action "from the heart" produces work that is of high quality and is pursued for "the right reasons", which, importantly, feels good! Good work—heartful work—is good for others but it is also good for us.

RESONANCE — Heartfulness

What does heartfulness look like in practice? Emily Foulkes, the director of the Singing for Health Network, describes how she invokes heartfulness with her singing groups:

At the start of each session, we begin with social connection through guided sharing. Participants are invited to share something they love, enjoy, or find meaningful—like a favourite place, song, or musical piece.

This practice activates what we call "heartfulness"—dropping into a space of connection, gratitude, and positive intention.

While we validate when people need to express frustrations (like healthcare challenges), we gently guide mindsets toward positive action: "What can we do right now? What do we feel grateful for?" This is especially important for participants with chronic health conditions who often feel unheard or invalidated.

We use metaphor extensively to help people express themselves. Instead of asking directly how they're feeling, we might ask, "If you were to describe how you're feeling right now as a landscape, what landscape would it be?" or "What genre of music are you feeling like?" This approach helps gauge where people are emotionally, while avoiding negative language. For example, one woman described feeling like she was "walking through quicksand"—an image that resonated with others without explicitly focusing on pain or limitations.

Emily draws on her own heartfulness—her own strengths in action— when leading her singing for health groups. How do we know this? Because Emily is fully engaged when she leads her singing groups:

> I never really knew what flow was until I started doing this work and finding my way with it and feeling, as I grew in confidence with it. I still struggle with singing, performing to sing in front of others, but when I'm facilitating a singing group, I don't have any problem at all. No problem at all. It's like I just step into something completely different. It's just amazing.

Importantly, heartfulness is both interpersonal and *intra*personal—that is, we act from heartfulness towards others and ourselves (Niemiec, 2017). This means that our strengths "can and should be directed to ourselves and it's anything but selfish to do so because it makes us stronger and hence more available and present to others" (Niemiec, 2017, p. 127).

In the next chapter, we will explore how Emily's experience of flow is contributing to her own sense of wellbeing. We will explore a positive psychology framework to understand what contributes to wellbeing (the PERMA model), and we'll discuss evidence-based practices to support our wellbeing as leaders (self-care). By taking care of ourselves, we are in a better position to help others thrive, flourish, and connect.

RESONANCE—Remaining curious

The final word on self-leadership for this chapter goes to community music practitioner Allison Girvan: "If you can embody one word, it's curiosity … It keeps you from knowing in advance what's going to happen." This openness to experience becomes a powerful practice, removing judgment, and creating space for growth. "If you're just wondering what's going to happen", Girvan notes, "something happens, and you can't say that was wrong because the goal was to be curious ... Whatever happens then is neither right nor wrong, it's just more information."

As you begin your journey of positive self-leadership, try to cultivate this spirit of curiosity. Like Allison, stay open to discovering new aspects of yourself, your practice, and your potential to create positive change through music. The path of self-leadership, like music itself, unfolds most beautifully when we remain genuinely curious about what might emerge.

Refrain

As we've explored throughout this chapter, self-leadership is a powerful tool for musicians looking to expand their impact, find greater fulfilment, and navigate the ever-changing landscape of music practice. By developing a deep understanding of your character strengths, interests, aspirations, values, abilities and talents, and environmental resources (Du Plessis, 2019), you're equipping yourself with the self-awareness needed to lead yourself effectively. Remember, self-leadership is not about perfection, but about continuous growth and alignment. It's about making conscious choices that reflect your authentic self and your highest aspirations. The journey of self-leadership is ongoing, requiring regular reflection, adjustment, and commitment, but the rewards are great. By cultivating self-leadership, you're not just becoming a better musician; you're becoming a more impactful leader, capable of using your musical gifts to create positive change in the world.

Call and response

You've been asked to reflect a lot throughout this chapter, so no more questions! Instead, here's a bonus tool for building self-awareness. This tool reflects Allison Girvan's advice that we should always remain curious and reserve judgment.

The ABCD choice process

As you begin to apply the self-leadership principles we've discussed, you may find yourself in situations where you need to make quick decisions under stress. The ABCD choice process is a valuable tool for maintaining self-awareness and exercising self-leadership in the moment.

This useful shortcut process comes from the book, *Change Your Questions, Change Your Life* by Marilee Adams (2010). It is designed to develop self-awareness moment to moment:

> Become **A**ware of your mindset, taking a moment to step back and **B**reathe, break, back off, getting **C**urious about yourself, and **D**eciding what to do next.

The next time you find yourself losing your cool, becoming anxious, or even angry, see if you can time a moment to run through the ABCD choice process. The more often you do this, the deeper your self-awareness will become.

References

Adams, M. (2010). *Change your questions, change your life*. ReadHowYouWant.

Boniwell, I., & Tunariu, A. D. (2019). *Positive psychology: Theory, research and applications*. McGraw-Hill Education.

Cameron, K. S. (2018). *Positive leadership: Strategies for extraordinary performance* (2nd edition). Berrett-Koehler.

Cameron, K. S. (2021). *Positively energizing leadership: Virtuous actions and relationships that create high performance* (1st edition). Berrett-Koehler.

Csikszentmihalyi, M. (2002). *Flow: The classic work on how to achieve happiness* (revised edition). Rider.

Du Plessis, M. (2019). Positive self-leadership: A framework for professional leadership development. In L. E. van Zyl & S.RothmannSr (eds), *Theoretical approaches to multicultural positive psychological interventions* (pp. 445–461). Springer. doi:10.1007/978-3-030-20583-6_20.

Forbes, M., & Bartlett, I. (2020). "This circle of joy": Meaningful musicians' work and the benefits of facilitating singing groups. *Music Education Research, 22*(5), 555–568. doi:10.1080/14613808.2020.1841131.

Friedman, S. D. (2008). *Total leadership*. Harvard Business Review Press.

Gambill, T., & Carbonara, S. (2021). *Getting it right when it matters most: Self-leadership for work and life*. Business Expert Press.

Gardner, H. (ed.). (2007). *Responsibility at work*. Jossey-Bass.

Gardner, H., Csikszentmihalyi, M., & Damon, W. (2001). *Good work: When excellence and ethics meet*. Basic Books.

Goleman, D. (2013). *What makes a leader a leader: Why emotional intelligence matters*. More Than Sound.

Goleman, D., & Senge, P. (2014). *The triple focus: A new approach to education*. More Than Sound.

Haslam, S. A., Reicher, S., & Platow, M. J. (2020). *The new psychology of leadership: Identity, influence and power*. Routledge.

Imru-Mathieu, S. (2018). Self-leadership, a buzz word or science?9 October. www.leaderstoday.co/2017/07/10/self-leadership-a-buzz-word-or-science26a2fa68.

Linley, P. A., Nielsen, K. M., Gillett, R., & Biswas-Diener, R. (2012). Using signature strengths in pursuit of goals: Effects on goal progress, need satisfaction, and well-being, and implications for coaching psychologists. *International Coaching Psychology Review, 5*(1), 6–15.

Luthans, F., Avolio, B. J., Avey, J. B., & Norman, S. M. (2007a). Positive psychological capital: Measurement and relationship with performance and satisfaction. *Personnel Psychology, 60*(3), 541–572. doi:10.1111/j.1744-6570.2007.00083.x.

Luthans, F., Youssef, C. M., & Avolio, B. J. (2007b). *Psychological capital: Developing the human competitive edge*. Oxford University Press.

Murnak, R., & Kirsner, N. (2023). *Positive psychology for music professionals: Character strengths*. Routledge.

Niemiec, R. M. (2017). On heartfulness. In M. A. White, G. R. Slemp, & A. S. Murray (eds), *Future directions in well-being: Education, organizations and policy* (pp. 123–128). Springer. doi:10.1007/978-3-319-56889-8_22.

Peterson, C., & Seligman, M. E. P. (2004). *Character strengths and virtues: A handbook and classification*. American Psychological Association.

Ryff, C. D., & Singer, B. H. (2008). Know thyself and become what you are: A eudaimonic approach to psychological well-being. *Journal of Happiness Studies, 9*(1), 13–39.

Stander, F. W., & van Zyl, L. E. (2019). The Talent Development Centre (TDC) as an integrated leadership development and succession planning tool. In L. E. van Zyl & S. Rothmann (Eds.), *Positive psychological intervention design and protocols for multi-cultural contexts* (pp. 33–56). Springer.

Westerlund, H., & Karttunen, S. (2024). The protean music career as a sociopolitical orientation: The mutually integrated, non-hierarchical work values of socially engaged musicians. *Musicae Scientiae, 28*(3), 502–519. doi:10.1177/10298649231222548.

Wrzesniewski, A., & Dutton, J. E. (2001). Crafting a job: Revisioning employees as active crafters of their work. *Academy of Management Review, 26*(2), 179–201. doi:10.5465/amr.2001.4378011.

3 Tuning your instrument

Self-care for positive music leaders

Introduction

We've all heard the safety brief before flying that advises us to fit our own oxygen masks before helping others. While this analogy has merit, it falls short in one crucial aspect—self-care should be a regular practice, not a last-minute emergency measure (Donahue, 2018). When viewed as an ongoing habit, self-care is a vital component of self-leadership. We can't effectively lead others if we're not taking care of our own wellbeing.

It's important to note up front that the term "self-care" is sometimes viewed as problematic. Singing leader Jane York argues that self-care can reinforce individualistic, capitalist mindsets that place all responsibility on individuals rather than broader social structures. Jane explains, "Of course, we need to take care of ourselves, but not in the absence of community care. We need to do a lot less self-care if we have community in place." Jane's perspective reminds us that while individual practices are important, they should ideally exist within broader networks of community support. Jane also points out that "self-care" is complicated by the fact that leaders may sometimes be dealing with their own health issues. In the post-COVID-19 era, music leaders must make conscious choices about managing the physical health risks. This might mean making difficult decisions about indoor rehearsals, the implementation of safety measures, and the adaption of practice to protect both leader and participant wellbeing. Jane says that sometimes self-care means setting clear boundaries about what work you can safely undertake in a given space.

Positioned against this backdrop, and noting from the outset the complexity that surrounds self-care, this chapter has two primary goals:

1   to build music leaders' wellbeing literacy by providing an overview of the widely adopted PERMA model for wellbeing (Seligman, 2011); and
2   to equip music leaders with concrete self-care strategies based on both positive psychology and music leaders' practices.

These tools can support music leaders' wellbeing, establishing a strong foundation for leading others.

DOI: 10.4324/9781003426509-5

Positive psychology offers both a scientific framework and evidence-based interventions to enhance wellbeing. While the first sections in the chapter present an overview of the PERMA model and the importance of musicians' wellbeing, the later sections outline practical strategies for music leaders to support their wellbeing. These interventions are the "bottom line" for positive psychology, as its promise is only truly realised through personal experience (Seligman et al., 2005, p. 413).

If you find the number of Positive Psychology Interventions (PPIs) in this chapter overwhelming, start by choosing just one and test it out as a personal experiment. Experiencing these practices firsthand is the best way to understand their value. As a special bonus, if you completed the VIA character strengths survey from Chapter 2, you've already engaged in one of the most effective PPIs, which is evidenced to increase happiness and even decrease depressive symptoms (Seligman et al., 2005, as discussed in Boniwell & Tunariu, 2019).

Importantly, all the strategies offered in this chapter are designed to be implemented without the help or guidance of a professional. They are simple positive practices designed to enhance your wellbeing so that you can enact self-leadership and lead others to the best of your ability. They are not intended to take the place of therapy.

Before we explore the PERMA wellbeing model and outline various PPIs, it's crucial to understand the wellbeing challenges faced by professional musicians. Acknowledging these challenges helps underscore why taking ownership of our wellbeing as music leaders is a vitally important aspect of our professional and personal practice.

Musicians' wellbeing

In recent years, there has been growing concern that despite music's wellbeing benefits, paradoxically, performing musicians themselves may not be reaping the rewards (Musgrave, 2023). The Musical Care International Network has highlighted how musicians often experience suboptimal wellbeing and face complex challenges to physical and psychological health (Spiro et al., 2023). Members of the network make it clear that notions of "musical care" must also extend to musicians themselves.

In their book *Can Music Make You Sick?*, Sally-Anne Gross and George Musgrave demonstrate that musicians in the British music industry experience high levels of mental distress relative to the general population (Gross & Musgrave, 2020). Musicians must cope with precarious working conditions, constant pressure to remain "relevant", and the need to adapt to digital disruption. Gross and Musgrave's work details the dire consequences for mental health and wellbeing when something as personal as making music is commodified. Similarly, Musgrave et al. (2024) argue that, because of the poor return on investment, musicians' pursuit of a career is analogous to gambling, and musicians' optimism is, in fact, a form of "cruel optimism" that keeps musicians on a potentially harmful and even traumatising trajectory.

One way to reorient a music career is to diversify into working in community contexts. In this way, musicians too can reap the social and emotional wellbeing benefits of music making (Forbes & Bartlett, 2020). The transition to community work, however, brings its own challenges, including finding and securing opportunities (especially for paid work), building new networks, and developing knowledge and new skills (Forbes et al., 2025).

Moreover, community musicians and arts workers face their own wellbeing challenges. These can include lack of professional supervision, exploitation due to chronic underfunding, and the strain of hidden emotional and financial costs, including the working of unpaid hours (Belfiore, 2022; Spiro et al., 2023; Throsby & Petetskaya, 2024). These hidden costs are not factored into cultural policy or funding provision, and are shouldered by artists who feel a moral responsibility towards the people they work with, some of whom are socially isolated or disadvantaged. Belfiore (2022, p. 61) argues this is a "moral failure of cultural policy" because such policy allows for the exploitation of artists' genuine motivations for positive impact.

This is where co-facilitation or shared leadership can be a valuable model for community arts interventions. Co-facilitation not only helps to share the workload, but it can be a vital source of energy and inspiration for the facilitators as much as the participants. Indeed, interdisciplinary arts and health researcher and community music facilitator, Naomi Sunderland, identifies co-facilitation as a "delicate dance". However, when it works, Naomi asserts, "it can create all the things that we love and hope for in community music". Naomi explains, "I would hope that the facilitators come out feeling better than they did when they went in, especially because there's such vulnerability, and community musicians are often solo practitioners." The co-facilitation model can address the isolation of leading a group solo and can amplify the benefits of participatory music making for music leaders themselves.

While there are undoubtedly critical structural issues that must be addressed to better support music leaders, in this chapter we will focus on what individual musicians can do to support their own wellbeing. This is not to place the burden of fixing systemic issues on individuals, but rather to provide concrete strategies for gaining agency over one's wellbeing or, at least, as much agency as possible. For this reason, it is vitally important that musicians who are transitioning into community work prioritise caring for themselves.

The following sections contain a mix of both theory and practical exercises to build your wellbeing literacy and your repertoire of self-care practices. Naturally, not all practices will be universally appealing. The best strategy is to start with one practice that appeals to you and progress from there (indeed, these interventions are most effective when practised intentionally and consistently).

Positive self-care strategies for musicians

Positive psychology interventions (PPIs) are evidence-based practices that are designed to promote wellbeing. Rather than focusing on what is "wrong", PPIs build on what is strong—our innate strengths—and thus recognise that we all need to build positive relationships, find meaning and accomplishment, and feel positive and engaged.

Regardless of whether you try one PPI or a few, the message to take away is that even just a few minutes of positive practice each day can yield significant long-term benefits (Hart, 2021). For example, a study of the "three good things" PPI—writing down three good things that went well that day, and their causes, over a week—found that participants experienced increased happiness and decreased depressive symptoms that lasted up to six months (Seligman et al., 2005). In a meta-analysis of 51 PPIs with over 4,000 participants, researchers found that even brief interventions produced meaningful improvements in well-being and reductions in depressive symptoms (Sin & Lyubomirsky, 2009).

Intentional activities offer the best "bang for buck" for sustainable increases in happiness. According to Lyubomirsky et al. (2005), we each have a "chronic happiness level"—a "set point", if you will—which is determined by genetics, circumstances, and intentional activities (Lyubomirsky et al., 2005). While changing circumstances can provide a short-term happiness boost, we quickly return to our set point. We can guard against this return to our baseline by using a variety of PPIs; however, much like any other practice (learning to play golf, for example, or perfecting a recipe), these interventions must be the right fit for us, and they require consistent effort to yield the best results (Lyubomirsky et al., 2005).

The PERMA model of wellbeing

The PERMA model of wellbeing, the brainchild of Martin Seligman (2002, 2011), provides a useful framework for understanding wellbeing. In this chapter, we will use the PERMA model to structure our exploration of self-care.

To begin, each letter in the word "PERMA" represents a different element of wellbeing:

- Positive emotions,
- Engagement,
- Relationships,
- Meaning, and
- Accomplishment.

While no single element defines wellbeing, each contributes to it, and each can be independently measured (Seligman, 2011). The character strengths and virtues that we discussed in Chapter 2 underpin the PERMA theory of wellbeing. When viewed through a positive psychology lens, self-leadership requires high self-awareness to align our potential with our signature strengths, values, and motivations. Using our strengths to meet our greatest challenges can lead to an increase across all elements of PERMA, building wellbeing and allowing us to flourish (Seligman, 2011). When we flourish, we experience better health, increased resilience, improved performance, and greater life satisfaction (Seligman, 2011).

P—*Positive emotions*

Positive emotions, experienced subjectively, are a key component of wellbeing. While emotions are complex and nuanced, experiencing mostly positive emotions significantly contributes to our health and wellbeing (Fredrickson, 2010).

According to the "broaden and build theory" (Fredrickson, 2004), positive emotions encourage exploration and learning, broadening our "thought–action" repertoire, meaning the range of responses we have access to in any given moment. Over time, increasing positive emotions (relative to negative ones) builds a reservoir of personal resources (relationships, knowledge, and resilience) that we can draw on during challenges. These resources can be enduring, lasting long after the initial positive emotion (Hart, 2021). For music leaders, positive emotions can enhance creativity and problem-solving abilities. Conversely, negative emotions narrow our thought–action repertoire, usually limiting our actions to confronting, escaping, or dismissing (Fredrickson, 2004, 2010; Hart, 2021).

It is important to consciously cultivate positive emotions to counterbalance our innate "negativity bias"—our tendency to pay more attention to negative experiences and information (Baumeister et al., 2001). While this bias may have evolutionary origins in its ability to enhance our chances of survival, in today's world, we need to make a conscious effort to increase positive experiences and emotions such as gratitude and joy (Baumeister et al., 2001; Fredrickson, 2010).

The following simple practices will support you to increase positive emotions.

Gratitude

While gratitude, in some contexts, has spiritual dimensions (such as expressing thanks through prayer), the simple act of expressing gratitude for everyday things can enhance wellbeing. In this sense, it is possible to think of gratitude simply as "a felt sense of wonder, thankfulness, and appreciation for life" (Emmons & Shelton, 2001, p. 460).

Gratitude is also dispositional in the sense that it is considered a personality trait and somewhat stable within individuals (Wood et al., 2010); however, gratitude can be cultivated through specific practices. Research shows, for example, that simple gratitude exercises can significantly increase positive emotions and reduce negative ones (Emmons & McCullough, 2003; Lambert et al., 2012). In relationships, expressing gratitude can strengthen bonds and promote prosocial behaviour (Algoe et al., 2010). In the workplace, gratitude is associated with increased job satisfaction and reduced burnout (Lanham et al., 2012; Waters, 2012).

While further research is needed to fully unravel the mechanisms behind the wide-ranging benefits of expressing gratitude, the existing evidence provides a compelling case for incorporating simple gratitude practices into our daily lives, such as keeping a gratitude journal or practising mindfulness.

- Gratitude journal. Using a journal or a diary, write down three things you're grateful for each day, no matter how small. Reflect on their circumstances and their meaning (Boniwell & Tunariu, 2019; Rashid & Seligman, 2018; Seligman, 2011). Reflect on why you're grateful for each thing. Was it a small act of kindness that you experienced? Or perhaps you are grateful for having a positive impact on someone else? Was it something new that you learned? For ongoing benefits, practise for about a week, then continue voluntarily if you find journalling beneficial (Boniwell & Tunariu, 2019; Gander et al., 2013).
- Gratitude letter. Write a detailed, heartfelt letter expressing gratitude to someone who has been particularly kind to you, but who you have never properly thanked (Seligman, 2002). The letter should be specific, describing the actions the person took and the ways in which they made a difference. Even simply writing the letter will generate positive emotions and promote a sense of connection and appreciation (Toepfer & Walker, 2009).
- Gratitude visit. Take your letter writing exercise one step further! Deliver your letter in person and read it aloud to the recipient. This face-to-face expression of gratitude strengthens the emotional impact of the intervention, fostering a profound sense of connection and evoking positive feelings for both the giver and receiver (Seligman et al., 2005; see also Gander et al., 2013).

Joy

Joy is a distinct positive emotion characterised by sudden, intense feelings of pleasure or delight. According to Fredrickson (2013), joy promotes play and engagement with our surroundings. When we experience joy during learning, the skills we acquire become durable resources (Fredrickson, 2013; Hart, 2021). Positive emotions like joy have an "upward spiral" effect and have even been shown to improve physical health (Fredrickson, 2013; Hart, 2021).

- Acts of kindness. Help someone else do something, or volunteer in your community. Practising kindness has been shown to increase happiness and other positive emotions (Lyubomirsky et al., 2005). Performing five acts of kindness throughout one day each week appears to be most beneficial (discussed in Lyubomirsky et al., 2005). The positive effects of acts of kindness flow to the giver and receiver, even when they are complete strangers (Curry et al., 2018)!
- Savouring. Consciously focus on appreciating a positive experience with all your senses (Bryant & Veroff, 2007). This can include savouring past, present, or anticipated future events. If you're feeling creative, you could try capturing a savouring experience through a song, poem, or short story.

- Using your strengths. Actively using your signature strengths has been linked to increased happiness and wellbeing (Seligman et al., 2005). Engaging in activities that align with your strengths can be intrinsically rewarding and promote feelings of joy, meaning, and accomplishment. For example, if you discover one of your signature strengths is humour, think of ways to incorporate humour into your community music practice. You may wish to start your sessions with some silly games or jokes. Allowing yourself to play to your strengths means that you will be authentic with your participants, who in turn will appreciate your efforts, creating "upward spirals" of positive emotions like joy, fun, and gratitude.

Hope

Hope is a nuanced positive emotion that often arises when we are faced with challenges. For musicians who confront failed auditions, practice plateaus, or financial struggles, maintaining hope is crucial. As Fredrickson (2010, p. 43) confirms, "Deep within the core of hope is the belief that things can change. No matter how awful or uncertain they are at the moment, things can turn out better. Possibilities exist." Hope counters our negativity bias and provides a braking mechanism on our unique human ability to imagine the future, including our own mortality. It prompts action to improve our situation, building long-term resources of optimism and resilience (Hart, 2021; Fredrickson, 2013).

RESONANCE—A new door opens

Emma Dean describes her transition from solo performer to community choir leader as passing through an open door. After striving for many years to "make it" as a solo artist—a struggle that felt like "knocking on doors and just having them slammed in your face"—Emma started her community choir "Cheep Trill". For Emma, Cheep Trill is a way to heal herself and help others:

> Cheep Trill been the one thing in my life that has flow. It's been probably the one career thing in which I haven't had to hustle. So, the challenges are much less in the Cheep Trill space than they are in my other things. It's been like an open door. It's just like, "Oh, there's a bigger door there".

Emma's establishment of Cheep Trill is the perfect example of "one door closes, another opens". By remaining open to other possibilities beyond a certain level of success as a solo performer, Emma has created a new pathway for her own practice, which is having a tremendous positive impact on her, and others.

PRACTICE POINTS

- "One door closes, another opens." Reflect on a negative experience (the closing door), then shift your focus to potential positive outcomes (the opening doors) (Boniwell & Tunariu, 2019; Rashid & Seligman, 2018). Consider what you've learned from this experience and contemplate new possibilities for personal growth. There is evidence this practice can increase happiness (Gander et al., 2013).
- Best possible self. Imagine and write about your best possible future self, achieving desired goals and realising your full potential. Consider where you'd like to be in 10 years if everything goes well. Write about this daily for a week, then reflect on your life's mission. This practice has been shown to increase optimism, positive emotions, and self-efficacy (King, 2001; Sheldon & Lyubomirsky, 2006).
- Goal setting and planning. Pursuing our goals is a key way to satisfy our most fundamental psychological needs (Deci & Ryan, 2000). Set clear, achievable goals and develop action plans to reach them. This fosters a sense of agency, hope, and optimism. Pursuing and achieving goals gives life purpose, meaning, and a sense of accomplishment. If you're not a natural goal-setter, start small. To guide your process, use a popular goal-setting model such as SMART (Specific, Measurable, Attainable, Realistic, Timely) or GROW (Goal, Reality, Options, Way forward).

E—Engagement

As a musician, have you ever lost track of time while practising or performing, feeling completely absorbed in the music? This state of heightened engagement is known as *flow,* and it is a powerful tool for enhancing your wellbeing. You may recall from Chapter 2 that intentionally undertaking tasks that use our signature strengths and talents is an effective way to experience engagement (Seligman et al., 2005). The experience of complete absorption is the "flow state", or more simply, "flow".

Mihaly Csikszentmihalyi, a founding father of positive psychology, dedicated much of his career to defining and exploring flow (Csikszentmihalyi, 2002; Nakamura & Csikszentmihalyi, 2009; Seligman, 2011). Flow has nine dimensions, including the pre-conditions for flow (a balance of challenge with skill level, clear goals, immediate feedback) and experiential characteristics (focused concentration, intrinsic reward, time distortion, the merging of action and awareness, a loss of self-consciousness, and a sense of control) (Cohen & Bodner, 2019). Flow is a "Goldilocks" state where the respective challenge must be "just the right" match to our skill level in order to avoid both anxiety (when the challenge is too hard) and boredom (when the challenge is too easy) (Nakamura & Csikszentmihalyi, 2009).

Interestingly, music is one of the most researched activities in connection with flow (Tan & Sin, 2021). For musicians, seeking flow experiences can "sweeten" the journey to mastery (Tan et al., 2021). Flow contributes to a sense of meaning and accomplishment, particularly in improvised contexts such as jazz (Forbes,

2021; Hytönen-Ng, 2013). Leaders of community singing groups often report experiencing the flow state. As one music leader explains, "I enter into the music and just lose myself … the hour and a half goes by so quickly, and then I come out of it feeling better, like the others [group participants] do" (Forbes & Bartlett, 2020, p. 562).

Singing for health practitioner–researcher Emily Foulkes reflects on how her work brings her into the flow state:

> I never really knew what flow was until I started doing this work and finding my way with it and feeling, as I grew in confidence with it … I still struggle with singing, performing to sing in front of others, but when I'm facilitating a singing group, I don't have any problem at all. No problem at all. It's like I just step into something completely different. It's just amazing.

For music leaders, cultivating flow can enhance personal wellbeing and improve the quality of the music making experience for community music groups.

Practice points

Challenge yourself to cultivate flow experiences in your daily musical practice. How might you redesign your routine to incorporate these elements of engagement?

- Music practice sessions. Design personal practice sessions with clear, achievable goals that stretch your skills just beyond your current level.
- Playing with improvisation. Experiment with improvisation in your preferred genre to experience flow through spontaneous creation. Start simple!
- Flow in groups. Think about how you could explore the principles of flow in a community music setting. Try to match the challenges that you set your group to their level of experience (or make the challenge slightly harder than their current skillset). Provide clear goals and lots of immediate and encouraging feedback. If you, as a leader, find yourself getting into flow when working with the group, there is a good chance group members will experience flow too.
- Dedicate time for creative play. One common challenge for music leaders is that they often juggle multiple roles beyond those associated with their community group. Singing leader Jane York suggests allocating administrative tasks to specific time blocks to prevent from overwhelming and thwarting creative energy. Similarly, protecting uninterrupted time for creative work— arranging, composing, or developing new material—is essential for maintaining engagement and preventing burnout.

R—Relationships

Positive relationships are another key component of the PERMA model (Seligman, 2011). Relationships impact our thoughts, feelings, and behaviours, and can be both positive and negative, and based on either close or weak ties. In today's digital age, relationships span both virtual and real-world interactions. While close relationships are crucial for our wellbeing, we benefit from various relationships in our workplaces and communities (Killam, 2024; Hart, 2021).

In fact, our fundamental need to belong (Baumeister & Leary, 1995) drives us to pursue relationships for their own sake (Seligman, 2011). When we experience belonging, we feel accepted and part of something larger than ourselves (Siegel & Drulis, 2023). Unmet belonging needs can have severe consequences for our mental health (Allen, 2021; Hart, 2021).

Social health refers to our need for human connection and positive relationships, and its importance is "vastly underappreciated" (Killam, 2024, loc. 58). We are currently facing a global crisis of social disconnection (Way et al., 2018), but just like food and water, our relationships are fundamental to our survival (Allen, 2021; Killam, 2024). Establishing, maintaining, and nurturing positive relationships with others is one of the most effective and important things we can do for our health and wellbeing.

For music leaders working with community groups, there are unique opportunities to build social connections—even between strangers—that can contribute to wellbeing. Research on group singing has demonstrated that the relationships formed in these settings are crucial to both the individual's enjoyment of the activity and their wellbeing. Music leaders have described these relationships as transcending typical work relationships, often characterising these connections as familial, loving, and empowering (Forbes & Bartlett, 2020). Group singing provides an opportunity to "perform healthy relationships" between group members and leaders (Camlin et al., 2020).

Interestingly, "love" and "care" are increasingly associated with musicians' work in community settings (Camlin, 2023; Spiro et al., 2023). Barbara Fredrickson's concept of "Love 2.0" suggests that love can be experienced in micro-moments of connection, even with strangers, contributing to overall wellbeing and resilience (Fredrickson, 2013). Fredrickson's perspective on love challenges the traditional view that love is confined to close, enduring relationships, and suggests that we can cultivate love and connection in our daily interactions with others.

Community music researcher Brydie-Leigh Bartleet (2019) describes how music enables "micro-kindnesses"—small but significant acts of connection that occur naturally through shared music making. These acts of micro-kindness might include teaching someone a song, listening deeply to another's musical contribution, or collaborating on a new piece. While these moments may seem minor, they gradually build trust, respect, and care, even amongst those with different cultural values and backgrounds. For music leaders, this suggests that fostering positive relationships does not require grand gestures but rather comes from creating regular opportunities for these small musical exchanges and connections to occur.

Fredrickson's concept of Love 2.0, and the broader music research on love, reiterates the importance of both creating opportunities for positive social interactions and fostering a sense of shared humanity in our everyday lives. With that in mind, here are some ideas to help you foster positive relationships with others.

Practice points

- **Self-compassion.** The foundation of empathy is our own ability to show kindness and compassion to ourselves. Develop kindness towards yourself to enhance resilience and improve your relationships with others (Neff, 2011). Self-compassion involves treating yourself with kindness, care, and understanding during difficult times, rather than judging yourself harshly (Neff, 2003). By treating ourselves with kindness and by recognising our shared humanity, we are better able to cope with life's challenges and to maintain a sense of perspective. When we are self-compassionate, we are less likely to become absorbed in our own emotional dramas, which suggests that self-compassion may be even more beneficial to us than healthy self-esteem (Leary et al., 2007; Neff, 2011). This is because "self-compassion provides greater emotional resilience and stability than self-esteem, but involves less self-evaluation, ego-defensiveness, and self-enhancement than self-esteem" (Neff, 2011, p. 1).
- **Loving-kindness meditation (LKM).** Try LKM by cultivating warm feelings towards yourself and others. Research shows LKM increases positive emotions and builds personal resources (Fredrickson et al., 2008). Sit quietly and repeat: "May I be happy, well, safe, peaceful, and at ease". Then, extend these wishes to others, your community, and the world. You might even consider adapting this practice to a group exercise that could be undertaken by a community music group. Many groups begin and end with a short song or incantation which brings the group together and expresses gratitude for the companionship of fellow members. Explicitly expressing the desire for others to be safe, peaceful, and at ease is one way to foster a group identity with it its own psychological resources (see Chapter 6 for more detailed discussion on social identity and identity leadership).

M—Meaning

To find life meaningful, we need to feel that we belong to, and that we serve, something bigger than ourselves (Seligman, 2011). Meaning arises when our lives feel coherent, when we have clear goals, and when we believe our existence matters (Hart, 2021; Heintzelman & King, 2014).

For this reason, a key aim of this book is to help musicians find meaning in their work. In a 2020 study of singing group leaders, participants reported their work as deeply meaningful (Forbes & Bartlett, 2020). Leaders described their work as "profound", "a privilege", and "part of something bigger" (Forbes & Bartlett, 2020). These responses are textbook experiences of "meaning"—feeling like one's work really matters, that we are in the right place, doing the right work, contributing to something bigger than ourselves, and being valued for our unique contributions.

While work is one source of meaning, we can also derive meaning from relationships, spirituality, and self-acceptance (Wong, 1998, as cited in Hart, 2021). While our modern society places a lot of emphasis on accumulating wealth as a source of meaning, the relationship between meaning and financial status is complex. According to Lyubomirsky et al. (2005), only 10% of our happiness comes from life circumstances, including income. The concept of "hedonic adaptation" suggests that increased income may not lead to lasting happiness, as we quickly adapt to higher levels of comfort (Hart, 2021). Even though we become habituated to these higher levels of comfort, we continue to strive ever higher with little or no reward. Thus, we find ourselves on the "hedonic treadmill" (Hart, 2021), traversing over the same terrain and getting nowhere!

In terms of "bang for buck", it seems best to focus on intentional activities that promote positive emotions and a sense of satisfaction, but with a final caveat that there is considerable variability in how people adapt to the hedonic treadmill and the benefits they gain from intentional activities like PPIs.

Practice points

- **The PURE model.** While originally developed for use in therapeutic contexts (specifically "Meaning Therapy"), the PURE model can be used to guide reflection on one's own life (Wong, 2010). Reflect on Purpose, Understanding, Responsible action, and Evaluation to enhance life meaning. Key questions include:

  1 Purpose: "What are my strengths and what can I do best?"
  2 Understanding: "What kind of person am I?"
  3 Responsible action: "What is the right thing to do?"
  4 Evaluation: "Am I satisfied with how I live my life?"

- **The gift of time.** You can strengthen your relationships by dedicating quality time to others. This can involve engaging in activities together or doing something special for someone else without expecting anything in return. By giving the gift of time, you can create positive experiences, deepen you connection with others, and potentially improve others' wellbeing. This, in turn, can increase your happiness over time (Gander et al., 2013).
- **Legacy reflection.** Consider how you'd like to be remembered and what positive contributions you want to make. What will people say about you at your funeral? (Boniwell & Tunariu, 2019; adapted from Rashid & Seligman, 2018).

A—Accomplishment

Accomplishment refers to the different ways over time that we pursue goals by using our skills and our own effort (Hart, 2021). It involves a sense of progress, working towards and reaching targets, and feeling capable and effective in what we do. Accomplishment includes external objective markers of success as well as the intrinsic satisfaction and pride we feel when we achieve something for its own sake (Seligman, 2011). Pursuing our goals will involve challenges, setbacks, and the need for perseverance, but overcoming these challenges builds resilience.

There is an obvious connection between accomplishment and engagement because we often experience flow when striving to achieve a goal where our skills are matched to the task at hand (Hart, 2021). Accomplishment is also closely linked to positive emotions (because we are likely to feel pride and satisfaction when we achieve a goal), and meaning (that is, the satisfaction and fulfilment that we feel when we contribute to something larger than ourselves).

Practice points

- **Create achievable milestones.** Break down musical goals into manageable steps that allow groups to experience regular wins. This might mean mastering a simple song before tackling more complex pieces or celebrating when different vocal parts come together successfully.
- **Reframe "performing" as "sharing".** Framing the public sharing of music in less pressured ways can make accomplishment more accessible and enjoyable. Consider informal sharing sessions, family gatherings, or community events rather than formal concerts.
- **Celebrate collective achievements.** Acknowledge both big and small group accomplishments. This could be successfully learning a new harmony, maintaining steady rhythm together, or simply everyone showing up consistently.
- **Document progress.** Consider recording sessions occasionally (with permission) so groups can hear their improvement over time. This provides concrete evidence of accomplishment that can boost confidence and motivation.

Let's give the final word on accomplishment to Jane York:

> [Singing leader] Stephen Taberner talks about a "near life experience" when we sing together, and it's the perfect description of singing in a group. For me, the near life experience is so often not in the performing setting but in the rehearsal before the performance when everyone's across the material and we can make something great sounding and everyone feels really accomplished.

Refrain

This chapter has emphasised the importance of self-care for musicians, particularly those transitioning into community-focused work. We began by acknowledging the unique challenges that musicians face, from the pressures of performance to the precarity of music work. We introduced the PERMA model of wellbeing, exploring each element—positive emotions, engagement, relationships, meaning, and accomplishment—as well as positive psychology interventions (PPIs) to enhance wellbeing and resilience.

A key takeaway for this chapter is that self-care is not selfish or indulgent, but a fundamental aspect of effective leadership. Through regular self-care, music leaders are better equipped to lead and inspire others, contributing positively to the social health of their communities.

Interestingly, some researchers argue that the letter H for health should be added to the PERMA(H) model because physical health is also fundamental to our wellbeing. While it is beyond the scope of this chapter to directly address strategies for physical health, the importance of physical health for effective self-care is acknowledged. For music leaders, this will include getting sufficient sleep, eating a well-balanced diet, and engaging in some form of exercise that is both enjoyable and sustainable over time. For music leaders who sing, this will also include looking after their vocal health. Many community music sessions occur during evening mealtimes, so planning nutrition around these scheduling realities is crucial for maintaining energy and focus. Finally, for busy music leaders, effective energy management is crucial for sustaining positive emotional states. This includes practical considerations like spacing rehearsals appropriately and ensuring sufficient recovery time between sessions.

As we transition to Part II of the book, we're now prepared to explore how this foundation of self-care and positive psychology can be leveraged by musicians in participatory music settings to promote the social health of group members.

Call and response

1   Consider your current approach to self-care. How might reframing self-care as an essential component of leadership change your priorities and habits?
2   Think about a challenging aspect of your musical practice or career. How could you apply the PERMA (or PERMAH) model to transform this challenge into an opportunity for growth and increased wellbeing?

Suggested readings

The following references from the list below provide further information and advice about the issues discussed in this chapter: Csikszentmihalyi (2002), Fredrickson (2010, 2013), Neff (2015), and Seligman (2002, 2011).

References

Algoe, S. B., Gable, S. L., & Maisel, N. C. (2010). It's the little things: Everyday gratitude as a booster shot for romantic relationships. *Personal Relationships, 17*(2), 217–233.
Allen, K.-A. (2021). *The psychology of belonging.* Routledge.
Bartleet, B.-L. (2019). How concepts of love can inform empathy and conciliation in intercultural community music contexts. *International Journal of Community Music, 12*(3), 317–330. doi:10.1386/ijcm_00003_1.
Baumeister, R. F., Bratslavsky, E., Finkenauer, C., & Vohs, K. D. (2001). Bad is stronger than good. *Review of General Psychology, 5*(4), 323–370. doi:10.1037/1089-2680.5.4.323.
Baumeister, R. F., & Leary, M. R. (1995). The need to belong: Desire for interpersonal attachments as a fundamental human motivation. *Psychological Bulletin, 117*(3), 497–529. doi:10.1037/0033-2909.117.3.497.
Belfiore, E. (2022). Who cares? At what price? The hidden costs of socially engaged arts labour and the moral failure of cultural policy. *European Journal of Cultural Studies, 25* (1), 61–78. doi:10.1177/1367549420982863.

Boniwell, I., & Tunariu, A. D. (2019). *Positive psychology: Theory, research and applications.* McGraw-Hill Education.

Bryant, F. B., & Veroff, J. (2007). *Savoring: A new model of positive experience.* Psychology Press.

Camlin, D. A. (2023). *Music making and civic imagination.* Intellect Books.

Camlin, D. A., Daffern, H., & Zeserson, K. (2020). Group singing as a resource for the development of a healthy public: A study of adult group singing. *Humanities and Social Sciences Communications, 7*(1), article 1. doi:10.1057/s41599-020-00549-0.

Chowdhury, M. R. (2019). 19 top positive psychology interventions + how to apply them. https://positivepsychology.com/positive-psychology-interventions.

Cohen, S., & Bodner, E. (2019). Flow and music performance anxiety: The influence of contextual and background variables. *Musicae Scientiae, 25*(1), 25–44. doi:10.1177/1029864919838600.

Csikszentmihalyi, M. (2002). *Flow: The classic work on how to achieve happiness.* Rider.

Curry, O. S., Rowland, L. A., Van Lissa, C. J., Zlotowitz, S., McAlaney, J., & Whitehouse, H. (2018). Happy to help? A systematic review and meta-analysis of the effects of performing acts of kindness on the well-being of the actor. *Journal of Experimental Social Psychology, 76,* 320–329. doi:10.1016/j.jesp.2018.02.014.

Deci, E. L., & Ryan, R. M. (2000). The "what" and "why" of goal pursuits: Human needs and the self-determination of behavior. *Psychological Inquiry, 11*(4), 227–268. doi:10.1207/S15327965PLI1104_01.

Donahue, K. (2018). Why "put your oxygen mask on first" is not the best metaphor for self-care and what to do instead. www.kellydonahuephd.com/blog-1/2019/3/2/why-put-your-oxygen-mask-on-first-is-not-the-best-metaphor-for-self-care-and-what-to-do-instead.

Emmons, R. A., & McCullough, M. E. (2003). Counting blessings versus burdens: An experimental investigation of gratitude and subjective well-being in daily life. *Journal of Personality and Social Psychology, 84*(2), 377–389. https://pubmed.ncbi.nlm.nih.gov/12585811.

Emmons, R. A., & Shelton, C. M. (2001). Gratitude and the science of positive psychology. In C. R. Snyder & S. J. Lopez (eds), *Handbook of positive psychology* (pp. 459–471). Oxford University Press.

Forbes, M. (2021). Giving voice to jazz singers' experiences of flow in improvisation. *Psychology of Music, 49*(4), 789–803. doi:10.1177/0305735619899137.

Forbes, M., & Bartlett, I. (2020). "This circle of joy": Meaningful musicians' work and the benefits of facilitating singing groups. *Music Education Research, 22*(5), 555–568. doi:10.1080/14613808.2020.1841131.

Forbes, M., Dingle, G. A, Aitcheson, N., & Powell, C. (2025). Music from performance to prescription: A guide for musicians and health professionals. *Music & Science,* Advance online publication. doi:10.1177/20592043251338013.

Fredrickson, B. L. (2004). The broaden-and-build theory of positive emotions. *Philosophical Transactions of the Royal Society B: Biological Sciences, 359*(1449), 1367–1378. doi:10.1098/rstb.2004.1512.

Fredrickson, B. L. (2010). *Positivity: Groundbreaking research to release your inner optimist and thrive.* Penguin.

Fredrickson, B. L. (2013). *Love 2.0: Creating happiness and health in moments of connection.* Penguin.

Fredrickson, B. L., Cohn, M. A., Coffey, K. A., Pek, J., & Finkel, S. M. (2008). Open hearts build lives: Positive emotions, induced through loving-kindness meditation, build consequential personal resources. *Journal of Personality and Social Psychology, 95*(5), 1045–1062. doi:10.1037/a0013262.

Gander, F., Proyer, R. T., Ruch, W., & Wyss, T. (2013). Strength-based positive interventions: Further evidence for their potential in enhancing well-being and alleviating depression. *Journal of Happiness Studies, 14*(4), 1241–1259. doi:10.1007/s10902-012-9380-0.

Gross, S. A., & Musgrave, G. (2020). *Can music make you sick? Measuring the price of musical ambition.* University of Westminster Press.

Hart, R. (2021). *Positive psychology: The basics.* Routledge.

Heintzelman, S. J., & King, L. A. (2014). (The feeling of) meaning-as-information. *Personality and Social Psychology Review, 18*(2), 153–167. doi:10.1177/1088868313518487.

Hytönen-Ng, E. (2013). *Experiencing "flow" in jazz performance.* Ashgate.

Killam, K. (2024). *The art and science of connection: Why social health is the missing key to living longer, healthier, and happier.* Piatkus.

King, L. A. (2001). The health benefits of writing about life goals. *Personality and Social Psychology Bulletin, 27*(7), 798–807. doi:10.1177/0146167201277003.

Lambert, N. M., Fincham, F. D., & Stillman, T. F. (2012). Gratitude and depressive symptoms: The role of positive reframing and positive emotion. *Cognition & Emotion, 26*(4), 615–633.

Lanham, M., Rye, M., Rimsky, L., & Weill, S. (2012). How gratitude relates to burnout and job satisfaction in mental health professionals. *Journal of Mental Health Counseling, 34*(4), 341–354.

Leary, M. R., Tate, E. B., Adams, C. E., Batts Allen, A., & Hancock, J. (2007). Self-compassion and reactions to unpleasant self-relevant events: The implications of treating oneself kindly. *Journal of Personality and Social Psychology, 92*(5), 887–904. doi:10.1037/0022-3514.92.5.887.

Lyubomirsky, S., Sheldon, K. M., & Schkade, D. (2005). Pursuing happiness: The architecture of sustainable change. *Review of General Psychology, 9*(2), 111–131. doi:10.1037/1089-2680.9.2.111.

Musgrave, G. (2023). Music and wellbeing vs. musicians' wellbeing: Examining the paradox of music-making positively impacting wellbeing, but musicians suffering from poor mental health. *Cultural Trends, 32*(3), 280–295. doi:10.1080/09548963.2022.2058354.

Musgrave, G., Gross, S. A., & Klein, M. (2024). The dark side of optimism: Musical dreams, belief, and gambling. *Musicae Scientiae, 28*(4), 634–648. doi:10.1177/10298649241230673.

Nakamura, J., & Csikszentmihalyi, M. (2009). Flow theory and research. In S. J. Lopez & C. R. Snyder (eds), *Oxford handbook of positive psychology* (pp. 195–206). Oxford University Press.

Neff, K. D. (2003). Self-compassion: An alternative conceptualization of a healthy attitude toward oneself. *Self and Identity, 2*(2), 85–101. doi:10.1080/15298860309032.

Neff, K. D. (2011). Self-compassion, self-esteem, and well-being. *Social and Personality Psychology Compass, 5*(1), 1–12. doi:10.1111/j.1751-9004.2010.00330.x.

Neff, K. D. (2015). *Self-compassion: The proven power of being kind to yourself.* HarperCollins.

Rashid, T., & Seligman, M. P. (2018). *Positive psychotherapy: Clinician manual.* Oxford University Press.

Seligman, M. E. P. (2002). *Authentic happiness: Using the new positive psychology to realize your potential for lasting fulfillment.* Free Press.

Seligman, M. E. P. (2011). *Flourish: A visionary new understanding of happiness and well-being.* Simon & Schuster.

Seligman, M. E. P., Steen, T. A., Park, N., & Peterson, C. (2005). Positive psychology progress: Empirical validation of interventions. *American Psychologist, 60*(5), 410–421.

Sheldon, K. M., & Lyubomirsky, S. (2006). How to increase and sustain positive emotion: The effects of expressing gratitude and visualizing best possible selves. *The Journal of Positive Psychology*, *1*(2), 73–82. doi:10.1080/17439760500510676.

Siegel, D. J., & Drulis, C. (2023). An interpersonal neurobiology perspective on the mind and mental health: Personal, public, and planetary well-being. *Annals of General Psychiatry*, *22*(1), 5. doi:10.1186/s12991-023-00434-5.

Sin, N. L., & Lyubomirsky, S. (2009). Enhancing well-being and alleviating depressive symptoms with positive psychology interventions: A practice-friendly meta-analysis. *Journal of Clinical Psychology*, *65*(5), 467–487. doi:10.1002/jclp.20593.

Spiro, N., *et al.* (2023). Perspectives on musical care throughout the life course: Introducing the musical care international network. *Music & Science*, *6*. doi:10.1177/20592043231200553.

Tan, J., Yap, K., & Bhattacharya, J. (2021). What does it take to flow? Investigating links between grit, growth mindset, and flow in musicians. *Music & Science*, *4*. doi:10.1177/2059204321989529.

Tan, L., & Sin, H. X. (2021). Flow research in music contexts: A systematic literature review. *Musicae Scientiae*, *25*(4), 399–428. doi:10.1177/1029864919877564.

Throsby, D., & Petetskaya, K. (2024). Artists as workers: An economic study of professional artists in Australia. https://creative.gov.au/advocacy-and-research/artists-as-workers-an-economic-study-of-professional-artists-in-australia/.

Toepfer, S. M., & Walker, K. (2009). Letters of gratitude: Improving well-being through expressive writing. *Journal of Writing Research*, *1*(3), 181–198.

Way, N., Ali, A., Gilligan, C., & Noguera, P. (eds). (2018). *The crisis of connection: Roots, consequences, and solutions*. NYU Press.

Waters, L. (2012). Predicting job satisfaction: Contributions of individual gratitude and institutionalized gratitude. *Psychology*, *3*(12A), 1174–1176.

Wong, P. T. P. (1998). Implicit theories of meaningful life and the development of the personal meaning profile. In P. T. P. Wong & P. S. Fry (eds), *The human quest for meaning: A handbook of psychological research and clinical applications* (pp. 111–140). Lawrence Erlbaum Associates.

Wong, P. T. P. (2010). Meaning therapy: An integrative and positive existential psychotherapy. *Journal of Contemporary Psychotherapy*, *40*(2), 85–93. doi:10.1007/s10879-009-9132-6.

Wood, A. M., Froh, J. J., & Geraghty, A. W. A. (2010). Gratitude and well-being: A review and theoretical integration. *Clinical Psychology Review*, *30*(7), 890–905. doi:10.1016/j.cpr.2010.03.005.

Part II
Ensemble

4 Revitalising social health through positive music leadership

Introduction

Vocal leader James Sills had a transformative experience when visiting Ghana that shifted his understanding of the purpose and function of music making. James recalls:

> When I met someone new for the first time there, they would immediately share their name, church, ethnic group, and language. There's an incredible sense of rootedness that we've largely lost in the West. When I returned home to the UK, I saw more clearly how we're becoming increasingly atomised. Traditional structures that once fostered belonging are breaking down—whether that's the workplace, organised religion with its tradition of communal singing, or in my country, the decline of local pubs. Add to this greater geographical mobility, with people no longer living where they grew up, and you see these connections fraying. While these societal changes aren't necessarily negative in themselves, alongside the rise of social media and remote work, people find themselves paradoxically connected everywhere but belonging nowhere. They have many light connections, an impression of connection, but lack that deep sense of belonging. This is why I see my work as creating spaces where people can truly belong, where they can say "these are my people". Even if it's just for an hour or two each week, for some people that's enough. In the homeless choir I run, many participants tell me it's the only place where they feel they truly belong.

James recognises that human beings are hard-wired for social connection (Baumeister & Leary, 1995)—it's part of our biology. This is why forming quality relationships with others is a key pillar of wellbeing. You may recall from Chapter 3 that the "R" in Seligman's (2011) PERMA model for wellbeing stands for relationships. Building and maintaining positive relationships is critical to our sense of wellbeing, and a necessary precursor to flourishing or optimal functioning.

Our social connections are more than just "nice to haves"—they are fundamental to both mental and physical health. A ground-breaking meta-analysis (a study of other studies) involving 148 studies and 308,849 participants found that people with robust social ties had a 50% greater likelihood of living longer than

DOI: 10.4324/9781003426509-7

those who were more socially isolated (Holt-Lunstad et al., 2010, p. 14). This effect is comparable to well-established risk factors for mortality like smoking and alcohol consumption and even exceeds the impact of factors such as physical inactivity and obesity (Holt-Lunstad et al., 2010, p. 14).

Despite the very serious consequences poor social relationships have on longevity, our understanding of the importance of our social relationships is generally quite poor (Killam, 2024). The meta-analysis by Holt-Lunstad et al. (2010) demonstrates that the influence of social relationships on our health and longevity is substantial and should be taken as seriously as other major risk factors that affect our mortality. In general, many of us fail to recognise or understand the threat posed to our health by loneliness and social disconnection (S. A. Haslam et al., 2018b).

There is now mounting evidence that group-based musical activities can foster social connection, group identity, and a sense of belonging among participants (Dingle et al., 2021). These social connections appear to be a key mechanism through which musical activities promote wellbeing across diverse populations and settings. Music activities offer a rich resource for enhancing social health and wellbeing for people of all ages and backgrounds (Dingle et al., 2021).

As we explored in the "Overture" chapter, positive leaders seek to bring out the best in themselves and in others; they promote the health and wellbeing of themselves, and those they work with, and they create the conditions for people to connect with each other (Lucey & Burke, 2022; Cameron, 2018, 2021). To set the scene for the role that positive music leaders play in promoting the social health of others, let's take a reality check. The following section briefly examines what has been referred to as "the global crisis of connection" (Way et al., 2018) so that we might understand how positive music leadership might revitalise our social health and renew our relationships with ourselves and with each other.

The global crisis of connection

We currently live in a world where people are more disconnected than ever before; some warn we are living through a global crisis in social connection (Ending Loneliness Together, 2022; Murthy, 2023; Way et al., 2018). Across the world, one in four older adults is socially isolated (World Health Organization, 2023). The World Health Organization has mobilised its resources to address these issues because social isolation is such a serious risk to health.

Music leaders frequently hear from their participants—particularly older adults—that group music making provides a vital lifeline of social connection. As musician Kym Dillon observes:

> People in my groups will tell me, "This is the one thing I come out of my house for". When you consider how difficult it can be for someone experiencing isolation to overcome the inertia of staying home, the fact that they make the effort to attend week after week suggests these music groups are filling a profound need for connection. Through regular participation, people forge new friendships and social bonds. While these groups typically include diverse

age ranges, this social connection seems especially valuable for older adults who might otherwise face increasing isolation.

But why *are* we more socially isolated? Aren't we supposed to be globally connected through technology and social media?

Despite our technological advances, we have become increasingly atomised at the community, environmental, familial, and individual levels. In his book *Bowling Alone*, American political and social scientist Robert Putnam argued that the decline in civic life and social capital in the United States is having significant impacts on community health, education, and democratic participation (Putnam, 2000). "Social capital" refers to the networks of relationships among people who live and work in a particular society, enabling that society to function effectively (Putnam, 2000). Putnam charts in meticulous detail declining participation in religious institutions, labour organisations, parent-teacher bodies in schools, social clubs and civic organisations. He attributes this decline to the modern pressures to make a living, time poverty, suburbanisation, the rise of technology and generational change. Putnam calls for a revival of civic engagement and community participation to rebuild America's social capital. In a documentary about his life and work, *Join or Die* (Davis & Davis, 2024), Putnam regretfully admitted that his calls for re-engaging in civic life have largely gone unheeded.

In *The Connection Cure*, Julia Hotz considers our disconnection from our environment from an evolutionary perspective:

> Movement, nature, art, service, and belonging were once staples of our daily lives. But since our survival no longer requires these five ingredients, we no longer structure our lives around them. Instead of moving our bodies, observing nature, creating art, serving our neighbors and seeking belonging among fellow humans, most of us spend most of our time sitting, observing screens, consuming "content", obsessing over our stuff, and seeking belonging among superficial sources. Instead of connections in our environments, we fill our waking hours with their substitutes.
>
> (Hotz, 2024, location 169)

Here, Hotz observes that we are now more engaged with *representations* of reality, than with reality itself. And while strictly speaking our physical survival may not require connecting with "the real world", or health and happiness does.

The decline in social capital across our civic organisations and social institutions has increased alienation and individualism (Putnam, 2000). The COVID-19 pandemic exacerbated existing issues of disconnection and social media has polarised public discourse. Furthermore, we are degrading our natural ecosystems and competing for ever-diminishing resources. In short, our modern world is one characterised by *dis-integration*, where the wholeness of things has been sacrificed for the parts, for the benefit of a few. As we've seen from the research evidence, the disintegration of our social fabric has dire implications for our health.

RESONANCE—Taking a stand against social atomisation

Musician and social inclusion choir leader Kym Dillon sees community choirs as resistance against the increasing commodification of music in the digital age:

> With artificial intelligence now capable of creating pop music and people consuming music through platforms like Spotify that commodify music, maintaining music as a communal activity feels like holding the line. When we create music together, we're standing up for music as a living, breathing thing rather than just content to be consumed. These choirs represent resistance against cultural forces pushing us toward isolation and passive consumption. We're actively reminding ourselves of our humanity, not through words but through living it. People respond to this instinctively because I think we all hunger for this kind of authentic connection.

While Kym reflects on the role of technology and commercialisation in de-personalising music and music making, in the following RESONANCE box, Nsamu Moonga suggests it is also our physical disconnection from place which contributes to our sense of social atomisation.

RESONANCE—Disconnection from place

Nsamu Moonga, music therapist, psychotherapist, and educator identifies the role that migration and loss of sense of place plays in social disconnection and declining mental health:

> Migration takes away belonging, whether it's intended migration or it's conquest, there's something that when we leave a home, depending on how we leave, there's something that is lost and we overcompensate by conquest, by conquering and putting other people down. That was their flaw. That's always been the flaw of colonialism. So, we beat people down so that we feel that we've taken over. So, I think it's a human need that is expressed and the human experience tells us—when did we start talking about mental health and mental issues? Right at the turn of the Industrial Revolution. Suddenly people got separated from their land and places of being and mental health became a thing and it's not getting any easier. It's not getting—it's not lessening. So mental health for me, it's not so much of the deficit of what is happening between somebody's ears. It's the deficit of belonging or place.

Nsamu's and Kym's reflections capture the quietly rebellious spirit of positive music leadership—it is a stance against the forces that would seek to disconnect us from ourselves and each other, from a sense of place, and from our humanity.

Social prescribing

Social prescribing is a public health model which seeks to respond to the connection crisis and our disintegrating social fabric. The rise of social prescribing globally presents an opportunity for positive music leaders whose aim is to support community social health (Chatterjee et al., 2018). A social prescription is a nonmedical intervention where healthcare providers or community workers connect people to activities and resources in their community to improve their wellbeing. Rather than prescribing medication, they might "prescribe" participation in social activities, like joining a community choir or exercise group, particularly for those experiencing loneliness or other social issues that impact their health (Muhl et al., 2023).

Social prescribing programs seek to address the social determinants of health (e.g. housing, education, socioeconomic status, social inclusion) to improve health (World Health Organization, 2022). First popularised in the United Kingdom where it is now part of the National Health Service, social prescribing has spread internationally over the last decade, and there are now social prescribing programs in countries across Europe, Asia, and North America (Morse et al., 2022).

Social prescribing supports but doesn't replace the medical model (Hotz, 2024.) For example, a patient who presents with aches and pains may be prescribed pain killers and referred to a physical therapist. A conversation between the patient and their doctor may also reveal other issues which could be influencing or even causing their physical pain (e.g. the recent loss of a loved one). In addition to treating the physical symptoms medically, a social prescription may be given to reconnect the patient to their source of wellness. Someone who has previously been involved in musical activity but dropped off due to physical or other health issues could be prescribed to join a local music group, as an example. Hotz (2024) explains that instead of only asking "What is the matter with you?" a doctor adopting a social prescribing approach will also ask "What matters *to you*?" (see Barry & Edgman-Levitan, 2012).

Music activities on prescription are a form of "arts on prescription" and take diverse forms (Bungay & Clift, 2010; Forbes et al., 2025). Music activities on prescription are different to other open community music programs: there is a referral pathway and participants' progress is monitored by a healthcare professional, participants are offered tailored support, and the focus for participants is improving health and wellbeing (as opposed to education or enjoyment) (Forbes et al., 2025).

Many music leaders are already working in contexts where they are using their positive leadership skills to support the social health of their communities. As various countries move to formalise social prescribing as part of the public health infrastructure, music leaders may find there are increasing opportunities to develop and lead programs which support social health.

Why these leadership frameworks?

As we move into Part II of this book, I want to briefly justify the choice of leadership theories/frameworks covered in these chapters. The number of approaches to leadership is overwhelming, so why the focus on positively energising leadership (Chapter 5) and identity leadership and the social cure approach to health (Chapter 6)?

Leadership is a broad church, and many theories of leadership focus on how to get people to follow in a particular way to improve performance. Other leadership theories focus more on leadership as a way to live out our greatest potential as individuals, in groups, or as organisations. Within the context of music leadership to support social health, we are not so much focused on getting people to follow instructions and produce certain results, as we are seeking to cultivate musical engagement as a positive experience which promotes wellbeing through positive emotions, relationships, and belonging.

Therefore, the two frameworks which follow in Chapters 5 and 6 have been chosen for application to music leadership because, while they can certainly be adopted to enhance performance and drive results (e.g. within an organisation) they are highly amenable to more experiential leadership contexts where the focus is enhanced health and wellbeing. Some may argue that there are also many therapeutic approaches which achieve similar results, and of course, this must be acknowledged. However, when working within non-therapeutic contexts where the aim is positive flourishing rather than addressing pathologies, conceptualising this work as a form of leadership (rather than therapy) seems appropriate.

Both positively energising leadership (Chapter 5) (Cameron, 2018, 2021) and social identity/social cure approaches (Chapter 6) (C. Haslam et al., 2018a; S. A. Haslam et al., 2020) align well with positive psychology principles. The focus in both frameworks is on the leader's role in recognising strengths, fostering positive emotions, and promoting inclusion, belonging and connection. Positively energising leaders encourage us to tap into our best selves, fostering personal growth and self-actualisation through positive interactions and virtuous behaviours. Core to identity leadership is cultivating a sense of purpose and belonging in followers, which, according to the social cure approach to health, becomes a psychological resource for group participants (C. Haslam et al., 2018a). Both frameworks consider the whole person (be they leader or follower), not just their role or output, and they acknowledge the interconnectedness of personal wellbeing, positive relationships, and effective leadership.

In summary, the leadership frameworks that follow have been chosen because they are particularly relevant to musicians, who often work in collaborative environments where positive personal expression and healthy group dynamics are paramount. The chosen leadership frameworks provide a firm foundation for leading activities which build meaningful relationships and foster a sense of belonging and social connection.

Moreover, the two frameworks are complementary. Positively energising leadership operates at the individual level and provides a foundation for building positive relationships within the group. Identity leadership operates at the group level and offers specific approaches for building group cohesiveness and social identity which promotes social connection and belonging.

These frameworks align with emerging trends in leadership theory and thinking around music education that emphasise the importance of emotional intelligence, social responsibility, and civic mission as increasingly crucial to musicians' practice in a VUCA world—a world which is volatile, uncertain, complex, and ambiguous (Gaunt et al., 2021; Grant, 2019; Westerlund & Karttunen, 2024). The approaches are presented as both a future-orientation for musicians' leadership within community and as a way to capture and understand the current practices of the wonderful music leaders interviewed for this book.

Alignment with trauma-informed approaches

Practising from a trauma-informed stance means you are dedicated to preventing re-traumatisation and promoting healing, and within the fields of arts in health there has been a growing call for this approach (Sunderland et al., 2023). The topic of trauma-informed practice is complex and beyond the scope of this book. However, I want to briefly acknowledge this large and important field and provide an example of how trauma-informed practice is aligned with positive music leadership.

Naomi Sunderland is a community music facilitator and interdisciplinary arts-health researcher who has, with colleagues, published interim guiding principles on trauma aware and anti-oppressive practice (Sunderland et al., 2023). These principles were produced with First Nations resources in the foreground. The principles provide guidance for arts in health practitioners and community arts practitioners (such as music leaders) and are designed to facilitate healing, health and wellbeing.

Some key principles outlined by Sunderland et al. (2023) which we will discuss in the following chapters (albeit not directly identified as trauma or culturally informed approaches) are:

- care-giving (creating a caring, compassionate and understanding environment);
- supporting participant choice and agency (giving participants options regarding activities and their level of engagement, and giving them permission to opt-out or step away if needed);
- safety (establishing clear ground rules and ensuring participants can step out when needed); and
- using multi-sensory and embodied approaches (e.g. grounding) (see Sunderland et al. 2023 for a full discussion of these and other approaches).

As a practitioner, Naomi has undertaken We Al-li's (2025) culturally informed trauma integrated healing approach (see www.wealli.com.au). Naomi gave an example of how she might use these principles, when a group member checks out of participating in collaborative song writing activities:

> One person completely removed themselves from the process. I engaged in deep listening and remained non-judgmental. These are trauma informed

practice principles. I just got curious, asked questions and emphasised and applauded and congratulated that person for exercising their self-sovereignty. I thanked them and just tried to open it up, another time down the track—just said, "I'm just noticing that you seem to be resisting some of the stuff, is that something you want to talk about? All feedback is welcome." I tried to keep a non-defensive open space and herald everything as a choice. It is optional.

In this example, Naomi practises care, support, and respects participant agency. Naomi remains open and curious rather than tending to judgment.

As we will see in the following chapters, the leadership approaches presented are well-aligned with trauma-informed and anti-oppressive principles. They call for leaders to create positive and safe environments where participants can exercise their creative agency in ways that are meaningful for them.

Refrain

The evidence is clear—strong social relationships are as vital to our wellbeing and longevity as physical health factors. In this context, positive music leadership emerges as a powerful tool for revitalising social health. By harnessing the unique ability of music to foster connection, integration, and belonging, positive music leaders can play a crucial role in addressing this global challenge. Whether through formal social prescribing programs or community-based grass-roots initiatives, collective music making led by skilled, positive leaders offers a path to reconnect with our shared humanity. As we move forward, we'll explore specific leadership frameworks that can guide music leaders in this vital work of rebuilding our social fabric and promoting holistic wellbeing through the transformative power of music.

Call and response

1   How might your role as a musician change if you viewed your work through the lens of public health and social prescribing? What new opportunities or challenges might this perspective bring?
2   Reflecting on your own musical experiences, can you recall a time when music helped you feel deeply connected to others?
3   Consider the "magic moments" you've experienced or witnessed in group music making. What made these moments magical? If you could bottle this magic, what would the label say? What would be the recommended dosage? How might you explain the active ingredients to someone who's never experienced it? (Hint—these issues are covered in more detail in Part III!)

References

Barry, M. J., & Edgman-Levitan, S. (2012). Shared decision making—The pinnacle of patient-centered care. *New England Journal of Medicine*, *366*(9), 780–781. doi:10.1056/NEJMp1109283.

Baumeister, R. F., & Leary, M. R. (1995). The need to belong: Desire for interpersonal attachments as a fundamental human motivation. *Psychological Bulletin, 117*(3), 497–529. doi:10.1037/0033-2909.117.3.497.

Bungay, H., & Clift, S. (2010). Arts on prescription: A review of practice in the UK. *Perspectives in Public Health, 130*(6), 277–281. doi:10.1177/1757913910384050.

Cameron, K. S. (2018). *Positive leadership: Strategies for extraordinary performance* (2nd edition). Berrett-Koehler.

Cameron, K. S. (2021). *Positively energizing leadership: Virtuous actions and relationships that create high performance* (1st edition). Berrett-Koehler Publishers.

Chatterjee, H. J., Camic, P. M., Lockyer, B., & Thomson, L. J. M. (2018). Non-clinical community interventions: A systematised review of social prescribing schemes. *Arts & Health, 10*(2), 97–123. doi:10.1080/17533015.2017.1334002.

Davis, P., & Davis, R. (2024). *Join or die* [film]. Silkworm Studio.

Dingle, G. A., *et al.* (2021). How do music activities affect health and well-being? A scoping review of studies examining psychosocial mechanisms. *Frontiers in Psychology, 12*, article 3689. doi:10.3389/fpsyg.2021.713818.

Ending Loneliness Together. (2022). Strengthening social connection to accelerate social recovery: A white paper. https://endingloneliness.com.au/ending-loneliness-together-white-pap er-social-connection-to- accelerate-social-recovery.

Forbes, M., Dingle, G. A, Aitcheson, N., & Powell, C. (2025). Music from performance to prescription: A guide for musicians and health professionals. *Music & Science, 8*. doi:10.1177/20592043251338013.

Gaunt, H., Duffy, C., Coric, A., González Delgado, I. R., Messas, L., Pryimenko, O., & Sveidahl, H. (2021). Musicians as "makers in society": A conceptual foundation for contemporary professional higher music education. *Frontiers in Psychology, 12*. doi:10.3389/fpsyg.2021.713648.

Grant, C. (2019). What does it mean for a musician to be socially engaged? How undergraduate music students perceive their possible social roles as musicians. *Music Education Research, 21*(4), 387–398. doi:10.1080/14613808.2019.1626360.

Haslam, C., Jetten, J., Cruwys, T., Dingle, G. A., & Haslam, S. A. (2018a). *The new psychology of health: Unlocking the social cure.* Routledge.

Haslam, S. A., McMahon, C., Cruwys, T., Haslam, C., Jetten, J., & Steffens, N. K. (2018b). Social cure, what social cure? The propensity to underestimate the importance of social factors for health. *Social Science & Medicine, 198*, 14–21. doi:10.1016/j.socscimed.2017.12.020.

Haslam, S. A., Reicher, S., & Platow, M. J. (2020). *The new psychology of leadership: Identity, influence and power.* Routledge.

Holt-Lunstad, J., Smith, T. B., & Layton, J. B. (2010). Social relationships and mortality risk: A meta-analytic review. *PLOS Medicine, 7*(7), article e1000316. doi:10.1371/journal.pmed.1000316.

Hotz, J. (2024). *The connection cure: The prescriptive power of movement, nature, art, service and belonging.* Headline.

Killam, K. (2024). *The art and science of connection: Why social health is the missing key to living longer, healthier, and happier.* Piatkus.

Lucey, C., & Burke, J. (2022). *Positive leadership in practice: A model for our future* (1st edition). Routledge.

Morse, D. F., et al. (2022). Global developments in social prescribing. *BMJ Global Health, 7*(5), article e008524. doi:10.1136/bmjgh-2022-008524.

Muhl, C., Mulligan, K., Bayoumi, I., Ashcroft, R., & Godfrey, C. (2023). Establishing internationally accepted conceptual and operational definitions of social prescribing through expert consensus: A Delphi study protocol. *International Journal of Integrated Care*, 23(1), article 3. doi:10.5334/ijic.6984.

Murthy, V. H. (2023). Our epidemic of loneliness and isolation: The US Surgeon General's advisory on the healing effects of social connection and community. www.hhs.gov/sites/default/files/surgeon-general-social-connection-advisory.pdf.

Putnam, R. D. (2000). *Bowling alone: The collapse and revival of American community*. Simon & Schuster.

Seligman, M. E. P. (2011). *Flourish: A visionary new understanding of happiness and well-being*. Simon & Schuster.

Sunderland, N., Stevens, F., Knudsen, K., Cooper, R., & Wobcke, M. (2023). Trauma aware and anti-oppressive arts-health and community arts practice: Guiding principles for facilitating healing, health and wellbeing. *Trauma, Violence, & Abuse*, 24(4), 2429–2447. doi:10.1177/15248380221097442.

Way, N., Ali, A., Gilligan, C., & Noguera, P. (eds). (2018). *The crisis of connection: Roots, consequences, and solutions*. NYU Press. www.jstor.org/stable/j.ctv12pnr8w.

Westerlund, H., & Karttunen, S. (2024). The protean music career as a sociopolitical orientation: The mutually integrated, non-hierarchical work values of socially engaged musicians. *Musicae Scientiae*, 28(3), 502–519. doi:10.1177/10298649231222548.

World Health Organization. (2022). A toolkit on how to implement social prescribing. https://iris.who.int/handle/10665/354456.

World Health Organization. (2023). WHO commission on social connection. www.who.int/groups/commission-on-social-connection.

5 Building connection through positively energising leadership

Introduction

"All human beings flourish in the presence of positive energy and languish in the presence of negative energy, or they orient themselves toward that which is life-giving and away from that which is life-depleting" (Cameron, 2021, loc. 255). In this quotation, world-renowned positive leadership scholar Kim S. Cameron invokes the "heliotropic effect"—the tendency of all living things to orient towards light.

Yet paradoxically, we are biologically wired to pay more attention to the negative—remember, bad is stronger than good (Baumeister et al., 2001). While negative experiences may dominate our emotions and immediate attention due to our survival instincts, research shows that positive energy has a more profound impact on behaviour (Cameron, 2021). To overcome our negativity bias, we must consciously cultivate and direct our attention towards the positive, just as a gardener might position plants to receive optimal sunlight.

Musician and community choir leader Emma Dean recognises the heliotropic effect in her work as a counterforce to the challenges we face in modern societies:

> I often think that choir is this light filled space that is such a feel-good thing for people. People need it. They need that light, to follow that joy, to follow that spark because life is really heavy for a lot of us. There's a lot of struggle.

Throughout this chapter, we will explore Cameron's strategies for "positively energising leadership" (PEL), one of the most prominent and evidence-based models for positive leadership. Positively energising leaders help people thrive and flourish (Cameron, 2018, 2021). You will see how this approach naturally aligns with musicians' energetic, embodied, and relational practice, and learn how to harness the energy of positive relationships created through music making to support others' social health.

You will recall from the Prologue that community music leader Allison Girvan describes her work as "conducting energy". Allison says that she has come to embrace the word "conductor" as "somebody who is channelling energy rather than dictating what happens ... somebody who is channelling energy or allowing energy to pass through them in order to direct it in a specific way". Allison's

DOI: 10.4324/9781003426509-8

evocative, insightful metaphor with its clever wordplay on traditional notions of conducting within music perfectly aligns with positively energising leadership.

Along similar lines, interdisciplinary arts and health researcher and community music facilitator Naomi Sunderland says the intention underlying her work is "to make people feel like a million bucks if I can. That's what I've learnt really, it's been role modelled to me from Aboriginal Elders. Affirmation, compliments." Naomi acknowledges this can be "a fine line" and that "sometimes if you're doing too much of that and it's not coming across as authentic it can be counterproductive". Naomi identifies that bringing a positive energy into a community music space needs to come from a place of genuine appreciation for participants' contributions to music making. And what is Naomi's intended outcome of her positive, strengths-based approach? "I always like people to walk out feeling better than they did when they walked in."

While positively energising leadership emerged from organisational psychology, its application in participatory community music settings requires some consideration of context. As singing leader Jane York observes, leading voluntary communities differs fundamentally from corporate leadership:

> There's a different relationship when you are working with volunteer communities, or communities who are coming to you of their own will to participate in something. That's a very different social contract than "you are my employees, and you have to do what I say and I'm paying you".

Jane humorously illustrates this distinction from corporate settings: "I'm not going to fire the sopranos because they're singing flat!"

At the same time, Jane notes how leadership roles naturally encourage positive behaviour: "Leadership, by its nature, if people are looking to you, does improve your behaviour." She likens it to parenting, where leading by example proves more powerful than dictating instructions. This aligns with PEL's emphasis on virtuous behaviours, but in community music settings these behaviours emerge not from organisational mandates, but from the intimate, voluntary nature of the relationships involved.

In this chapter we will consider PEL as it relates to musicians' practice as an approach highly amenable to revitalising the social health of our communities. While PEL was born within the field of organisational scholarship, the practice of PEL can apply equally to any walk of life, from families, to relationships, education, and serving communities (Cameron, 2021). PEL is a theory of leadership that readily applies to musicians' work, particularly when it is driven by a desire to use music as an agent of positive change.

Let's explore the PEL framework in more detail and then consider some practical applications of the core strategies within music making for social connection.

Positively energising leadership

Positive leadership (the precursor to PEL) has its beginnings in strengths-based approaches drawn from positive psychology which focuses on strengths and virtues in teams rather than problems and weaknesses. Positive leaders promote health—they create healthy environments, healthy communication, and healthy relationships (Lucey & Burke, 2022). They prioritise connection with and between others, and deepen these connections over time (Lucey & Burke, 2022).

Kim Cameron's most recent book *Positively Energizing Leadership: Virtuous Actions and Relationships that Create High Performance* (2021) evolves "positive leadership" to "positively energising leadership". PEL emphasises the role of leaders in creating and spreading positive energy in organisations. The book focuses on how virtuous actions and positive relationships can lead to extraordinary or "positively deviant" performance. While deviance usually carries a negative connotation, Cameron uses the term "positive deviance" to communicate the extent to which positive leadership can create results which are far beyond our expectations: these outcomes are *positively deviant*, that is, deviant, in a good way!

How are these outcomes achieved? The foundation for positive leaders lies in virtuous behaviours such as compassion, forgiveness, gratitude, and kindness, all embodied in positive relationships (Cameron, 2018, 2021). Cameron (2021) draws on the Latin and Greek origins of the word "virtuousness", which equate it with "excellence": "More recently, virtuousness has been described as representing the best of the human condition, the most ennobling behaviors and outcomes of people, the excellence and essence of humankind, and the highest aspirations of human beings" (Cameron, 2021, loc. 847).

Cameron's four core positive leadership strategies were introduced in *Positive Leadership: Strategies for Extraordinary Performance* (2018): positive leaders create a positive climate, build positive relationships, engage in positive communication, and help others experience positive meaning. Let's explore these strategies and consider their application to music making with others for social connection.

Core strategies for positive leaders

Building a positive climate, relationships, and meaning for participants using positive communication is fundamental to music leaders' practice when seeking to build social connections between participants: " … community music facilitators must attend to multiple layers of relationship and interaction between themselves and participants, between participants, and between each person and the musical material as it evolves" (Howell et al., 2017, p. 606). The core strategies for positively energising leaders provide concrete actions to help navigate these multiple layers.

Positive climate

A positive climate is one in which "positive emotions predominate over negative emotions" (Cameron, 2018, loc. 322). The idea of creating a positive climate draws on Fredrickson's (2004, 2010) "broaden and build" theory of positive emotions which says that positive emotions *expand* our possibilities for thought and action, whereas negative emotions *narrow* the possibilities (see **Chapter 3**). As with positive self-leadership explored in Part I, there are simple practices music leaders can cultivate with their groups to create a positive climate.

PRACTICE POINTS

- Begin or end a music making session with a simple **gratitude** reflection. For example, ask your group to close their eyes and focus on something *about the group* for which they are grateful. It could be the opportunity to simply take a break from the business of everyday life, or for the companionship of someone in the group, or the chance to be expressive. Nothing is too small to notice.
- Express **gratitude** to your group regularly for their contributions—acknowledge someone's help in setting up the room, or participants' strong voices in a particular section of a song. Again, nothing is too small to notice!
- Get creative with your group and compose a simple **gratitude song** which you perform as a ritual for your group, thanking the leader/s, the participants, and any volunteers who support the group.
- Listen to a piece of music with your group and marvel at the gift of music, cultivating a sense of **gratitude** for the positive role music plays in our lives.
- Model **compassion** towards yourself and others in the group. Acknowledge your own mistakes as a leader and make light of them to promote a growth mindset in the group—reframe mistakes as information to help the group learn and improve (Coyle, 2009). When someone is struggling to grasp a particular idea or skill, demonstrate compassion and patience rather than engage in critique.
- **Compassion** is particularly important when a group member suffers some personal loss or pain. Rather than failing to acknowledge this (which is very common in regular workplaces), a positive leader will facilitate the group's collective noticing, feeling, and response to the pain experienced by a group member (Kanov et al., 2004). Simply acknowledging the humanity of such a situation is a virtuous action a positive leader can take to build a positive climate of trust, care, and concern.
- If the practice of **compassion** in music making strikes a chord with you, you may wish to explore this topic in depth in the book *Compassionate Music Teaching* by Karin S. Hendricks (2018). The six ingredients for compassionate music teaching are trust, empathy, patience, inclusion, community, and authentic connection. Just like Cameron's positive leadership, Hendricks's compassionate teaching framework draws on virtuous behaviours like trust and empathy as the foundation for positive relationships with others.
- Balance **confidence** in your musical skills and abilities with a **vulnerability** to consider others' views and the admit when you've got it wrong!

RESONANCE—Creating a safe space

Every music leader interviewed for this book emphasised the importance of creating a positive climate for their groups, a space which is safe for people to be themselves and free from judgment.

Musical inclusion advocate Graham Sattler describes it as follows:

[As a music leader] you have to create a judgment free environment. Absolutely. It's being capable of being able to genuinely welcome people into a space in which they are able to feel safe, they are able to feel vulnerable, and that they're able to experiment, that they can try. That it is judgment free, that it is hospitable in the true sense of the word, and a space also in which they feel they can question or challenge—and challenge you as the leader. This requires confidence on the part of the leader, compassion, and a willingness to be vulnerable but to balance that vulnerability with knowledge and capability, and to see vulnerability as the opposite of failing.

This emphasis on creating psychological safety takes different forms for different leaders. James Sills describes it as "realising that what I really love to do is bring people together, to hold the space, to create the space", while musician Gillian Howell emphasises leaving space for agency: "In every creative decision, you're just leaving space in front of people—space for them to step into if they choose ... never crowding someone out—not crowding out their energy, not making assumptions."

Group songwriting facilitator Naomi Sunderland speaks of taking on a persona that is high energy with "body language that sort of role models that lack of shame ... without going too overboard ... there's a lot of role modelling and then ... gradually lowering people down the cliff face with small steps first and to build confidence". When leading a songwriting group, Naomi might start with some grounding or breathing to "get in the same room at the same time" and then move into sense-bound image making (using the senses to come up with song lyric ideas): "It's stuff that's accessible to all of us. We all have bodies. That's also where a lot of the healing or therapeutic outcomes can be intensified by bringing people back into their bodies and having positive embodied experience at the same time."

Singing leader Jane York sees safety as foundational to music leadership, especially when working with vulnerable populations. "I want people to feel safe to be in that room firstly, and that's not a given for people that I work with", she explains. For Jane, this means "depressurising the experience" and recognising that participation can take many forms: "It's about making a space that's going to encourage participation whatever way that person's capable of on that day." This might mean offering a cup of tea, exchanging greetings, or simply providing a rare moment of respite where no demands are made.

RESONANCE—Setting the rules

When leading a group songwriting session, Naomi Sunderland discusses how she sets three rules or protocols for participating. Naomi learned the process of simple rule setting from Kristina Jacobsen, who's an ethnographic songwriter, ethnomusicologist and anthropologist at the University of New Mexico. She learned deeper practices of setting shared protocols through We Al-li training in culturally informed trauma integrated healing.

Naomi begins by saying that everyone is welcome, then expresses the rules so the group understands the parameters within which they are creating. For example, "if someone shares a story, it's not your story. It's still their story. You don't get to repeat it." Naomi explains to participants:

> You are in charge of your level of participation. If you need to sit down and rest, you rest. If you don't want to participate, you can stand and support in any way you like. You can roll around on the floor. You can squeal, whatever, it's all welcome here.

Then Naomi usually intuits the final rule based on the setting and the group. Another rule Naomi learned from Kristina is "we say yes":

> When there's a creative fire starting to kindle, we don't want to dampen that fire by going no, I don't think that's a good idea. We say yes to every idea. We follow it and if it's not going to work out it will just naturally fall to the forest floor as fertiliser for our creative work together. So, don't worry if you don't like the idea that someone puts forward. Just say yes and let your inner critic go and have a little walk and sit by the fire. We love them but they can sit over there for now ...

These insights from music leaders demonstrate how creating a positive climate goes far beyond simply maintaining an upbeat atmosphere. It requires a deep understanding of psychological safety, a willingness to be vulnerable as a leader, and the ability to create spaces where people feel truly welcomed rather than merely tolerated. When leaders successfully cultivate such environments, they tap into the heliotropic effect Cameron describes, creating conditions where people naturally orient themselves toward growth, connection, and flourishing.

Positive communication

It's communicating genuinely human-to-human.

—Graham Sattler, musical inclusion advocate

It's about lightness and playfulness and humour, but not making it about that. It's a balance.

—James Sills, vocal leader

How we talk is hugely important.

—Jane York, singing leader

Positive communication requires music leaders to become intentional about language and monitoring the number of positive statements we make relative to negative statements: "Positive statements are those that express appreciation, support, helpfulness, approval, or compliments. Negative statements express criticism, disapproval, dissatisfaction, cynicism, or disagreement" (Cameron, 2018, loc. 742). As positive leaders, we want to aim for positive statements to significantly outnumber negative statements if we are seeking to promote the best in ourselves and others.

RESONANCE—Fame not shame, let's all play the game!

To foreground positive communication, in her community songwriting workshops, Naomi Sunderland often tells the story of the Mulga Bore hard rock band from remote Central Australia.

Mulga Bore Hard Rock won the Battle of the Bands and ended up opening for mega group Kiss at a stadium gig on the Gold Coast in 2022, performing to thousands of heavy rock fans. The lead singer of Mulga Bore Alvin Manfong has a motto, "Fame not shame, let's all play the game!" Naomi uses this story and Alvin's motto to invite and role model positive and open communication within the group. In this way, Naomi is inviting participants to offer their ideas and provide positive support for everyone throughout the creative process, without fear of shame.

While the subject of positive communication—including having difficult or challenging conversations—is huge and the subject of many books and methods, the following are a few key things to try when leading music groups for social connection.

PRACTICE POINTS

- Provide consistent encouragement to your group through affirmative statements: "Wow, you are all sounding great!" or "I can really hear how much you are all paying attention to x".
- Acknowledge and celebrate members of the group, but with a caveat. As you get to know your group, you may have some members who prefer not to be publicly acknowledged in front of the group, but still appreciate you taking the time to acknowledge their contributions quietly. One study of music

leaders' experiences of working with a singing group for people with Parkinson's found that having strong interpersonal skills to pick up on nonverbal cues of participants was an important factor in making sure members were acknowledged in ways that were right for them (Forbes & Bartlett, 2020a).

- In situations where you need to provide a participant with feedback they may not want to hear, try "descriptive communication" (Cameron, 2018). Describe the behaviour dispassionately rather than evaluate it, identify the objective consequences of the behaviour, and suggest an acceptable alternative behaviour (Cameron, 2018). For example, singing group leaders will often come across a scenario where a member may be singing too loudly, affecting those around them. A way to handle this using descriptive communication would be: "Your volume is high relative to the other singers and we all need to hear each other. Try to match your volume to the others around you." This feedback is of course best given to the participant in private rather than in front of the whole group. A skilful positive leader will slip this feedback into conversation so that it does not seem like a big deal to the receiver.

RESONANCE—Turning challenges into opportunities through positive communication

Community music practitioner Allison Girvan demonstrates how positive communication can transform potential limitations into creative opportunities. Her approach is based on "setting intentions rather than expectations", allowing room for beautiful accidents and unexpected innovations: "Sometimes it can be simply a mistake that somebody makes where it's like, 'wow, that note sounds really great in that chord, let's keep that in there'."

This philosophy proved particularly powerful when working with participants with mobility challenges. When one member was concerned about using a cane during body percussion activities, Allison shared how another member had transformed their cane into a unique percussion instrument: "He ended up looking like the most badass person in the choir because he had this instrument that nobody else had access to!"

Allison's positive communication style consistently opens possibilities rather than imposing limitations: "We can't know at this point where this might go ... you are encouraged to explore what feels true for you and what might actually end up being a much more powerful experience than if you weren't there."

This collaborative approach extends to how she handles suggestions from group members:

> I've gotten much better at gently saying, "That's a great idea. Let's see if we can find a way to deploy that down the road." So that people feel emboldened to offer up suggestions and not feel beaten back ... Because I really do feel like if something sparks for somebody and they express it, there's something to it. It's got potential at some point.

Allison's approach illustrates how positive communication goes beyond simply offering praise or avoiding criticism. Positive communication transforms challenges into opportunities, validates diverse forms of participation, and creates an environment where everyone feels empowered to contribute. Through consistent encouragement, thoughtful acknowledgment of contributions, and skilful handling of feedback, positive music leaders use communication intentionally to nurture individual growth and group cohesion. The language music leaders choose shapes not just how participants feel in the moment, but their ongoing relationship with music making and their sense of belonging within the group.

Positive relationships

Building positive relationships is one of the core strategies of a positively energising leader to promote the health, wellbeing, and flourishing of those they work with. Positive relationships are fundamental to the practices outlined throughout this book, as they are foundational to building social connections, belonging, and better social health. As we've seen in earlier chapters, positive relationships are critical to our mental and physical health—remember, they are so important that they even impact our longevity!

Within Cameron's framework, positive relationships are nurtured through relational energy which is generated through virtuous actions of "generosity, compassion, gratitude, trustworthiness, forgiveness, and kindness" (Cameron, 2018, loc. 116). Cameron argues that relational energy does not deplete like other forms of energy; rather when it is consistently created through virtuous actions, positive relational energy intensifies (Cameron, 2021, loc. 327).

We've all experienced the beneficial effects of positive relational energy when we interact with someone who makes us feel energised, enthusiastic, buoyant, and uplifted. We've also experienced the opposite when an interpersonal interaction leaves us feeling defeated, depleted, or disheartened. Because positive energy is a "non-zero-sum game" it can be "infinitely expanded in a system" (Cameron, 2021, loc. 501).

Positive relational energy does not rely on the charisma or extroversion of the leader, nor does it rely on "superhuman attributes" (Cameron, 2021, loc. 813). Rather, positive relational energy is a learned behaviour which can be practised and developed through intentional and consistent application of positive practices based on virtuous behaviours. In other words, practising virtuous behaviours builds positive relationships which in turn creates self-reinforcing positive energy within a group (or organisation) (Cameron, 2021).

PRACTICE POINTS

Strength-based leadership

- Positive leaders focus on building on group members' strengths. For example, in the singing group for people with Parkinson's that I lead, we have one member who lost his wife to Parkinson's some years ago, yet he continues to attend our sessions. This member has been encouraged to continue attending, of course for the social support, but also because he has a lovely singing voice, and really helps to boost the group sound. He is one of our strongest singers, and this is remarked upon frequently, promoting positive relational energy.

- Positive leaders practice humility. They are focused on taking action to help others flourish which is its own reward. In a study of singing group leaders' experiences of their work, the positive relationships formed with and between group members was integral to the reward and meaning the leaders' received from their practice (Forbes & Bartlett, 2020b).

Intentional practice

- Notice how much time you spend during a group music session on building positive relational energy and how much time you spend giving instructions or seeking to influence participants. Consciously cultivate your practice to emphasise positive relational energy as the most important thing you can do as a music leader to foster wellbeing and connection.
- Celebrate the life-enhancing relationships of the group at each session by intentionally noting them, and the role they play in creating positive energy. Draw focus and attention to the playful, joyful moments of personal and musical interaction and celebrate these with the group.

Creating connection opportunities

- A very common practice to build positive relationships among community music groups for social connection is socialising together *outside* of group music time. For example, members might regularly go for coffee and cake after a group music session. While this additional socialising is not mandatory, for some people it is a vitally important source of social connection. These opportunities for "extra-curricular" get-togethers further solidify the positive relationships between group members.

RESONANCE—Building positive relationships through music

Community music practitioner Allison Girvan compares football and group singing to illustrate how music builds positive relationships. Both activities involve practising together, building skills, and working toward performance. However, as Allison observes, while sports are inherently adversarial— "you're always playing against another team"—group music making is purely collaborative: "There's no contrary force". This has implications for relationship building that flow when an activity is inherently cooperative rather than competitive.

According to Allison, this fundamental difference shapes how relationships develop within musical groups. Without competition driving the dynamic, participants can focus entirely on supporting each other and creating something beautiful together. The process involves what Allison calls "woodshedding"—working "hard on something over and over and over again" until the group achieves a magical synergy. She reflects that in our world of constant novelty and change, this shared commitment to practice helps to create unique bonds between people.

The journey from practice to performance further strengthens these relationships. Group members work intimately together, "mapping things out … understanding where to breathe, where not to breathe, what kind of sound to make", until they can present their work to others. This shared experience of dedication, discovery, and eventual celebration creates relationships built on mutual support rather than competition. Allison says the final performance becomes "that moment where the communication is complete"—not just between performers and audience, but between group members who have learned to trust and rely on each other throughout the creative process.

Allison's comparison of sports and music making illustrates Cameron's point about positive relational energy being "infinitely expandable" within a system. Unlike competitive activities where energy is often divided or depleted, collaborative music making creates an ever-expanding reservoir of positive relationships and connections. Each practice session, each shared breath, each moment of collective discovery adds to this renewable source of energy, creating what Cameron calls a "non-zero-sum game" where everyone benefits and no one's gain comes at another's expense.

Positive meaning

According to positive psychology, we experience something as meaningful when the focus is taken off us, and we feel we are contributing to something greater than ourselves (Seligman, 2011). Positive leaders seek to cultivate a strong sense of meaning for themselves and for those they work with (Cameron, 2018).

Creating meaning through music involves helping participants connect deeply with the material and recognising how their individual contributions contribute to collective success. These practices align with Cameron's (2018) emphasis on helping people find deeper purpose in their work and activities.

RESONANCE—Finding meaning through story and song

Community music practitioner Allison Girvan demonstrates how exploring the deeper meaning of song lyrics can transform both the musical experience and the sound itself:

> We've had lots of conversations about what these words [of a particular song] mean. [The song is] in Swedish so we need to translate it and talk about each word, what that picture looks like in their heads … what

does it feel like to have the wind under your wings? What does it feel like to sing as though that wind is under your wings?

Rather than focusing on technical corrections ("you're under pitch there"), Allison engages singers' imaginations and emotions through storytelling. This approach not only improves the musical outcome but creates a deeply meaningful experience for participants. As she observes, "As human beings we're so hard-wired not just to enjoy story but to need story, to actually require story in our lives".

By connecting singing to universal human experiences and emotions, Allison skilfully guides participants towards finding greater purpose in their music making.

PRACTICE POINTS

- When working with your group, draw attention to the positive impacts of the group on individual health and wellbeing. Emphasise that each and every member contributes to these positive outcomes—the group is nothing without its members, so every person has a vital role to play.
- Periodically discuss with your group your personal values, and how those values inform your practice. For example, if you personally value excellence, explain to your group how they help you achieve excellence in your music practice e.g. through their enthusiastic participation, their openness to learning new skills, or their generosity to fellow group members. Help your group members understand how their participation contributes to the group's "positively deviant outcomes".
- Periodically remind participants of the group's origins. Perhaps your group had humble beginnings and has gone on to achieve extraordinary things such as public performances, or individual successes. Emphasise to the group their role in achieving these positively deviant outcomes.
- Always recognise the contributions of group members to the day-to-day functioning of the group, and to the bigger picture successes such as providing social support, creating belonging, and being a group that values each person's unique strengths.

These positive practices will consistently reinforce to your group that when the group comes together in pursuit of shared values and goals, they can achieve extraordinary things. This can be a great source of meaning for you as a music leader, and for each member of your group.

Positively energising leadership and the PERMA model for wellbeing

Positively energising leadership is focused on positively deviant outcomes and promoting health, wellbeing, and human flourishing. How does positively energising leadership map to the elements of Martin Seligman's (2011) PERMA model for wellbeing (explored in Chapter 3)?

Positive emotions

PEL emphasises creating and fostering positive energy, which directly relates to positive emotions. Positively energising leaders consciously and intentionally cultivate environments where individuals experience more gratitude and compassion, joy and optimism. Recall Fredrickson's (2004, 2010) "broaden and build" theory of positive emotions which we explored in Chapter 3. Positive emotions broaden our possibilities for action and build psychological resources, helping us to be more resilient, hopeful, and happier (Fredrickson, 2004, 2010).

Engagement

PEL emphasises strengths, and when people can play to their strengths, they become highly engaged and may even experience flow, a state of optimal functioning where we lose track of time and feel highly energised afterwards.

Relationships

Positively energising leaders foster relational energy and build supportive relationships between those they work with. This directly aligns with the R in PERMA, which emphasises the importance of building and maintaining positive relationships for wellbeing.

Meaning

By leveraging strengths, positively energising leaders help people find purpose and meaning. By enacting virtuous behaviours and creating a positive culture, these leaders imbue others with a sense of meaning and purpose. Positively energising leaders help us understand that when we come together, we create something bigger than ourselves.

Accomplishment

Positively energising leaders seek to create positively deviant outcomes that are beyond our expectations. This creates a sense of accomplishment and achievement, not just for individual participants but for the leader as well. Singing leader Jane York shares a powerful example of how these accomplishments can create expanding ripples of achievement:

> I often have people come to me who've never sung in a group, never done harmony singing. They'd come and they'd be in my group for a year, two years, and they'd build their confidence up to go on to perhaps a group that is

auditioned, more performance focused, to challenge themselves a bit. So, they'd sort of graduate and I'd say, "See you later!"

When one such member later performed with their new group and credited Jane for making it possible, her response exemplifies the humble appreciation characteristic of positive leaders:

Firstly no, *you've* worked really hard … You're the one singing, but just making possibilities for people to do music in a way that is a bigger part of their life, is something I'm very grateful for that opportunity, to be a part of that journey for people.

Jane's story demonstrates how positively energising leadership creates a sense of accomplishment at multiple levels—the immediate accomplishments within the group, the longer-term growth in participants' capabilities and confidence, and the leader's own sense of meaningful achievement in supporting others' journeys.

Research perspective

A systematic review of the research on the skills and attributes of singing group leaders (referred to as facilitators in the review) supports the strategies outlined in this chapter as effective ways to foster social connection and social health (Irons et al., 2024). The review found that effective leadership qualities include being democratic, collaborative, and compassionate rather than authoritarian or dictatorial. Group leaders need to balance providing structure with being flexible and adaptive to the needs of the group and leadership skills involve empowering participants, encouraging different forms of participation, and developing a sense of collective ownership. Further, effective leaders create an enthusiastic, positive, and motivating atmosphere.

Perhaps most importantly, the review supported the idea of cultivating positive relationships as being central to the role of leader. Group leaders show genuine interest and concern for members, create a warm, welcoming, and accepting environment, foster social connections and a sense of belonging among group members, and treat singers with respect using positive communication to provide constructive feedback.

Overall, this systematic review emphasises that effective group singing facilitation involves a combination of musical competency and strong interpersonal/leadership skills to create positive, energising experiences and foster meaningful social connections among participants. The strategies of positively energising leadership outlined in this chapter can help guide emerging and established music leaders towards these positively deviant outcomes.

Overcoming challenges

Remember, positive approaches to leadership do not deny the existence of challenges; rather, they acknowledge challenges while seeking to maintain a positive bias (Cameron, 2018, 2021). Some key challenges positive music leaders will face include honouring diversity, equity, and inclusion in their groups, managing compassion fatigue, and the hidden costs of working within funding systems which do not extend support (to either the leader or participants) beyond the life of the project (if indeed, funding is available at all).

Music leaders work in diverse contexts with diverse participant groups. Are the strategies of positively energising leadership broadly applicable? Yes. In fact, Cameron (2018, loc. 682) argues that the strategies of positive leadership are *crucial* to creating "a culture of diversity, equity, and inclusion". How then do we balance a positive approach which takes participants at face value and focuses on their strengths, with the reality that, at times, music leaders work "exist[s] within a hierarchy of priorities" (Howell et al., 2017) which may often be culturally and socially determined, and in conflict with those of positive leadership?

Howell et al. (2017) raise the paradox of inclusion, in that groups for specific cohorts may exclude others. The commitment to inclusion is paramount and leaders need to be alive to any tendency for some group members to form "in groups" (and thus relegating others to "out groups"). This emphasises the challenge to maintain the dynamic nature of these groups, never allowing them to become exclusionary but at the same time, building a sense of cohesion: "facilitation involves a constantly reflexive and responsive act, and a willingness to weight and counterweight contrasting and sometimes conflicting needs of a group in musical and social terms" (Howell et al., 2017, p. 612).

In addition to honouring diversity and inclusion, there is also the challenge for positive leaders of managing what is referred to as "compassion fatigue". It is characterised by feeling less compassion over time and can lead to serious physical and mental exhaustion (Cocker & Joss, 2016). Music leaders working with diverse groups, which include vulnerable members of the community (those experiencing trauma, disadvantage, or health issues), need to be aware of the signs of compassion fatigue and prevention strategies. Symptoms include emotional exhaustion, reduced empathy, feeling hopeless or powerless, a decreased sense of accomplishment, irritability or anger, difficulty sleeping, and physical and emotional fatigue (Figley, 2002). Preventative strategies include practising self-care, maintaining work-life balance, seeking support from colleagues or professionals, setting realistic expectations and boundaries, and engaging in stress-reduction techniques (Mathieu, 2012; see Chapter 3).

RESONANCE—Embodied compassion and the universal heart

Singing for health practitioner–researcher Emily Foulkes reflects on how her work has evolved from empathy towards embodied compassion:

> There's research that shows that empathy lights up the same parts of the brain associated with pain. If we feel somebody else's pain, then we really feel it. That's when we end up with what was called compassion fatigue but is now often referred to as empathy stress. If we feel

compassion, which is really truly coming from a heartful space of compassion, then we should feel on top of the world. We should feel really amazing that we are helping somebody, and we're doing our best to help somebody.

Emily makes a distinction between her personal heart and universal heart:

If we're in our personal heart, then we are more likely to feel pain, and we are more likely to become really affected, and really upset, and really worn out, and drained, and burnt out. If we're tapping into this more universal heart and compassion, then that's less likely to happen because we've got those boundaries. We've got that in place that, yes, I'd feel you, but there's this permeable boundary around that enables me to still be able to give and do as much as I can but without feeling drained.

One final challenge is that socially engaged artistic leadership comes with additional, often unrecognised costs (Belfiore, 2022). Leaders of publicly funded participatory arts projects involving disadvantaged communities often feel a deep moral obligation to provide care for participants beyond their formal job requirements. This sense of duty stems from their understanding of participants' social challenges and their own ethical and political beliefs. However, the funding structure rarely provides adequate resources for leaders to fulfil these care responsibilities, both during and after the project. Belfiore (2022) contends that this represents a failure in cultural policy: public arts institutions and funders effectively sidestep meaningful care responsibilities, instead relying on artists' ethical principles and willingness to take on these extra duties. Given the power disparity between artists and funders, this reliance on unpaid discretionary effort is fundamentally exploitative (Belfiore, 2022).

Music leaders working in community settings may face similar challenges to those described by Belfiore (2022). The sense of moral obligation to care for participants beyond contracted duties, combined with inadequate resources and support, can lead to stress, burnout, and potentially compassion fatigue.

While these systemic issues require policy-level changes, positively energising leadership strategies can help music leaders navigate these challenges more effectively:

- **Cultivate positive meaning.** Reconnect with your core values and the purpose of your work (see Chapter 2). This can help maintain motivation and resilience in the face of challenges.
- **Build positive relationships.** Foster a support network with fellow music leaders or other community artists (see Chapter 2). Share experiences, strategies, and resources to collectively address challenges.

- **Practice positive communication.** Clearly articulate the value and impact of your work to funders and institutions. This may help in advocating for better support and resources (we will explore this in further detail in Part III).
- **Create a positive climate.** Implement self-care practices (see Chapter 3) and encourage the same in those you work with. This can help mitigate stress and prevent burnout.
- **Set boundaries.** While maintaining compassion, establish clear limits on your responsibilities to protect your own wellbeing (see Chapter 3).

These strategies are not intended to be trite solutions to serious systemic issues but rather are offered as tools to help music leaders maintain their wellbeing and effectiveness in the face of challenges.

Refrain

Positively energising leadership offers music leaders a transformative approach to fostering social connection and belonging through music. By focusing on virtuous behaviours, cultivating positive relationships, and creating environments where positive emotions flourish, music leaders can achieve "positively deviant" outcomes that go beyond ordinary expectations. This approach not only enhances the wellbeing of participants but also contributes to the leaders' own sense of purpose and fulfilment. As we tackle the global crisis of social disconnection, the principles of positively energising leadership provide a way forward, showing how music can be a powerful force for revitalising our relationships and our social health.

Call and response

1   Reflect on a time when you experienced or witnessed positively energising leadership in a musical context. How did it affect the participants and the overall atmosphere?
2   Consider the four core strategies of positively energising leadership. Which one do you feel most drawn to implement in your own practice, and why?
3   How might you apply the principles of positively energising leadership to address a specific challenge in your music leadership practice?
4   Think about a "positively deviant" outcome you'd like to achieve with your music group. Dream big! What steps could you take, using PEL strategies, to work towards this goal?
5   In what ways could you foster more positive relational energy in your music leadership practice? What might be the potential benefits and challenges of doing so?

References

Baumeister, R. F., Bratslavsky, E., Finkenauer, C., & Vohs, K. D. (2001). Bad is stronger than good. *Review of General Psychology, 5*(4), 323–370.

Belfiore, E. (2022). Who cares? At what price? The hidden costs of socially engaged arts labour and the moral failure of cultural policy. *European Journal of Cultural Studies, 25* (1), 61–78.

Cameron, K. S. (2018). *Positive leadership: Strategies for extraordinary performance* (2nd ed.). Berrett-Koehler.

Cameron, K. S. (2021). *Positively energizing leadership: Virtuous actions and relationships that create high performance* (1st edition). Berrett-Koehler.

Cocker, F., & Joss, N. (2016). Compassion fatigue among healthcare, emergency and community service workers: A systematic review. *International Journal of Environmental Research and Public Health, 13*(6), article 6. doi:10.3390/ijerph13060618.

Coyle, D. (2009). *The talent code: Greatness isn't born. it's grown. Here's how.* Random House.

Figley, C. R. (2002). Compassion fatigue: Psychotherapists' chronic lack of self care. *Journal of Clinical Psychology, 58*(11), 1433–1441. doi:10.1002/jclp.10090.

Forbes, M., & Bartlett, I. (2020a). "It's much harder than I thought": Facilitating a singing group for people with Parkinson's disease. *International Journal of Community Music, 13*(1), 29–47. doi:10.1386/ijcm_00009_1.

Forbes, M., & Bartlett, I. (2020b). "This circle of joy": Meaningful musicians' work and the benefits of facilitating singing groups. *Music Education Research, 22*(5), 555–568. doi:10.1080/14613808.2020.1841131.

Fredrickson, B. L. (2004). The broaden-and-build theory of positive emotions. *Philosophical Transactions of the Royal Society B: Biological Sciences, 359*(1449), 1367–1378. doi:10.1098/rstb.2004.1512.

Fredrickson, B. L. (2010). *Positivity: Groundbreaking research to release your inner optimist and thrive.* Penguin.

Hendricks, K. S. (2018). *Compassionate music teaching: A framework for motivation and engagement in the 21st century.* Rowman & Littlefield.

Howell, G., Higgins, L., & Bartleet, B.-L. (2017). Community music practice: Intervention through facilitation. In R. Mantie & G. D. Smith (eds), *The Oxford handbook of music making and leisure* (pp. 601–618). Oxford University Press.

Irons, J. Y., Bonshor, M., Tip, L., Boyd, S., Wydenbach, N., & Sheffield, D. (2024). What are the skills, attributes and knowledge for group singing facilitators? A systematic review. *International Journal of Community Music, 17*(2), 129–160. doi:10.1386/ijcm_00101_1.

Kanov, J. M., Maitlis, S., Worline, M. C., Dutton, J. E., Frost, P. J., & Lilius, J. M. (2004). Compassion in organizational life. *American Behavioral Scientist, 47*(6), 808–827. doi:10.1177/0002764203260211.

Lucey, C., & Burke, J. (2022). *Positive leadership in practice: A model for our future* (1st edition). Routledge.

Mathieu, F. (2012). *The compassion fatigue workbook: Creative tools for transforming compassion fatigue and vicarious traumatization.* Routledge. doi:10.4324/9780203803349.

Seligman, M. E. P. (2011). *Flourish: A visionary new understanding of happiness and well-being.* Simon & Schuster.

6 Activating the power of social identity for connection

Introduction

As human beings, we all share a fundamental need to belong, to feel part of something larger than ourselves. This innate drive for connection is a crucial component of our overall health and wellbeing. In the previous chapter, we explored how positively energising leadership founded in leaders' virtuous behaviours can foster positive relationships within our groups and enhance connection and wellbeing. In this chapter we examine how the group itself can become a powerful source of social connection and belonging.

Even under extremely challenging circumstances, collective music making can create a valuable new health-enhancing *social identity* which builds connection and belonging. In a research study I conducted with carers in the "Park 'n Songs" singing group for people with Parkinson's, participants reflected that caring for a spouse with Parkinson's had diminished their *personal* identity—much of their existence had been subsumed into the caring role. However, participating in the singing group generated a new, expansive *social* identity, creating a wellspring of psychological resources: the group increased their agency, renewed their purpose, and provided social support and belonging. Carers truly felt a part of the Park 'n Songs community (Forbes, 2021). One of the carers in the group, Edward (a pseudonym), eloquently described this transformation:

> Life can be fairly empty … you can get sidelined and you can become insular. [The group has] meant that the gravity or drift into that has not been as strong. And that we're pushing back against those things, and re-engaging with people, and relationships in a situation which was otherwise just closing in, diminishing.

For Edward, being a member of Park 'n Songs created a new social identity, one which helped him "push back" against the forces of Parkinson's.

Drawing on theories from social psychology, this chapter equips you to harness the power of social identity and provides strategies to help your group members feel they truly belong to something meaningful. You will learn how to cultivate a shared social identity that goes beyond individual connections, creating a collective

DOI: 10.4324/9781003426509-9

"we" that can provide group members with vital psychological resources. By understanding and applying social identity principles, you can transform your music groups into sources of connection, support, and enhanced wellbeing for your participants, just as the Park 'n Songs group did for the spouse carers.

The social identity approach: Understanding group dynamics

Your identity is a complex tapestry; some threads represent your individual characteristics such as your personality, skills, and experiences. But woven throughout are also threads that represent the groups you belong to, like your family, profession, and community. Understanding the interplay between individual and group identities is at the heart of the social identity approach.

The social identity approach has been applied in both the domains of health and leadership, and combines two influential theories: social identity theory (Tajfel & Turner, 1986) and self-categorisation theory (Turner et al., 1987). Together, these theories provide a powerful framework for understanding how group memberships shape our sense of self and our behaviour, and impact our health and wellbeing.

At its core, the social identity approach suggests that our group memberships profoundly influence who we are and how we behave (Reynolds et al., 2020). It's not just about who we are as individuals, but also about the "we" that we become when we're part of a group:

1   We categorise ourselves as members of various groups (e.g. "I'm a musician", "I'm part of the community choir").
2   We adopt the values and norms of these groups.
3   Our behaviour starts to align with these group norms.

The process of social identification can happen naturally, but as a music leader, you can actively nurture it. By intentionally cultivating a strong group identity, you can unlock powerful health benefits for your group members. This is where two specific social identity perspectives come into play:

1   the social cure approach to health, which explores how group memberships can act as a "social cure", boosting health and wellbeing (Haslam et al., 2018); and
2   the social identity approach to leadership, which explores how leaders can shape and strengthen group identities to benefit members (Haslam et al., 2020).

RESONANCE—The voice as a source of shared identity

The social identity approach suggests that our sense of self is profoundly shaped by our group memberships. Community music practitioner Allison Girvan offers a compelling perspective on how the voice—both literal and metaphorical—can serve as a powerful tool for building shared identity:

Voice is one of the most inclusive ways to bring people together. We each have a voice as part of our identity. When we use our voices collaboratively, we need to be attuned to what the group is doing. If your voice is a certain colour, you can blend yours with another colour and come up with something greater than the sum of its parts. Voice is a birthright. Babies sing sometimes before they speak ... but I don't know how many adults I've come across who say "I can't sing" because they were told at some point, usually by some choral director in elementary school, that they couldn't sing and to please just mouth the words. This is about reclaiming something which I think is a birthright.

Allison's reflections point to several key principles of social identity formation. Her description of voices blending like colours to create "something greater than the sum of its parts" perfectly captures how individual identities can merge into a new collective whole without losing their distinctive qualities. When leading a choir, Allison speaks of being "attuned to what the group is doing," describing the delicate balance between individual expression and group cohesion.

Perhaps most importantly, her framing of singing as a "birthright" suggests that the capacity for group belonging is innate and common to our human experience—we just need the right conditions and leadership to activate it and draw us together.

Allison's practice is motivated by a deep desire to bring people together, not despite their differences, but because of them. She harnesses the wonderful unifying forces of singing and the energy we create when we sing together to bridge divides. She says, "My life's practice is how to bridge gaps, how to bring people together using music and specifically the voice. Using voice as a binding medium for people who may feel very differently to each other."

In the following sections, we will dive deeper into social identity approaches to health and leadership, and provide you with practical strategies to harness the power of social identity in your music groups.

The social cure approach to health

While we all probably understand that we have a personal identity unique to us that we share with the world (Breakwell, 2023), we may not necessarily appreciate that we also have various social identities. Social identity refers to "internalised group membership that serves to define a person's sense of 'who they are' in a given context" (Haslam et al., 2018, p. 15). For example, at the individual level, I identify as "Melissa" with certain personal attributes. At the social level, I identify as female, Australian, a practitioner–researcher, a member of the Park 'n Songs singing group, to name a few examples. These social identifications mean I am cognitively and emotionally attached to these groups (Reynolds et al., 2020). The extent of my attachment depends on how much I value and find meaning in my membership (Haslam et al., 2018).

There is mounting evidence that social identification impacts our health. Haslam et al. (2018) present a range of hypotheses about group membership, social identity, and health. The key hypothesis for this current chapter is that "a person will generally experience the health-related benefits or costs of a given group membership only to the extent that they identify with that group" (Haslam et al., 2018, p. 17).

The social cure perspective emphasises the critical role of social identification in promoting health outcomes. When individuals strongly identify with a group, they experience multiple benefits: a sense of connection and belonging, a deepened sense of purpose, increased motivation to support fellow group members, and enhanced personal agency and control (Greenaway et al., 2016; Haslam et al., 2018).

At the heart of social identification is transforming "other" into "self"—we develop a sense of "us-ness" (Haslam et al., 2018). This forms the basis of group behaviours and important social processes like communication, trust, social connection, and leadership (Haslam, 2004).

For music leaders, understanding these principles can help you intentionally foster health-enhancing group identities in your ensembles, potentially amplifying the wellbeing benefits for your participants.

As a music leader, be aware that personal identities may conflict with the adoption of a new social identity. For instance, as Allison noted, many people believe they "can't sing". Remember, group members won't identify with a group they don't value or feel they could never belong to. If you are leading a community singing group, for example, your role is to create a space where even self-identified "non-singers" can learn to enjoy singing, understand their contribution, and eventually identify as group members. Consider gentle education about the rarity of true tone-deafness and the role of social conditioning in developing a "vocal identity". However, always respect individual choice—promoting social identity should never mean coercing unwilling participants.

In arts and health, the social identity approach has been used in numerous studies, demonstrating how identification with arts groups can improve mental health and wellbeing in adults with chronic health conditions (Dingle et al., 2013, 2017; Williams et al., 2019a, 2019b). Crucially, mere participation is not enough; benefits are tied to the extent of group identification. This underscores the importance of music leaders employing specific strategies to facilitate group identification.

With this understanding of social identification and its health implications, let's explore how music leaders can develop identity leadership skills to harness the group's power for enhancing social health.

The social identity approach to leadership

Graham Sattler, musical inclusion advocate, has seen the power of social identity first-hand:

The sense of membership is, I think, a really important feature of the sense of safe and rewarding community. Self-esteem and group esteem are incredibly important outcomes of community music making. But group esteem can only develop when there's a clear sense of group identity and community. Once that identity forms, it builds confidence and social cohesion—all positive outcomes that stem from people feeling they truly belong to something.

Effective leadership in community music settings often emerges not from standing apart from the group, but from embodying its values and creating spaces where people feel free to be themselves. Musician Kym Dillon describes how this works in practice:

> I lead by being myself and creating a space where people can feel free to be themselves, and by modelling that music is all about enjoying it. In this way, *I am one of them*. I show that I believe in this community and its importance. When you have a group where people can just be themselves and enjoy their music, so much else flows naturally from that. People these days can tell when someone isn't being real, when they're trying to be something they're not in their leadership style. I feel like I'm always just being myself, and people respond to that. Especially in this kind of group, where being yourself is the name of the game. This is probably part of the reason people want to keep coming back, even if it's the one thing they do in their week.

Kym's intuitive approach and Graham's observations capture what social psychologists call "the social identity approach to leadership". In contrast to conventional leadership theories that emphasise how leaders stand out through their individual traits and actions, identity leadership posits that effective leaders should emphasise their similarities with followers rather than their differences (Haslam et al., 2020). This perspective suggests that leadership emerges from the interplay between leaders and followers within a specific context, fostering a sense of unity. Leadership is "a relationship between leaders and followers *within a social group*" with a strong sense of "we" (Haslam et al., 2020, p. 45, emphasis in original). This marks a departure from most prevailing approaches to leadership which have generally focused on the individual qualities of the leader rather than their capacity to build a sense of the collective.

To put these ideas into practice, let's explore four key strategies, known as the "4 I's of identity leadership":

1 Identity entrepreneurship: Crafting a shared identity—the leader creates "a sense of us".
2 Identity prototypicality: Embodying the group's identity—the leader is "one of us".
3 Identity advancement: Promoting the group's interests—the leader is "doing it for us".
4 Identity impresarioship: Devising activities that promote and sustain social identity—leading activities that "make us matter" (Haslam et al., 2020; Haslam et al., 2024).

For music leaders, identity entrepreneurship and identity advancement are especially important to practice in order to ensure groups are meaningful for participants (Haslam et al., 2024, p. 10, citing Robertson et al., 2023; Tarrant et al., 2020). By mastering these approaches, you'll be able to foster the kind of strong, health-enhancing group identities we discussed in the "social cure" section and amplify the wellbeing benefits of your music groups by creating a sense of belonging, social support, agency, and purpose.

Identity entrepreneurship—crafting "a sense of us"

Identity entrepreneurship involves creating a shared sense of "we" and "us". It requires leaders to find ways to make individuals feel that they are part of the group, and to be inclusive. Leaders need to define core values, norms, and ideals in order to establish what the group stands for (Haslam et al., 2020). Leaders as identity entrepreneurs actively work to create, shape, construct, and promote a shared social identity within their group or organisation. These leaders don't just passively represent an existing group identity. Instead, they actively construct and manage the group's identity, helping to define "who we are" and "what we stand for" as a collective (Haslam et al., 2020).

RESONANCE—Crafting a sense of "us" by cultivating belief in the group's potential to achieve

Singing for health practitioner–researcher Emily Foulkes crafted a strong "sense of us" when working with a small group of singers in the small town of Penzance, England. Through a dogged belief—on the group's behalf—of their potential, Emily led them towards successful three-part harmony singing:

> I used to travel down to Penzance once a week and meet with a very small group of maybe four or five women, and none of them professed to being singers or being able to sing, but they loved it. They just loved singing. It never crossed my mind ever that they couldn't do a three-part harmony. It just didn't. It was like, this is what we're doing, this is what we're doing. They loved that. They loved just the fact that I just didn't even question because actually most of that small group had said to me, I was told I couldn't sing, the age-old story that I hear so many times. I was told to shut up at primary school. I was told to mouth the words. I was told I was tone deaf. That's what I heard in this little group in Penzance ... I would say to them, "We're going to do this!" There were people that couldn't hold parts, so I would sing with the people that couldn't hold the parts, but there were some that could. We played to strengths and we found a way of making it work that they could actually feel really proud of the sound.

Note Emily's use of inclusive language—"this is what *we're* doing"/ "*we're* going to do this!"—and the group's positive response—"they loved that". Through crafting a sense of us and shared ability, Emily was able to lead the group towards an incredible sense of achievement: "Do you know what? They did it. They did it and they felt just—they couldn't believe that they could do it." This sense of group achievement also fuelled Emily's self-belief as a singing leader: "That's how I felt, like, I can do this. Isn't this amazing?"

This shared sense of "us" is vitally important within Emily's singing for health groups as well, because it contributes to participants' sense of social support and belonging:

> One of the comments we had from a mindfulness and singing research project was that somebody said, everybody listens and nobody's judgmental. Everybody understands because they're all going through the same thing. We're all here because we are going through a similar thing. It's that shared understanding. Even though everybody's different and we have had quite considerable differences within groups, but it's still that, I can say this here because you get it.

Emily says the musical activities play a role on crafting this sense of "us": "that shared experience of we are doing these exercises and these songs together and that gives us something to anchor that relationship around more than just the health condition that brought me here".

Practice points

- When leading your group, consistently use inclusive language by referring to "us", "we", "our group".
- Get "buy-in". Work to establish the vision, purpose, and ideal behaviours for your group. It's important to encourage participation in these planning discussions because this will ultimately impact the strength of a member's identification with the group and hence their openness to adopting the group's values, norms, beliefs and beneficial behaviours (Haslam, 2004; Reynolds et al., 2020). Empowering members to take ownership of the group's direction is a great way to craft a "sense of us".
- Beyond planning, look to involve members in decision-making on an ongoing basis, where possible. For example, within community music groups, repertoire is one of the most frequently visited issues which requires decisions. What repertoire does the group perform? Who gets to decide/choose? What happens when there are differences of opinion? These are all issues of collective decision-making which a music leader can actively harness to build a group sense of "us" and "how we deal with things together".

- Co-write a group song to represent what the group stands for (collectively agreed-upon values, goals, aspirations) and sing the song at the start or end of a session.
- Devote some group time to allowing people to share their stories or to share a celebration like a birthday or anniversary. This demonstrates collective care for members' lives outside of group activities and communicates that we are "in this together".
- Highlight unique aspects of the group's identity. For example, in my Park 'n Songs group, I consistently remark on the wonderfully strong collective sound they make when singing, despite the fact that many in the group have vocal impairment from the effects of Parkinson's. I emphasise to the group that without each other, making such a wonderful sound would not be possible. The ability to sing out and sing loudly—despite the very real physical limitations—is an important aspect of our group's identity. In this respect, we are supported by a loyal and dedicated group of community musicians and volunteers who contribute to the strong group sound. I find it important to remark on this in each session and acknowledge these collective contributions which make us "us".
- Celebrate collective achievements. This is particularly important where groups of amateur musicians perform in public—this is a significant achievement and one to be celebrated! Beyond these grander achievements, take care to comment frequently on the little things: a nicely performed phrase, some lovely dynamics, or the delivery of lyrics which beautifully captures a particular emotion. Nothing is too small to notice (Haslam et al., 2020).
- Organise social events outside regular sessions. This could be as simple as a quick tea/coffee after a group session or might extend to a whole day excursion together doing something completely different to the usual musical activity.
- Consistently highlight how members' efforts contribute to group success.
- Actively facilitate interaction between group members. Where appropriate, sort participants into parts or sections and let them take ownership of their work. When everyone re-groups, thank each section for their work and contributions.
- Create roles within the group or seek volunteers for certain tasks. Establish opportunities for members to take on different responsibilities, like leading warm-ups or organising sheet music. This allows members to contribute to the group's functioning in various ways.
- As a group, decide to what extent you would like to share your group activity with supportive others. For example, a family and friends afternoon is a great opportunity to "perform" or show off the group's work for an appreciative crowd, which can bring a sense of pride and accomplishment for group members, reinforcing a sense of "us" and collective achievement. Inviting others to participate also enables them to experience the power and energy of the group.

RESONANCE—Crafting a sense of "us" and feeling part of the team

Musician and social inclusion choir leader Kym Dillon reflects on the ways in the attitudes of her group's members evidences a sense of "us":

> There are many things which show how members feel they are part of the team. They may begin to network with other members and they make friends or perhaps volunteer to help with a certain thing. When people commit to coming week to week, which is no small thing especially these days, it's because they feel they're part of it. It's particularly articulated when someone is hanging back after choir for the supper that we have afterwards and is choosing to say hello to people and get to meet new people. It sort of weaves them into the group nicely. While I make performance attendance very much a casual thing—if you can make it, you can make it, that's great, but it's not a compulsory thing. If you didn't come to rehearsals, that's fine. But then people will make an effort to tell me if they can't come. That tells me how important they think it is and that they feel that they're part of it, they're part of the team.

Kym's reflection demonstrates that group members have a strong sense of commitment to group activities and go out of their way to build a sense of us beyond the music making activities. This is because Kym actively engages in identity entrepreneurship, building a sense of what the group stands for, and its norms and ideals of inclusion and mutual support.

Identity prototypicality—being "one of us"

Prototypicality is about embodying the group's identity and values. It means that, as a music leader, you stand *for* the group rather than apart from it (Haslam et al., 2020, p. 71). For a music leader to be representative of unique qualities of the group and what group membership means (and in turn, positively influence group behaviour), leaders need to be seen as "one of us". This means music leaders need to be "an exemplary model member of the group" (Steffens et al., 2014, p. 1003).

Making your representativeness (or prototypicality) apparent to your group is an active rather than a passive process (Haslam et al., 2020, p. 99). Anything that clearly sets a music leader apart from the group is likely to undermine your ability to positively influence group dynamics. This is because "distance between the leader and the group is not only bad for leader effectiveness, but it is also bad for the effectiveness of the group as a whole" (Haslam et al., 2020, p. 74).

Singing for health practitioner–researcher Emily Foulkes is a firm believer in playfulness in her leadership practice—this sense of fun is intentional as it breaks down perceived barriers between leader and group. For the group members, this approach shows that Emily is "one of us":

We do these silly exercises but it makes us laugh, it breaks the ice and it's really good fun, and we do it together, we're in it together. People think, it's not just me she's making do these exercises, we're all doing it, we're all in the same boat.

Practice points

- Create a non-judgmental and inclusive environment. Move away from deficit-based approaches common in traditional music training. As a music leader you can demonstrate "prototypicality" by being inclusive, and normalising—even welcoming—mistakes. Musician Allison Girvan says, "When everybody can make a mistake and feel good enough to actually sing a wrong note or make a terrible sound or something … That's when things start getting really exciting because then things can move faster." For Allison, mistakes generate more energy and creativity, which then creates a positive feedback loop for participants.
- Model lifelong learning. Adopt a "beginner's mindset" (known as *shoshin* in Japanese) to emphasise what you and your group have in common. This approach identifies you as someone committed to ongoing learning rather than someone who has all the answers.
- Embody aspirational identity. Represent the identity the group strives for, particularly in early stages of group formation. This is especially relevant when group members may feel unsure about their musical skills or ability to participate meaningfully (Steffens et al., 2021; Robertson et al., 2023).
- Balance creativity with group interests. You can be different or creative in your approaches, but make sure that in doing so you stay true to interests of the group (Adarves-Yorno et al., 2006, 2007; Haslam et al., 2020, p. 74). For example, you may personally really want to get your group improvising, but perhaps this has never been discussed as a core interest or value of the group, and when you attempt it with your group, you may sense some genuine resistance. A scenario like this is an opportunity to revisit group values and whether including some improvising could in fact be an opportunity for learning—both for the group and for you as a leader as well. By demonstrating your prototypicality (as Allison demonstrates in the above example, welcoming mistakes and using them as creative fodder), you have a better chance of moving your group in new directions (Haslam et al., 2020, p. 99).

RESONANCE—Being "one of us"

When a highly trained musician seeks to represent a community music group which may be comprised of amateur—and sometimes even reluctant—participants, prototypicality presents a unique challenge to music leaders. How does a trained musician convey to amateur musicians that they are "one of them"?

Musician and community choir leader Emma Dean provides some insight:

> I don't think my training to be a performer helped me when it came to community choir work. A lot of the technical stuff that I know, I think I probably started in a pretty gung-ho way wanting to share that knowledge with the choristers. But a lot of it is redundant. Like a lot of it I use and my accompanist uses and we have our own language, but it's not necessarily important to be using that [with the group]. I think finding a language between you and the choir that we all understand is super important. I don't think that my training helped with that. That was very much trial and error and years of refining that and figuring out what works and what doesn't.

Emma's experience is one of adapting the musical skills and language she had been trained in to suit the group. Through a process of trial and error, Emma understood she need to represent the group—to be seen as "prototypical"—and using the language of a highly trained musician with her community choirs was counterproductive to that goal.

Vocal leader James Sills emphasises the importance of language in conveying a sense that the leader is "one of us" and that new group members are also "one of us":

> I'm very, very intentional about the language that I use around singing these days as well. There's nothing quicker to alienate people or to think that singing isn't for them than to use certain language. An example might be if someone plucks up the courage to walk through the door of an open access community choir for the first time and the leader says, "Oh, hello there. Are you an alto or a soprano?" That person may think, "Oh, I haven't even sat down and I don't know what I'm doing!" There is a challenge where maybe there are groups that appear to be open access and community based but actually, when you get inside, are still reinforcing the same stereotypes or the same coded language of, say, choral societies. I think that is actually a problem because then you're creating a false expectation.

James's reflections show that the language we use as leaders can be inviting and inclusive, or alienating and exclusionary. Practising identity leadership therefore requires trained musicians to communicate with group members in ways that avoid alienating them and actively cultivates a sense that "we are all in this together".

Similarly, musician Kym Dillon, who leads choirs for social inclusion says:

> It's important for me to demonstrate that I am just one of the group. So, I'm going to be chatting to people afterwards if there's some vacuuming

that needs doing, I'm happy to go and vacuum. I really believe in that kind of leadership and that's something I hold very close to my heart.

Kym explains further:

I have the skills to lead from the front, but in the end, I'm just here getting the same thing out of it you are. Which is genuinely true. I often have a bad mental health day on a Monday or something, but I'll get there and sing and feel better afterwards. So, I need it as much as everyone else does. So, I think that's a particular leadership strength that I regard about myself, is that ability to communicate that you are just like everyone else. You don't think of yourself as knowing more than them or higher than them. Even though obviously I have different musical skills, but I think being able to communicate with that. But the thing that people say is that they feel welcome and included from their very first visit and I think that comes from my joy at doing what we're doing and, I guess, engaging with the room too as you're teaching.

The reflections from Emma, James, and Kym demonstrate that identity proto-typicality—being one of us—is vitally important for skilled musicians to embody when leading participatory music groups. This is quite a departure from the training many musicians receive within the master-apprentice model, where overtly demonstrating mastery to the learner has traditionally been seen as an important aspect of the pedagogy.

Identity advancement—"doing it for us"

To move a group in a common direction, music leaders must be seen by group members as working *for* the group. Music leaders who aren't "doing it for us" will be seen as "doing it for themselves". It is therefore important for music leaders to stand up for their group, promote group interests, and champion the group, sometimes in situations beyond the immediate group activities (Haslam et al., 2020, p. 101). Below are some practice points for music leaders to demonstrate that their leadership serves the group rather than their own interests.

Practice points

- Be responsive to participants' needs and feedback. As noted above, crafting a "sense of us" means involving the group in collective decision-making. Music leaders have an opportunity to practice identity advancement by being open to group feedback and sensitive to members' needs. This openness and flex-ibility shows that as a music leader, you are willing to do what is right for the group in that particular time and place, rather than imposing your own pre-conceived ideas about the best way to do things. When faced with challenges to achieving group objectives, the way you respond as a music leader will demonstrate whether you are "for the group" or "for yourself".

- Represent the group outside of usual activities. For example, you may seek funding for your group from a local government authority which requires you to advocate for group needs as part of the application process. The group may ask you to speak in public forums to promote the group to gain broader membership or to spread the word about the health-enhancing benefits of group music making. You may be approached by media to do an interview about your group. These are all wonderful opportunities to demonstrate that as a music leader, you are working to advance group interests, and you are "doing it for us".
- The work to advance the identity of the group beyond usual group activities has the potential to be time-consuming. It is therefore important for you to balance this form of identity leadership with self-care and professional boundaries, or you may risk compromising your own wellbeing in the interests of group advancement.

Identity impresarioship—"making us better"

Identity impresarioship involves implementing structures and coordinating events and activities that allow group members to "live out" their membership (Haslam et al., 2020). It's about creating a tangible reality for the group, making it visible both to members and outsiders (Haslam et al., 2020). For music leaders, identity impresarioship means crafting experiences that bring the group together, arranging events that help the group function effectively, and creating structures that are useful for and support group members (Haslam et al., 2024).

Practice points

GROUP STRUCTURE AND ROUTINE

- Establish regular meeting rhythms. Set up a consistent schedule for group sessions. Regular sessions provide routine and predictability and help embed the group's existence into members' lives.
- Design sessions to progressively build cohesiveness over time (Tarrant et al., 2018). Work simultaneously on short-, medium-, and longer-term goals such as learning new repertoire, to build a sense of achievement and group accomplishment.
- Create roles within the group. Establish opportunities for members to take on different responsibilities, like leading warm-ups or organising sheet music. This allows members to contribute to the group's functioning in various ways.
- Establish group rituals. Develop opening and closing rituals for each session, like a welcome song or a closing reflection circle. These rituals can become powerful markers of group identity.

GROUP IDENTITY AND VISIBILITY

- Organise performances or sharing sessions. Arrange opportunities for the group to showcase their work, either to each other or to a wider audience. This gives tangible outcomes to work towards and makes the group's achievements visible both to themselves and others.
- Create group artifacts. Develop materials that represent the group's identity, such as a group name, logo, YouTube videos, T-shirts, or even a signature song. These tangible symbols can strengthen group cohesion.

MAINTAINING CONNECTION

- Use digital platforms. Use online tools to keep the group connected between sessions. This could be a social media group, a shared playlist, or a group chat for sharing music-related content.
- Document the group's journey. Keep a record of the group's activities and progress, perhaps through photos, recordings, or a social media page. This creates a tangible history of the group's existence and achievements, helping you as a leader to monitor and reinforce the development of group identity and cohesiveness.

These structures and activities provide numerous ways for members to engage with the group, reinforcing their sense of shared identity and belonging. Remember, the goal is to make the group matter to members by making it a significant and visible part of members' lives.

RESONANCE—Identity leadership in action

Vocal leader James Sills says adapting your approach as a leader to the group in front of you is vitally important:

> My approach adapts to the context and participants—whether it's a lunchtime wellbeing choir, homeless choir, or corporate workshop. While the core skills remain the same, I structure each session based on who's in front of me and what they need. Sometimes this means directly acknowledging potential resistance, like in corporate settings where I might say, "I know you've already decided you hate me!"—getting a laugh because I've recognised their discomfort. Other times, it means responding with deep sensitivity to group experiences, such as when my homeless choir lost a prominent community member. In those moments, creating space for silence or shared reflection comes before any music making. It's about establishing that crucial sense of "us" from the very beginning.

This reflection captures the essence of identity leadership in action. When James acknowledges corporate participants' scepticism about singing, he demonstrates identity prototypicality by showing he understands exactly what they're thinking and feeling (James is "one of us"). His willingness to adapt session structures for different groups shows identity advancement by putting group needs first rather than his own ("doing it for us"). By creating appropriate spaces for reflection and sharing experiences, James practises identity impresarioship, leading activities that are appropriately structured to strengthen group bonds ("making us better"). Most importantly, through all these approaches, he actively engages in identity entrepreneurship by crafting that vital "sense of us", uniquely tailored to each group, that underpins all successful collective experiences.

Connecting identity and positively energising leadership

As we've explored the various aspects of identity leadership, you may be wondering how this approach aligns with the positively energising leadership strategies we discussed in Chapter 5. Let's examine how these concepts can work together to create powerful group experiences.

The social identity approach to leadership offers a complementary perspective to positively energising leadership, which emphasises the virtuous attributes of individual leaders. Identity leadership suggests that a leader's virtuous behaviours become influential not simply because of their inherent value, but because they align with the group's prototypical qualities in a specific context (Haslam et al., 2020).

The effectiveness of a leader's virtuous behaviours is mediated by how well they represent the group's identity. In fact, experimental studies have shown that a leader's in-group prototypicality often plays a more crucial role in gaining followers' support than abstract leadership qualities (Haslam et al., 2020).

Taking identity leadership and positively energising leadership together suggests that effective leadership involves not just displaying positive attributes, but ensuring these attributes resonate with and represent the group's shared identity. By combining the virtuous behaviours emphasised in positively energising leadership with the identity-conscious approach of social identity leadership, music leaders can create a powerful, context-sensitive leadership style that both energises and unifies their groups.

As a result, group members are likely to experience enhanced feelings of belonging and social connection, which are fundamental to wellbeing (Haslam et al., 2018). The development of these positive relationships within the group can lead to increased social support, improved self-esteem, and a greater sense of purpose (Tarrant et al., 2016).

Furthermore, as group members come to see themselves as part of a valued social identity, they may experience increased confidence in their musical abilities and a stronger commitment to the group's goals. This can lead to improved engagement, motivation, and even personal growth beyond the musical context (Dingle et al., 2013).

By employing leadership strategies that are both positively energising and social identity-affirming, music leaders can create an environment where participants enjoy making music together and gain substantial psychosocial benefits that can positively impact their overall quality of life. This integrative approach allows you to harness the full power of group identity as a social cure, amplifying the well-being benefits of participatory music groups.

RESONANCE—The power of a shared language

The following example from Emma Dean demonstrates virtuous behaviours (and an "egoless" approach) to developing a shared language with a community choir:

> Gesture is so important, and physicality. Because a lot of times, people learn kinaesthetically and you've got to address all of the different learning styles. I use everyday gestures or things that everyone can relate to. "You know when you're going to vomit, you know that feeling? I want that sound." People go, "Okay, cool. I get it. Awesome." "You know that sound of raindrops on the window? Can we sing it a little bit like that?" And they'll think, "I get it". Staccato, no one knows what that is! That stuff excites me so much. Just saying something and seeing everyone's face go, "Oh, I get it." Then hearing the difference, oh my God, I love that so much.

Emma, a highly trained and skilled musician, relies on physical gesture rather than technical musical directions, when working with her group. Emma's ability to meet her group where they are—and inject some humour into her communication style—is a wonderful example of both positively energising leadership and identity leadership. By adapting her communication style, she creates a positive climate, and a strong sense of prototypicality ("one of us") by using everyday imagery to communicate musical ideas, in a highly relatable and accessible way.

Community choir leaders and researchers Dave Camlin and Tiri Bergensen Schei echo Emma's positive, values driven, and identity-affirming approach to leadership:

> our intentions and values as leaders clearly shape how participants experience the phenomenon of group singing, and as leaders, we therefore have a primary responsibility for shaping, modelling and expressing those intentions and values. A serious and professional attitude, while at the same time being relaxed and aware, present and attentive to the situation of the here-and-now, is of greatest importance to set the table for a welcoming choral experience.
>
> (Camlin & Schei, 2024, p. 12)

Final thoughts

As we conclude this chapter, it's important to acknowledge that some readers may view the social identity approach as potentially manipulative. After all, the idea of intentionally shaping group identities might seem at odds with authenticity or individual autonomy. However, it's crucial to consider this approach in the proper context.

First, social identities are not artificially created by leaders; they naturally form in any group setting. What the social identity approach offers is a way to consciously nudge these identities in a positive, health-enhancing direction to build social connection. Rather than manipulation, this is about fostering an environment where people can find belonging, purpose, and support.

Second, the ethical application of these principles relies on transparency and shared goals. As a music leader, your aim is to facilitate experiences that benefit group members, aligning with their own desires for connection and wellbeing. The strategies we have discussed are not about imposing an identity, but about collaboratively building one that resonates with all members.

Last, it is worth noting that all leadership approaches influence group dynamics in some way. The social identity approach simply makes this process explicit and intentional, allowing for more thoughtful and beneficial outcomes for leaders and group members alike.

By understanding and applying these principles ethically, music leaders can create spaces where individuals thrive, not in spite of group membership, but because of it. The goal is not to manipulate, but to maximise the natural healing power of social connection through music.

Refrain

Social identity is a powerful tool in the positive music leader's toolkit. By understanding and applying the principles of identity leadership, you can transform your music groups into vibrant communities that enhance belonging and social connection. As a positive music leader, your role extends beyond the musical; you are crafting shared identities that can serve as a social cure, building important psychological resources for your participants. As you lead, strive to create a strong sense of "us," embody the group's values, champion its interests, and create meaningful experiences that make the group matter to members. In doing so, you are using your personal and musical energy to "conduct connection", supporting the social health of our communities.

Call and response

1 Reflect on a time when you felt a strong sense of belonging in a group. How did this affect your wellbeing?
2 Consider the four strategies of identity leadership (entrepreneurship, prototypicality, advancement, and impresarioship). Which do you feel most comfortable with? Which might you need to develop further?

3   How might you balance the needs of individual group members with the goal
     of creating a strong group identity? Can you think of potential challenges and
     how you might address them?
4   Think about a music group you lead or participate in. What unique aspects of
     its identity could you highlight or develop to strengthen the group's sense of
     "us-ness"?
5   In light of the social cure approach, how might you reframe the goals of your
     music leadership? What new possibilities does this perspective open up?

References

Adarves-Yorno, I., Postmes, T., & Alexander Haslam, S. (2006). Social identity and the
     recognition of creativity in groups. *British Journal of Social Psychology*, 45(3), 479–497.
     doi:10.1348/014466605X50184.
Adarves-Yorno, I., Postmes, T., & Haslam, S. A. (2007). Creative innovation or crazy irre-
     levance? The contribution of group norms and social identity to creative behavior. *Journal
     of Experimental Social Psychology*, 43(3), 410–416. doi:10.1016/j.jesp.2006.02.013.
Breakwell, G. M. (2023). *Identity: Unique and shared*. Sage.
Camlin, D. A., & Schei, T. B. (2024). Reaping the harvest of joy: Practitioner enquiry into
     intercultural group singing. *Australian Voice*. 25, 1–15. doi:10.56307/DLAZ9779.
Dingle, G. A., Brander, C., Ballantyne, J., & Baker, F. (2013). "To be heard": The social
     and mental health benefits of choir singing for disadvantaged adults. *Psychology of Music*,
     41(4), 405–421.
Dingle, G. A., Williams, E., Jetten, J., & Welch, J. (2017). Choir singing and creative
     writing enhance emotion regulation in adults with chronic mental health conditions.
     British Journal of Clinical Psychology, 56(4), 443–457. doi:10.1111/bjc.12149.
Forbes, M. (2021). "We're pushing back": Group singing, social identity, and caring for a
     spouse with Parkinson's. *Psychology of Music*, 49(5), 1199–1214. doi:10.1177/
     0305735620944230.
Greenaway, K. H., Cruwys, T., Haslam, S. A., & Jetten, J. (2016). Social identities pro-
     mote well-being because they satisfy global psychological needs. *European Journal of
     Social Psychology*, 46, 294–307. doi:10.1002/ejsp.2169.
Haslam, C., Jetten, J., Cruwys, T., Dingle, G. A., & Haslam, S. A. (2018). *The new psy-
     chology of health: Unlocking the social cure*. Routledge.
Haslam, S. A. (2004). *Psychology in organizations*. Sage.
Haslam, S. A., et al. (2024). Tackling loneliness together: A three-tier social identity fra-
     mework for social prescribing. *Group Processes & Intergroup Relations*, 27(5).
     doi:10.1177/13684302241242434.
Haslam, S. A., Reicher, S., & Platow, M. J. (2020). *The new psychology of leadership: Iden-
     tity, influence and power*. Routledge.
Reynolds, K. J., Branscombe, N. R., Subašić, E., & Willis, L. (2020). Changing behavior
     using social identity processes. In K. Hamilton, L. D. Cameron, M. S. Hagger, N.
     Hankonen, & T. Lintunen (eds), *The handbook of behavior change* (pp. 225–236).
     Cambridge University Press. doi:10.1017/9781108677318.016.
Robertson, A. M., Cruwys, T., Stevens, M., & Platow, M. J. (2023). A social identity
     approach to facilitating therapy groups. *Clinical Psychology: Science and Practice*, 31(3),
     375–389. doi:10.1037/cps0000178.

Steffens, N. K., Haslam, S. A., Reicher, S. D., Platow, M. J., Fransen, K., Yang, J., Ryan, M. K., Jetten, J., Peters, K., & Boen, F. (2014). Leadership as social identity management: Introducing the Identity Leadership Inventory (ILI) to assess and validate a four-dimensional model. *The Leadership Quarterly*, *25*(5), 1001–1024. doi:10.1016/j. leaqua.2014.05.002.

Steffens, N. K., Munt, K. A., van Knippenberg, D., Platow, M. J., & Haslam, S. A. (2021). Advancing the social identity theory of leadership: A meta-analytic review of leader group prototypicality. *Organizational Psychology Review*, *11*(1), 35–72. doi:10.1177/2041386620962569.

Tajfel, H., & Turner, J. C. (1986). The social identity theory of intergroup behavior. In S. Worchel & W. G. Austin (eds), *Psychology of intergroup relations* (pp. 7–24). Nelson-Hall.

Tarrant, M., Code, C., Carter, N., Carter, M., & Calitir, R. (2018). Development and progression of group cohesiveness in a singing programme for people with post stroke aphasia: An evaluation study using video analysis. *Aphasiology*, *32*(51), 222–223. doi:10.1080/02687038.2018.1487527.

Tarrant, M., Warmoth, K., Code, C., Dean, S., Goodwin, V. A., Stein, K., & Sugavanam, T. (2016). Creating psychological connections between intervention recipients: Development and focus Group evaluation of a group singing session for people with aphasia. *BMJ Open*, *6*(2), 1–9. doi:10.1136/bmjopen-2015-009652.

Tarrant, M., Haslam, C., Carter, M., Calitri, R., & Haslam, S. A. (2020). Social identity interventions. In K. Hamilton, L. D. Cameron, M. S. Hagger, N. Hankonen, & T. Lintunen (eds), *The handbook of behavior change* (pp. 649–660). Cambridge University Press. doi:10.1017/9781108677318.044.

Turner, J. C., Hogg, M. A., Oakes, P. J., Reicher, S. D., & Wetherell, M. S. (1987). *Rediscovering the social group: A self-categorization theory*. Basil Blackwell.

Williams, E., Dingle, G. A., Calligeros, R., Sharman, L., & Jetten, J. (2019a). Enhancing mental health recovery by joining arts-based groups: A role for the social cure approach. *Arts & Health*, *12*(2), 169–181. doi:10.1080/17533015.2019.1624584.

Williams, E., Dingle, G. A., Jetten, J., & Rowan, C. (2019b). Identification with arts-based groups improves mental wellbeing in adults with chronic mental health conditions. *Journal of Applied Social Psychology*, *49*(1), 15–26. doi:10.1111/jasp.12561.

Part III
Tutti

7 Cultivating contextual awareness
Appreciating complexity

Introduction

Zambian-born music therapist, psychotherapist, and educator Nsamu Moonga provides insight into his experience of music and belonging: "In the way that we understand music from the African perspective, *musicking itself is belonging*" (emphasis added). Nsamu describes the relationship between growing up in the Batonga culture and the role of music making as akin to a "fish in water"—music making is like the water for a fish, ever-present and as natural as breathing. For Nsamu, making music is inextricably linked with a sense of belonging—music and belonging cannot be separated, or reduced to their parts. This deep sense of integration between music and being could not be further from the atomisation and disconnection which has infected Western cultures and is in part reflected in the removal of music making from everyday life.

In fact, Nsamu's experience encapsulates the central theme of this chapter: in order to understand how and why music builds social connection and belonging, we must consider it contextually and systemically to appreciate the complexity of these multifaceted interactions.

Simply put, we can't understand the fish without appreciating its relationship to the water.

This brings us to Part III, the final and overarching area of focus for positive music leaders, namely contextual awareness. The "Overture" chapter introduced this book's tripartite structure: the "triple focus" of music leaders. Leaders must simultaneously develop an awareness of self (Part I), others (Part II), and the broader context within which they work (Part III).

To recap what we've covered so far, in Part I ("Solo"), we explored how effective positive music leadership begins with self-leadership. This requires deep self-awareness and intentional self-care practices. We explored how understanding and leveraging your unique strengths, values, and aspirations, while actively nurturing your own wellbeing through positive psychology interventions, provides the foundation for leading others towards enhanced social health and connection through music.

In Part II ("Ensemble"), we turned to leading others and saw how positive music leaders can revitalise social health by intentionally cultivating energising

DOI: 10.4324/9781003426509-11

relationships and strong social identities within their groups. By employing strategies from positively energising leadership and the social identity approach, music leaders can transform their groups into powerful sources of belonging, support, and wellbeing for participants, helping to address the broader crisis of social disconnection.

Now in Part III ("Tutti"—an Italian term used in music to mean "all together"), we bring everything together to consider the broader context within which positive music leaders conduct their practice. This final section encourages you, as a positive music leader, to develop contextual awareness, so that you can be more intentional as a music leader and better understand how your work is shaped by your context and the world around you. We will end Part III and the book by discussing how the strategies and ideas presented throughout can empower you to convincingly champion the value of positive music leadership for social connection as a public health resource.

This chapter challenges our very human tendency towards reductionist thinking and argues that we must embrace a more integrated and interconnected understanding of music's role in renewing social connections and promoting social health. To do so requires us to explore the context for positive music leadership in a way which acknowledges complexity and encourages systems thinking.

Before we begin, a note on complexity and knowledge systems: As a white, middle-aged, middle-class woman writing primarily from within the Western academic paradigm, I acknowledge the limitations of my perspective in discussing complexity. Indigenous peoples worldwide have understood and lived with principles of interconnectedness and complexity for millennia. Throughout the book, we've heard from interviewees Nsamu Moonga and Naomi Sunderland who have provided invaluable Indigenous perspectives on music leadership. I encourage readers to engage directly with Indigenous thinkers and writers whose work offers deep wisdom about complexity and interconnectedness. Some suggestions for further reading are included at the end of the chapter. This chapter draws primarily on Western frameworks not because they are superior or the first to recognise these principles, but because they reflect my own learning journey and the limits of my cultural position.

What do we mean by "complexity"?

> If your voice is a certain colour, you can blend yours with another colour, and come up with something that is greater than the sum of its parts.
>
> —Allison Girvan, community music practitioner

Complexity recognises that in many systems—whether ecosystems, social groups, or even the cells in living organisms—multiple elements interact in ways that create unpredictable but meaningful patterns over time (Meadows, 2008). Unlike simple linear cause-and-effect relationships (such as A causes B), complex systems are nonlinear and involve many parts that influence each other simultaneously, often creating feedback loops and new behaviours that can't be predicted through a consideration of the individual parts alone (Meadows, 2008; Siegel & Drulis, 2023).

Systems thinking is an approach or methodology for understanding and working with complexity. It is "a perspective, a language, and a set of tools" (Monat & Gannon, 2015, p. 11), and a lens through which we can examine complex phenomena, focusing on relationships and patterns rather than isolated components. In this chapter, we will focus mainly on systems thinking as a *perspective*:

> Most sources agree that systems thinking is the opposite of linear thinking, and that it focuses on the relationships among system components, as opposed to the components themselves. It is holistic (integrative) thinking instead of analytic (dissective) thinking. The scientific method prevalent in the last two centuries has taught us that we must break up complex situations into smaller and smaller pieces to understand them: dissective thinking. While this has great benefits, it also has the great disadvantage of ignoring the relationships among system components; those relationships often dominate systems behavior. Systems thinking requires that we study systems holistically.
>
> (Monat & Gannon, 2015, p. 17)

According to Donatella Meadows's classic work *Thinking in Systems* (2008), a system consists of elements, their interconnections, and a purpose, all working together to achieve something. While we often focus on the visible elements, it is actually the interconnections and purpose of the system that most powerfully shape how a system behaves. While interconnections can be difficult to identify, a system's purpose can be even more elusive, which is best understood by observing behaviour rather than stated goals.

Meadows (2008) explains that systems can exist within larger systems, each with their own purpose but at the same time remaining in harmony with each other for the whole to function well. Interestingly, a system can maintain its identity even when its parts are replaced, as long as its interconnections and purpose remain intact. However, if you alter the relationships between the parts or if you change the system's purpose, you fundamentally transform the system. Meadows gives the example of changing the rules from football to basketball: "as they say, a whole new ball game" (Meadows, 2008, loc. 401). This systems view helps explain why focusing on individual elements alone often misses the bigger picture. The relationships *between* parts and the *overall purpose* truly illuminate how a system works.

Group singing is an example of a complex system in action (Camlin et al., 2020). Camlin et al. (2020) conceptualise group singing as a "complex adaptive system" which is comprised of many different mechanisms, none of which can be separated out as causal in and of themselves (see also Camlin & Schei, 2024). Rather, Camlin (2023, pp. 57–58) argues that music making is an "entangled state", irreducible to its parts, but certainly greater than their sum.

Singing together is about much more than individual voices joining to create a group sound. There is a constant dance of mutual influence happening. As we have seen throughout this book, participatory music making such as a community choir is about performing "relationships" (Camlin et al., 2020). Just like a complex system, the "personality" of a community choir is in large part a product of the interconnections or relationships between singers. Singers adjust their pitch and timing to each other; their breathing and heartbeats start to synchronise; their emotions are affected by others in the group; and the acoustic space and physical environment shape how they respond. To add to the complexity, our emotional, physical, and psychological states are influenced by innumerable factors, down to such apparent trivialities as what we had for lunch, or a passing remark someone made to us on the way to the rehearsal! We are constantly at the effect of our environment, and dynamically interacting with space, people, and time. All these factors contribute to the complexity of an activity like group singing.

For these reasons, it's not possible to reduce the power of group singing to any single factor, such as higher levels of "feel good hormones". Instead, all these elements—the physiological act of singing, the social connections, the shared emotions, even the setting itself—interact with each other to create something new and powerful. This "something new" echoes the idea of "emergence" in philosophy and systems theory, whereby a system exhibits behaviours or properties that the parts themselves do not.

Understanding these complex interactions goes some way to explaining why the experience of singing with others often feels "magical" or transformative in ways that are hard to explain by just isolating and measuring individual benefits. As a research participant in a study on group singing put it: "When we sing as one, we create something much, much, much bigger that goes out into the universe and changes things" (Camlin, 2024, p. 9). These words capture the complexity of the experience of singing with a group—the experience is not simply an accumulation of separate aspects of experience; it is about how those parts interact and transform each other to create something greater than the sum of its parts.

Using descriptors like "magic" to explain the experience of music making can get us into trouble in a world informed in large part by reductionist thinking (more on this in the following section). As we will see in Chapter 9, simply claiming that community music making is magical or miraculous—even if this is experientially true—will not cut it if we are trying to convince those "outside the tent" to support our work (see Bartleet, 2023). We need robust and rigorous frameworks to convey the impact of participatory music making on music leaders and participants alike. The great challenge, as Naomi Sunderland puts it, is, "How do you describe the ocean?" For Naomi, this question arose when she was researching the role of music in diverse First Nations peoples' lives: should experience be codified? Or does codification strip the experience and research findings of their potency? Again, we will return to these issues in Chapter 9.

RESONANCE—Working with complexity within a community choir

The complexity of leading participatory music making is illustrated in the subtle art of repertoire selection. Community music practitioner Allison Girvan describes how choosing appropriate music to learn and perform requires a deep understanding of the "collective instrument" formed by the unique blend of voices in any given group. As Allison explains:

> The path to success is programming—understanding what instrument you have and programming for it. If it's a group of inexperienced singers, you're going to program something very different. You're not going to sing a Bach Cantata; it's just setting somebody up for failure. The person who is in front of the group needs to understand that collective instrument and love it. Then, find something that reflects the strengths of that particular group.

Allison's insights reveal how positive music leaders must navigate multiple interacting elements—individual vocal abilities, group dynamics, degrees of musical challenge, and different confidence levels—to create impactful experiences for group participants and, where relevant, audiences. Rather than applying a one-size-fits-all approach, leaders must appreciate how these elements combine uniquely in each group. As Allison notes, "Nine times out of ten, it's going to sound great because the intention is clear; you set people up with a way for their collective instrument to shine, and then you just need to get out of the way and have them do their thing."

Understanding the "collective instrument" is about more than simply identifying how each individual singer works; it requires an appreciation of what is possible—what might "emerge"—when all the different elements of the various systems involved interact with each other interdependently and multi-directionally.

This nuanced approach to repertoire selection exemplifies how positive music leaders embrace complexity rather than trying to simplify or control it. By understanding and honouring the intricate interplay between individual capabilities and group potential, leaders can create conditions where emergence—that magical "something greater than the sum of its parts"—becomes possible.

(Re)connection: The need for holistic thinking

Having an awareness of systems thinking and complexity can help you position your work as an antidote to some of society's most pressing ills. In an era of unprecedented technological connectivity, paradoxically, we find ourselves more disconnected than ever. In a recent survey conducted by Gallup (2023), nearly one in four people across 142 countries described themselves as fairly or very lonely. (Interestingly, this research was conducted in partnership with Meta, the parent company of Facebook, and a company which many claim is directly contributing to the loneliness pandemic.) We spend nearly seven hours a day staring at screens, often at the expense of face-to-face interactions (DataReportal, 2024). Meanwhile, membership in community organisations has plummeted by more than 50% since the 1960s (Putnam, 2000). These alarming trends point to a profound crisis of connection, one that threatens the very fabric of our society (Way et al., 2018; World Health Organization, 2023).

In fact, Wong et al. (2024) argue that we find ourselves facing a "polycrisis" or "metacrisis". The convergence of multiple crises—loneliness and social isolation, pandemics, wars, political turmoil, poverty, and deprivation—forms an intricate web that profoundly impacts both our collective psyche and our social systems. As Wong and colleagues note, this complexity, and each new crisis, can divert our already fragmented attention from critical health issues, including our fundamental need for social connection. As such, Wong et al. (2024) advocate for a "global health diplomacy" with multi-disciplinary practitioners leading the way for collaborative innovation. Accordingly, investment in leadership is critical to move beyond traditional public health models to align "health initiatives with broader political and social objectives" (Wong et al., 2024, p. 2).

While investment in leadership is vital, others beyond the public health sphere are going further, arguing we need to fundamentally re-examine our way of being in the world. In the midst of the polycrisis, or perhaps because of it, according to eminent British psychiatrist Iain McGilchrist (2021, 2024), we have forgotten *what is means to be human*. McGilchrist asks provocatively: How did we get to a place where we no longer know who we are as a species?

To explore this question, McGilchrist turns to psychiatric and neuroscientific research, and points (at first blush) to an unlikely culprit for the polycrisis—the left hemisphere of our brains. In his examination of decades of studies from neuroscience and psychiatry, McGilchrist (2009, 2021, 2024) argues that the left hemisphere is, in fact, far less reliable than we have been led to believe; it is prone to delusion and frequently engages in confabulation to maintain a position (anyone who has witnessed adversaries posting on social media will be familiar with this phenomenon!).

McGilchrist also debunks myths about brain lateralisation—for example, the idea that the "reliable" left hemisphere deals in reason and language, and that the "flighty" right hemisphere traffics in emotion. Rather, McGilchrist (2024, n.p.) argues that the right hemisphere "is a far superior guide to reality". However, public discourse and modern life is dominated by left hemisphere thinking which breaks reality down into representations of parts, stripping experience of its vitality and wholeness. The right hemisphere sees the whole as greater than the sum of the parts, and can apprehend "living presence" and potentialities, while accepting that nothing can ever be known fully or with certainty:

> The things that used to alert us to the inadequacy of our reductionist theories are fading away. They were: the natural world; the sense of a coherent shared culture; the sense of the body as something we live, not merely possess; the power of great art; and the sense of something sacred that is real but transcends everyday language.
>
> (McGilchrist, 2024, n.p.)

RESONANCE—Participatory music as joyful resistance to social fragmentation and isolation

There's a compelling argument that the dominance of left-hemisphere thinking is deeply entwined with colonial history. Ian Martin (2023) ventures as far to suggest that the European conquest of the Americas and the metaphorical "conquest" of the right hemisphere by the left hemisphere were mutually reinforcing processes. The reduction of land, resources, and Indigenous peoples to commodities that could be exploited aligned perfectly with left-hemisphere tendencies toward abstraction, control, and utility.

Meanwhile, Indigenous ways of knowing, which emphasise relationships, context, and interconnectedness, much like the right hemisphere's more holistic perspectives, were systematically devalued and destroyed. This historical parallel offers another lens for understanding our current challenges—that healing our relationship with complexity requires addressing both colonial legacies and our over-reliance on left-hemisphere thinking.

Singing leader Jane York reflects that colonial and capitalist systems thrive by dividing communities into isolated units, making populations easier to control and exploit: "European culture, colonialist culture, is all about fragmenting everyone and creating the individual, and that's very good for controlling populations and exploiting us because we are powerful collectively."

Jane's response to this destructionist tendency is to use participatory music making as a type of joyful resistance. During COVID-19, Jane witnessed how her singing groups transformed into mutual aid networks, with members supporting each other practically and emotionally. Jane sees community music making as an embodied practice of reclaiming collective power: "We use our voice, we practise using our voice and speaking—and it's not a metaphorical thing, we actually do it literally." Importantly, Jane says that serious purpose doesn't preclude joy: "We can have fun while we do that stuff [learning to sing together]. It's not always dry." This balance of purpose and pleasure exemplifies how positive music leadership, driven by strongly held values, addresses systemic issues of fragmentation and social isolation through enjoyment and authentic connection with others.

The left hemisphere's reductionist approach has left us ill-equipped to address the complex social challenges we face. Traditional public health models, often based on linear thinking, struggle to capture the multifaceted nature of our social health crisis. We need a new paradigm—one that embraces complexity, fosters social re-integration and connection, and values the power of music to play a significant role in a social "reset".

Music education, and the work of musicians and artists more broadly, has a profoundly important role to play in addressing these issues. Gaunt and colleagues observe that the contemporary zeitgeist is crying out for the creativity and humanity of music and the arts: their unique potential to uplift, heal, and engage people in expressing themselves, to help make sense of experience and challenge perspectives, and to contribute to building and sustaining communities.

(Gaunt et al., 2021, p. 3)

This recognition of art's power to reconnect us underscores the urgent need for holistic thinking in addressing our social fragmentation.

It will be tempting for those within the sway of left hemisphere thinking to dismiss a relational approach like positive music leadership as a way to respond to social disconnection, because it seems "airy fairy", "lacking in rigour", or too "artsy". The left hemisphere demands that reality be processed in easily digestible parts and measured to within an inch of its life; but this does not mean that reality *conforms* to this view, or that this is a "true" view of reality. It is *one view*, and a view, which McGilchrist argues, has gotten humanity into a bit of a pickle.

It is in this context that we turn to positive music leadership as a powerful tool for social (re)connection. Artists and musicians, with their unique ability to embody and communicate "living presence", offer a path back to our shared humanity (McGilchrist, 2021, 2024; Gaunt et al., 2021, p. 3). Through sound, gesture, metaphor, and narrative, artists reveal the interconnectedness of our world in ways that transcend the limitations of left hemisphere reductionist thinking (McGilchrist, 2021; Yankaporta, 2019).

Intentionally designed, positively led group music activities can guide us back to a primordial place of resonance, integration, and connection with others—and as we will see next, even our connection with the planet.

Beyond human connection: The ecological dimension

We sing and make music together to celebrate life's milestones, to worship and pray, and to connect with each other. We may even commune with nature when we make music and subsequently feel that we become one with the earth.

But what might it mean to sing *for* the earth?

Community music practitioner and researcher Dave Camlin (2024) posed this question in a research study of people who sing regularly in nature. What Camlin discovered underscores the complexity of group singing and reveals a new dimension to these experiences when nature itself becomes an agent within the complex system.

As Camlin (2024) reports, when people sing together in nature, they don't simply interact with each other and their environment; rather, they enter a complex web of relationships that can transform their personal relationship with the earth. In this respect, group singing represents more than just a collective musical activity—it offers a powerful response to our ecological crisis through "intra-action," where multiple elements combine to create effects greater than the sum of their parts.

Interestingly, Camlin's (2024) research participants made an important distinction between "singing *with* the earth"—a spiritual communion with nature—and "singing *for* the earth"—a political act of environmental advocacy. This dual approach suggests that group singing might help address what social ecologists see as the root cause of our environmental crisis: the attitude of domination within human society. McGilchrist would argue this domination mindset stems from an over-reliance on left hemisphere thinking without the moderating influence of the right hemisphere. By fostering connections between people and helping them attune to the rhythms of the natural world, group singing creates spaces where we can practise a different way of being, one based on reciprocity rather than domination and exploitation (Camlin, 2024).

Rather than reducing the experience of group singing into measurable components like hormone changes or distinct psychological benefits, Camlin embraces the inherent complexity of group singing. By accepting that multiple elements, including the physical act of singing, social connections, spiritual experiences, and ecological context are fundamentally entangled rather than separate, Camlin argues that we can better understand how these elements transform and amplify each other. This approach helps explain why singing in nature creates effects that are "greater than the sum of its parts", working simultaneously as both spiritual communion and political action.

Camlin's contribution to our emerging understanding of group singing (and by extension group music making) as a complex system draws in part on the work of American psychiatrist Dr Dan Siegel. Siegel's framework of interpersonal neurobiology (IPNB) offers a powerful way to understand how our minds emerge from the complex interactions between our brains, bodies, and relationships, and the world around us. IPNB brings together insights from multiple disciplines—including neuroscience, psychology, mathematics, and systems theory—to help us understand and appreciate human complexity rather than seeking to reduce it to constituent parts. Chapter 8 provides a detailed overview of this framework and suggests how positive music leadership can be enhanced by putting the principles of IPNB into practice.

Refrain

This chapter has positioned positive music leadership within the broader context of complexity and systems thinking. We've seen how participatory music making operates as a complex system where multiple elements—physical, social, emotional, and even environmental—interact in ways that create emergent properties that greater than the sum of their parts. Rather than trying to reduce these experiences to isolated components, positive music leaders work within complexity, embracing the interconnected nature of human experience.

Granted, this chapter barely scratches the surface of complexity and systems thinking, but the intention is to provoke thinking in new ways about your practice. Understanding complexity provides a crucial foundation for effective music leadership, but it also raises an important question: How can we practically work with this complexity to foster connection and belonging? The next chapter introduces interpersonal neurobiology (IPNB) as a framework that helps bridge theory and practice. IPNB offers positive music leaders concrete strategies to create transformative musical experiences that support social health and connection.

Call and response

1 Think about a time when you experienced group music making as something "greater than the sum of its parts". How would you describe this experience?
2 Consider how viewing your music leadership through a complexity lens might change your approach. What aspects of your practice might you pay more attention to? What might you do differently?
3 Think about a challenge you've faced in your music leadership. How might understanding it as part of a complex system, rather than an isolated problem, change how you approach it? What new possibilities for action emerge from this perspective?
4 To help you respond to question 3, here are some prompts to engage in systems thinking, which involves considering both spatial and temporal elements: "What circumstances and attitudes led to this point? What actions and behavior patterns led to this point? What are the likely attitudes, actions, and patterns going forward? What are the probable reactions of my: allies, enemies, competitors, neutral third parties, and the environment?" (Monat & Gannon, 2015, p. 17).

Suggested readings

The following references from the list below provide further information and advice about the issues discussed in this chapter: Absolon (2022), Cajete (2000), Kimmerer (2020), Martin (2023), McGilchrist (2009, 2021, 2024), Wilson (2008), and Yankaporta (2019).

References

Absolon(Minogiizhigokwe), K. E. (2022). *Kaandossiwin: How we come to know indigenous re-search methodologies* (2nd edition). Fernwood.
Bartleet, B.-L. (*2023*). A conceptual framework for understanding and articulating the social impact of community music. *International Journal of Community Music, 16*(1), 31–49. doi:10.1386/ijcm_00074_1.
Cajete, G. (2000). *Native science: Natural laws of interdependence.* Clear Light.
Camlin, D. A. (2023). *Music making and civic imagination.* Intellect Books.
Camlin, D. A. (2024). What does it mean to sing with the Earth? *Music Education Research, 26*(3), 209–222. doi:10.1080/14613808.2024.2347636.
Camlin, D. A., Daffern, H., & Zeserson, K. (2020). Group singing as a resource for the development of a healthy public: A study of adult group singing. *Humanities and Social Sciences Communications, 7*(1), article 1. doi:10.1057/s41599-020-00549-0.
Camlin, D. A., & Schei, T. B. (2024). Reaping the harvest of joy: Practitioner enquiry into intercultural group singing. *Australian Voice, 25,* 1–15. doi:10.56307/DLAZ9779.
DataReportal. (2024). Digital 2024: Global overview report. 31 January. https://datarep ortal.com/reports/digital-2024-global-overview-report.
Gallup. (2023). The global state of social connections. www.gallup.com/analytics/ 509675/state-of-social-connections.aspx.

Gaunt, H., Duffy, C., Coric, A., González Delgado, I. R., Messas, L., Pryimenko, O., & Sveidahl, H. (2021). Musicians as "makers in society": A conceptual foundation for contemporary professional higher music education. *Frontiers in Psychology, 12.* doi:10.3389/fpsyg.2021.713648.

Kimmerer, R. W. (2020). *Braiding sweetgrass: Indigenous wisdom, scientific knowledge and the teachings of plants.* Penguin.

Martin, I. (2023). The indigenous critique and the divided brain hypothesis: Ideas to postpone the end of the World. *Gragoatá, 28,* article e54159. doi:10.22409/gragoata. v28i60.54159.

McGilchrist, I. (2009). *The master and his emissary: The divided brain and the making of the Western world.* Yale University Press.

McGilchrist, I. (2021). *The matter with things: Our brains, our delusions, and the unmaking of the world.* Perspectiva Press.

McGilchrist, I. (2024). Resist the machine apocalypse. 1 March. www.firstthings.com/a rticle/2024/03/resist-the-machine-apocalypse.

Meadows, D. (2008). *Thinking in systems: A primer* (illustrated edition). Chelsea Green.

Monat, J. P., & Gannon, T. F. (2015). What is systems thinking? A review of selected literature plus recommendations. *American Journal of Systems Science, 4*(1), 11–26.

Putnam, R. D. (2000). *Bowling alone: The collapse and revival of American community.* Simon & Schuster.

Siegel, D. J., & Drulis, C. (2023). An interpersonal neurobiology perspective on the mind and mental health: Personal, public, and planetary well-being. *Annals of General Psychiatry, 22*(1), 5. doi:10.1186/s12991-023-00434-5.

Way, N., Ali, A., Gilligan, C., & Noguera, P. (eds). (2018). *The crisis of connection: Roots, consequences, and solutions.* NYU Press.

Wilson, S. (2008). *Research is ceremony: Indigenous research methods.* Fernwood.

Wong, B. L. H., Nordström, A., Piot, P., & Clark, H. (2024). From polycrisis to metacrisis: Harnessing windows of opportunity for renewed political leadership in global health diplomacy. *BMJ Global Health, 9*(4), article e015340.

World Health Organization. (2023). WHO commission on social connection. www.who. int/groups/commission-on-social-connection.

Yankaporta, T. (2019). *Sand talk: How Indigenous thinking can save the world.* Text.

8 Reconnecting through integration
The interpersonal neurobiology framework

Introduction

> It's an interesting point of our lives where our humanity and the environment and how we're inextricably linked to those things, our interconnectedness, has got to be the answer to all of our big problems—our dysfunction among ourselves and our feelings of supremacy over nature dominate over our connectedness.
>
> —Allison Girvan, community music practitioner

In the previous chapter, we explored how positive music leaders operate within complex systems where multiple elements interact in non-linear ways. This is nice to know in theory, but what are the practical implications of understanding the complex context within which music leaders operate? This chapter introduces interpersonal neurobiology (IPNB) as a practical framework that helps bridge theory and practice, offering positive music leaders concrete strategies for working with complexity to create powerful musical experiences that support social connection.

IPNB provides an elegant way to understand and work with complexity in human systems. Rather than trying to reduce human experience to isolated components, IPNB offers a holistic approach that acknowledges the complex interplay between brain, body, relationships, and our environment.

IPNB is a framework for understanding the complexity of the mind, mental health, and wellbeing. As a consilient framework which seeks to find common ground among disparate disciplines, IPNB synthesises knowledge from diverse fields including neuroscience, psychology, physics, mathematics, Indigenous knowledges, and contemplative practices to help us appreciate the complexity of human experience (Siegel, 2012, 2022; Siegel & Drulis, 2023).

IPNB proposes that the mind is not confined to the brain, but emerges from the interplay of brain, body, and relationships with others and the world around us. This perspective challenges traditional views of the mind as simply "what the brain does", offering instead a more holistic understanding that aligns with recent findings in cognitive science, embodied cognition, and neurobiology. In other words, our mental lives are more than what is "going on" in our heads: there is a *relational context* in which we experience our self, our identity, and our sense of belonging (Siegel & Drulis, 2023). IPNB emphasises the embodiment and

DOI: 10.4324/9781003426509-12

embeddedness of individuals within social worlds as being fundamental to understanding wellbeing.

Just as IPNB extends the mind beyond the brain, the framework extends beyond individual mental health to encompass public and even planetary wellbeing (Siegel, 2022). This echoes the work of Camlin's "singing for the earth" project which we explored at the end of the previous chapter. Viewing the mind as both embodied and relational has profound implications at multiple levels (Siegel & Drulis, 2023). At the individual or personal level, IPNB provides insights into how integration within our neural systems and in our relationships promotes individual health and resilience. At the public or societal level, the framework suggests that societal wellbeing is intrinsically linked to the quality of our interpersonal connections and the degree to which we are integrated within our communities. Perhaps most strikingly, IPNB extends to considering how our sense of integration (or lack thereof) impacts planetary health, proposing that our sense of self and our societal structures profoundly impact our relationship with the natural world.

Siegel suggests that the construction of the "solo-self" which is prevalent in modern, individualistic (Western) cultures may be at the root of many personal, social, and environmental challenges. This echoes the work of Iain McGilchrist (2009, 2021), by which the dominance of left-hemisphere reductionism (which extends to seeing each person as an individual rather than as part of an interconnected web of being) has left humans out of touch with their true nature, and disconnected from the natural environment. We can turn to John Donne to eloquently sum up the arguments of both Siegel and McGilchrist:

> No man is an island, entire of itself; every man is a piece of the continent, a part of the main. If a clod be washed away by the sea, Europe is the less, as well as if a promontory were, as well as if a manor of thy friend's or of thine own were: any man's death diminishes me, because I am involved in mankind, and therefore never send to know for whom the bells tolls; it tolls for thee.
>
> (John Donne, "Meditation XVII", 1624)

Donne was writing in the seventeenth century (and at a time when "man" was synonymous with "human"), however, the interconnectedness of reality described in these lines echoes both the modern framework of IPNB as well as ancient belief systems of Indigenous peoples (by his own acknowledgement, Siegel's work owes much to Indigenous knowledge systems). By fostering a more integrated view of self—one that recognises our deep interconnectedness with ourselves, others and with nature—IPNB offers a path toward not just individual healing, but also toward addressing broader societal issues and environmental crises. This systems perspective underscores the idea that personal, public, and planetary wellbeing are inextricably linked, and that positive change at any level can have far-reaching effects.

Therefore, within IPNB, the mind is defined as "an emergent, self-organizing, embodied and relational process that regulates the flow of energy and information" (Siegel & Drulis, 2023, p. 18). This definition emphasises the dynamic, interconnected nature of mental processes and their relationship to both internal bodily states and external social interactions.

IPNB's systems approach allows us to address complex phenomena that often elude more reductionist models, particularly the ways in which social connections can be enhanced to positively influence our wellbeing. By drawing on multiple disciplines, IPNB offers positive music leaders a comprehensive lens through which to view their work. The framework provides scientific grounding for understanding how participatory music making can foster social connection, not just through individual experiences, but through the complex interplay of neurological, physiological, and social processes. As we explore IPNB further, we'll see how this integrative approach can inform and enhance positive music leadership, offering new insights into the power of music to promote social health and connection.

Integration—Differentiation and linkage

A key principle of IPNB is the concept of *integration*— combining parts to form a whole. Music therapist, psychotherapist and educator, Nsamu Moonga speaks of his own lived experience in terms of integration, saying this sense of interconnection was there "before words":

> I didn't know anything else apart from just knowing that there's an integrated nature of existing in the world and relationships are built within that particular frame. Relationships are built with the animate and inanimate world, the above and the below, right, and the horizontal, the perpendicular, and the living and the non-living. So, it's all of that, it's part of how I was raised.

According to Nsamu, the fish only discovers that it has been swimming in water when there's no water. Nsamu reflects that colonial systems of education, religion, and capital metaphorically take our water away by making us believe "that growth and development is centred on how brilliant you are as an individual".

Siegel too argues that mental health and wellbeing arise from the integration of all aspects of experience—from the purely biophysical or neural to the interpersonal or relational. Integration involves linking differentiated elements while maintaining their unique qualities. This balance between differentiation and linkage is seen as crucial for optimal functioning and wellbeing. The opposites of integration are chaos and/or rigidity: in these states, which are typical of mental illness, we are no longer in the "flow" of life, and our mental health suffers significantly (Siegel & Drulis, 2023).

Siegel offers an elegant equation for integration (or wellbeing): Differentiation + Linkage. "Differentiation" refers to the ways in which parts of a system become specialised, unique in their growth, and individualised in their development; it can refer to different parts of a system within an individual or a group. "Linkage" refers simply to the connection of differentiated components to each other (Siegel, 2012, 2020; Siegel & Drulis, 2023).

This equation might seem abstract and paradoxically, reductionist, but in practice, as we will see from the RESONANCE examples in this chapter, fostering integration is as much an intuitive practice as it is one that can be prescribed— skilled music leaders intuitively create conditions for integration through their work. In the context of participatory music making, differentiation refers to, among other things, the unique contributions of each participant, while linkage represents the connections formed through collective music making. Integration, the result of this process, fosters wellbeing for both performers and listeners.

RESONANCE: Integrating voice, body, and mind

Singing leader Jane York's description of group singing beautifully illustrates IPNB's equation for integration (differentiation + linkage).

Jane describes how singing simultaneously grounds us in our individual bodies while connecting us to others. Jane observes how singing first creates physiological integration within individuals: "Singing puts us in our body ... our nervous system suddenly regulates ... we're breathing more deeply". This mindful, embodied experience differentiates participants from their usual "in our head" states. At the same time, the act of singing together creates powerful linkages between participants. Jane says, "there's an intimacy about everyone's voice and the differences", acknowledging both the uniqueness of each voice (differentiation) and how these distinct voices come together (linkage).

The result is what IPNB would recognise as integration or what Jane calls "the presence of our collective humanness". This integration manifests in the group's ability to share emotional experiences through music (linkage): "We can sing a love song and ... all relate to this perhaps and feel that story and share that moment together". The careful selection of musical material becomes crucial in maintaining this integration, as Jane notes that "the wrong material at the wrong moment can take people out of themselves", effectively disrupting the integrated state.

This RESONANCE example demonstrates how skilled positive music leaders can facilitate integration by creating conditions where individual embodied experience and collective musical expression combine to create meaningful connection, or integration.

Differentiation in practice

Both Emma and Kym in the box below recognise the inherent value of the individual members of their groups (differentiation) but also understand that the solo-self cannot realise its potential unless it is "linked" to others. This holds true within a community choir context as well as our lives more broadly. We need to be recognised as having inherent worth and dignity (Hicks, 2021), but we also need to belong to something beyond ourselves (Allen, 2021).

RESONANCE—Celebrating diversity in community choirs: The sound of humanity

Positive music leaders commonly talk about how the differences between community music group members is a strength. Differentiation in community music groups might involve recognising and valuing each participant's unique voice or instrumental contribution; acknowledging diverse musical backgrounds and skill levels; and encouraging individual expression within the group context.

Musician and community choir leader Emma Dean intuitively recognises the power of differentiation in the following passage:

> My philosophy—or one of the things I love talking about—is how cool it is that a choir is this space where people from literally all different backgrounds, all different genders, political leanings, sexualities, ages, cultural backgrounds, religions, come together to sing in harmony beautifully. That blows my mind because I'm like, what if parliament— every day they had a choir session? Wouldn't that be amazing?!

Musician Kym Dillon who leads social inclusion choirs makes a similar observation:

> Something I love about these choirs is that we don't try and smooth the sound out too much to create this kind of beautiful, heavenly, celestial thing that often – professional choirs are able to achieve that, and it's beautiful. But what I love about us is this kind of earthy – you can hear the individual voices and it's kind of rough here and – it's got this strange tex- ture to it which, for me, it's like the sound of humanity. That feels like when you have true inclusion where we haven't tried to sand this down into one ideal. But you just have a bunch of people of different shapes and sizes.

Linkage in practice

Community music making is arguably an inherently "linking" activity, although the success of such linkage will depend on the different group members, and the leaders' ability to successfully differentiate and leverage those parts. As community music practitioner Allison Girvan explains, group music making requires funda- mental agreements—what she calls "non-negotiable parameters", like rhythm, key, and breathing. But within these parameters lies deep potential for human con- nection. "Music opens up so much potential for communication that is in some ways simpler ... stripped down," Allison observes. When people make music together, they must constantly balance individual expression with group needs, learning to "communicate respectfully with other people" through elements like balance and blend.

RESONANCE—Finding common ground through music

What makes music so effective for creating linkage is that it transcends individual agendas, offering what Allison Girvan calls "a language that allows for some common understanding". Even something as simple as breath becomes a powerful tool for connection—whether breathing together in unison or consciously choosing different moments to breathe in order to support fellow singers. This illustrates how musical linkage creates interdependence while honouring individual contributions.

At the very least, as Emma Dean observes, there is an inherently linking or common purpose in these groups:

> The common thing is we all love music. We all love song. Definitely that's a common theme. Music is something we all share, like it's in all of us. It's in singing and dance and movement and creativity. It's our birthright. I really feel that. It's in each and every one of us. I think, maybe, there's a curiosity in most people about that. So, I think that's why music is the thing that draws people in.

Integration in practice—The "FACES flow" of integration

Let's explore what integration means by unpacking what Siegel refers to as the "FACES flow" of integration: a fully integrated system (be it an individual, or a group) is Flexible, Adaptive, Coherent, Energised, and Stable.

RESONANCE—The FACES flow of integration within a singing group for people with Parkinson's

FACES flow of integration often emerges during successful musical performances or practice sessions. The following is a reflection on my own experience as a music leader:

> I just returned from a session with my group Park 'n Songs. There were quite a few new faces today. It was a great session, and I played a game with the group: "Random Acts of Gratitude". At different points throughout the session, I turned to thank a volunteer for their commitment to our group, and acknowledged how their "behind the scenes" work helps the group to function and flourish. I then asked the group to join in to sing "For he/she's a jolly good fellow" ending with a rousing "hip, hip, hooray!" We also sang several new songs during the session but everyone—old members and new—joined in with gusto.
>
> Afterwards, I was chatting to our group's lead volunteer, and she mentioned how she thought the group had gotten vocally stronger and more confident over time, even though our membership is always

changing (albeit with a consistent core of members). I agreed, and said "It's as if the core energy of the group is getting stronger and stronger". I feel this is because as my own leadership has grown, and we have had the input of many other music leaders who share the role with me, the relationship between all parts of the group and the group's purpose has become clearer and stronger over time.

The Park 'n Songs group is an example of the FACES flow of integration: the group is *flexible* and *adaptive* (able to flexibly adapt to new members and different leaders), has a *coherent* and purposeful format, is *energised* through the leadership and membership, and is *stable* over time (we've been at it consistently for eight years!).

Kym Dillon's deeply intuitive understanding of linkage and "FACES flow" is evident in the following observations:

During performances, there's a three-way system of energy flowing between choir, audience, and leader. While I can't see the audience, I can tell from the choir members' faces when people are responding—they can't help but smile and laugh, even more than in rehearsal. People often describe wanting to be part of this energy, this electricity in the room. What makes choir unique is that every single person's voice contributes to creating this larger sound. While I help facilitate and hold it together, I can't make it happen without everyone else in the room. There's something deeply symbolic about this in terms of humanity and inclusion—literally every voice is being included in this bigger thing. When I see people getting swept away in performance or rehearsal, it's an affirmation that they're part of something larger than themselves.

This description perfectly exemplifies IPNB's formula for integration as differentiation + linkage. Each singer maintains their unique voice (differentiation) while simultaneously connecting with others (linkage) to create something greater than the sum of its parts. The "three-way system of energy" Kym describes demonstrates how multiple elements of a complex system—collective sound, audience response, and leadership—can integrate to create FACES flow: a system that is *flexible, adaptive, coherent, energised,* and *stable.* Kym intuitively recognises this "three-way system" as a complex system when she says, "it's an affirmation that they're part of something larger than themselves".

For positive music leaders, understanding IPNB can inform our understanding of why we structure our sessions the way we do, the repertoire choices we make, and how we interact with participants. By honouring each person's unique contribution (differentiation) while fostering connections within the group (linkage through participatory music making), we can create an environment conducive to the FACES flow of integration and wellbeing.

Playing your PART as a positive music leader

To effectively foster integration through differentiation and linkage, positive music leaders can embody the principles of PART from the IPNB framework which stands for Presence, Attunement, Resonance, and Trust. These elements, originally formulated by Siegel for application within the therapeutic relationship, are also relevant to participatory music making contexts. Leaders who enact the principles of PART can help create an atmosphere where participants "feel felt," fostering deeper connections and a sense of integration (see Camlin et al., 2020; Siegel & Drulis, 2023).

Presence is "the open awareness that engenders a receptive relational state" (Siegel & Drulis, 2023, p. 10). Presence is the very foundation of how we connect authentically with one another and requires us music leaders to be receptive to "what is". Presence takes a "bottom up" perspective rather than a "top down" view (that things should be a certain way). This is the very essence of a strengths-based, positive approach to working with others. Presence in a leader asks the leader to be vulnerable, responsive to the context, and welcoming of uncertainty.

Attunement involves focusing on inner experiences—both our own and others'—rather than just external behaviours. It requires developing sensitivity to participants' internal states without making assumptions about them (Siegel & Drulis, 2023). Emily Foulkes, singing for health practitioner–researcher, reflects on attunement:

> We have to listen, but we have to go beyond that. We have to do a whole body listening. It's like a whole being listening not just ears listening. It's sensing. Safety is like a felt sense. It's a very complex thing. We can't just apportion it to one sense. It's a whole experience. We have to use this attunement process and steps towards that include using mimicry, which we do unconsciously as well as consciously. If we're struggling to match with and attune with somebody, then we can use mimicry as a way into that.

Resonance is experiencing another's feelings, without taking them on as your own (Siegel & Drulis, 2023). For music leaders, this balance is crucial for maintaining boundaries while creating meaningful connections. Again, Emily Foulkes describes this as the difference between relating from the "personal heart" (where we might take others' experiences to heart) and the "universal heart" (in which we are able to honour others' experiences through compassion without taking them on as our own).

Trust "is that open state of feeling that the kind intentions and the availability of the other person are reliably present" (Siegel & Drulis, 2023, p. 10).

The following examples demonstrate how positive music leaders intuitively enact the principles of PART in their practices.

RESONANCE—Meeting participants "where they are"

Vocal leader James Sills is one of the pioneers of online singing groups, and his Sofa Singers have been meeting online since March 2020. Here, James describes his process to allow for different levels of engagement for his online singers:

> While teaching the main melodies and choruses, I'll offer optional backing vocals or harmonies that I've prepared beforehand. These might be a simple third above the melody or a call-and-response pattern—always designed for minimal effort but maximum musical impact. Participants can stick with the melody throughout if they prefer, or they can take on additional harmonic parts when they feel ready. I often provide both easier and more challenging options. This approach exemplifies my philosophy of meeting people where they are while leaving the door open for those who want to explore further.

James's approach demonstrates some of the key principles of PART. By being *present*, James is open to "what is" in terms of participants' capabilities and preferences. He is *attuned* to participants' inner states by anticipating and preparing for different levels of readiness and confidence. He demonstrates *resonance* through creating opportunities for participants to experience success and connection without becoming overwhelmed. And finally, James embodies *trust*—he offers options, providing clear structure (prepared harmonies, sing the melody) while allowing for autonomy in how participants engage.

The positive music leaders interviewed for this book spoke about meeting their groups "where they are at" rather than imposing a way of being on the group. This is a form of trust, an openness to the intentions of the participants in the group. Howell et al. (2017) describe this process of being receptive to "what is" in terms of improvisation: facilitating or leading community music making celebrates the diverse ways music can take, responding to whoever happens to be in the room at the time, and responds to the complexity of communities. The goal is to "allow the group's unique, time- and participant-specific response to emerge" (Howell et al., 2017, p. 613).

This improvisatory approach to leading community music groups beautifully captures the elements of PART within IPNB: taking an improvisatory approach requires leaders to remain open and present, to be attuned and sensitive to participant's energy while balancing participants' feelings with their own (resonance), and to cultivate trust by creating safe spaces where everyone is free to be themselves without judgment.

RESONANCE—Trust, uncertainty, and mistakes

Allison Girvan emphasises how trust, while initiated by the leader, must be actively tested and proven within the group. She explains: "Trust improves the music. The trust that's built up starting with you [as the leader] but then spreading throughout the group actually improves the music."

However, Allison acknowledges that creating a trusting environment requires more than just declaring a space "safe". Participants need opportunities to test that safety: "You can create the safest spaces you want but until you actually do something, dive in in a way that you need to be caught by that safe space … you don't really know." This testing of trust applies to everyone in the group, not just those who might appear to need extra support. As she observes, "The most successful [groups] are when everybody can make a mistake and feel good enough to actually sing a wrong note or make a terrible sound … that's when things start getting really exciting because then things can move faster."

This insight beautifully illustrates how trust within a music group operates as both a foundation for musical growth and a catalyst for deeper connection. When participants feel secure enough to take risks and make mistakes, the entire group benefits from increased freedom of expression and accelerated musical development. Further, Allison embodies the resonance of PART by allowing everyone to make mistakes but not take this on as a negative herself.

For positive music leaders, embodying the principles of PART can help to create group experiences that balance individual and collective musical expression. The goal is to avoid both the chaos of disconnected individualism and the rigidity of enforced uniformity. The foundation for achieving this is "relational integration", which emerges "as individuals are honored for their differences and connections are established with respectful, compassionate communication" (Siegel & Drulis, 2023, p. 9). What arises out of this integration is a sense of belonging and connection to self, each other, and even the world around us.

RESONANCE—Building trust by asking questions, allowing space, and never making assumptions

When working with Indigenous communities, musician Gillian Howell demonstrates how the elements of PART come together to create psychological safety through both physical presence and cultural protocols:

> In every creative decision, you're just leaving space in front of people—space for them to step into if they choose. It's about agency. That space might be facilitated or might just be a real literal empty space. But never crowding someone out—not crowding out their energy, not making assumptions.

This approach exemplifies *presence* through mindful awareness of space (both physical and metaphorical), keen *attunement* to participants' readiness to engage, and *resonance* with their energy levels. Most crucially, it builds *trust*. Gillian recalls how one of her collaborators said that feeling safe came from knowing she had consulted her Elders and that they had been involved in the process. This adherence to cultural protocols created the foundation for meaningful engagement.

The process requires patience and reciprocal trust-building, as Gillian reflects: "I also need to feel that sort of safety in this work, to feel like I have asked enough people, asked the right questions, given enough time for things to move and shift and settle."

These examples show how positive music leaders embody PART principles to create environments where genuine participation can emerge naturally. By being present without being overwhelming, attuned to individual states as well as social and cultural protocols, resonating with others without taking on others' emotional states, and being patient in building trust, leaders help establish the psychological safety necessary for meaningful musical engagement and social connection.

The principles of PART take on even deeper significance when we consider the rich diversity of human experience and cultural expression that positive music leaders encounter in their work. IPNB inherently acknowledges and values difference, which is a key reason why its application in the community music context is both illuminating and ethical. In the quest for consilience, the IPNB framework recognises the value of diverse ways of knowing, including Indigenous knowledge and contemplative practices. As Siegel and Drulis note:

> The wisdom of indigenous and contemplative teachings synergize with new contributions in the science of self, identity, and belonging. Though "modern culture" around the globe may teach that the Self is a separate, noun-like entity, Indigenous and contemplative teachings from around the world have independently offered a different view—of a self that is a more verb-like emergence embedded in all of humanity and in all of nature.
>
> (Siegel & Drulis, 2023, p. 13)

This respect for diverse perspectives within IPNB naturally leads us to consider the importance of cultural humility and culturally responsive leadership. Just as IPNB seeks to acknowledge, respect, and integrate knowledge from various disciplines and traditions, positive music leaders approach their work with an openness to different cultural understandings of music, community, culture, and wellbeing.

Cultural humility and culturally responsive leadership

If we are to truly embrace complexity in our practice as positive music leaders, we must acknowledge that one of the most significant manifestations of complexity lies in human diversity itself. Each person brings their own cultural background, lived experiences, and ways of understanding the world. Community music has a strong history and tradition of social justice and respect for diversity and inclusion (Higgins & Willingham, 2017). This context requires positive music leaders to practice cultural humility. Cultural humility extends beyond mere awareness of cultural differences. It involves a lifelong commitment to self-evaluation and critique, to redressing power imbalances, and to developing mutually beneficial partnerships with ourselves and our communities (Tervalon & Murray-García, 1998; see also Fisher-Borne et al., 2015). For positive music leaders, practising cultural humility is essential to creating inclusive, respectful, and truly integrative musical experiences that can support social health across diverse contexts.

Community music has always aimed to be inclusive and socially just, but achieving this is complicated by the long history of colonisation and racial inequality in many parts of the world. As more Indigenous and settler musicians work together, and as institutions try to become more culturally inclusive, an important question emerges: How can we make music together in ways that build genuine trust and respect across different cultures?

This question was discussed recently in a roundtable of community musicians. Facilitated by Canadian community musician Deanna Yerichuk, a panel of musicians and scholars from New Zealand, Canada, and Australia explored this question through the lens of cultural humility which recognises that we can never fully master another culture, but must instead commit to ongoing learning and cultivating respectful relationships (CMA Assembly, 2020). Rather than assuming expertise about other cultures, cultural humility emphasises building authentic connections, being accountable for our actions, and staying humble as we learn from each other.

RESONANCE—Moving from extraction to relationship in community music

Gillian Howell has worked extensively in cross-cultural contexts including with remote Indigenous communities. Gillian offers a powerful touchstone for critically reflecting on practice by distinguishing between extractive and relational approaches:

> For me it's extractivism versus relationship. When working cross-culturally, rather than asking "Am I benefiting too much from this?" or "Am I playing a white saviour role?", the more useful question is: "Is there something I'm extracting from this, or is my benefit coming because I'm actually in relation with these people?" If we're in right relations, then there should be good things that come back to us. That's what makes it sustainable.

This perspective challenges us to always keep genuine reciprocal relationships at the heart of practice—what matters is whether benefits for participants arise from authentic connections and fair exchanges rather than exploitation.

While cultural humility originated in healthcare settings, community music has developed its own framework through "culturally responsive leadership", as articulated by Higgins and Willingham (2017). Like cultural humility, culturally responsive leadership is informed by leaders' nuanced understanding of culture, ethnicity, race, and faith. Higgins and Willingham (2017, p. 55) suggest that "[o]ur participants must see themselves reflected in the experiences that community music provides". In this way, culturally responsive—and positive—leaders demonstrate they are "committed to the collective, not merely individual empowerment, such that the impact of this approach is directed towards making change for all members of society" (Higgins & Willingham, 2017, p. 55).

RESONANCE—The art of sitting alongside

When working with an Indigenous community in the Kimberley region, Gillian Howell emphasises the importance of literally and metaphorically "sitting alongside" community members:

> What really characterises the work is sitting alongside. Literally, we're generally sitting alongside each other—it's very rarely face-to-face. Sometimes my role is to be a scribe, noting down ideas. Sometimes it's thinking musically about maintaining consistency in rhythm that makes songs easy to learn and memorise. But always, I prioritise the relationships above everything. I try to carry myself with a huge amount of care and make sure I do what I say I will do. My preference is to approach with caution, I suppose. With care. Just with care, and recognising that I don't know all the rules of that community.

Gillian's work requires an openness to continuous learning and careful navigation between different perspectives. Her "sitting alongside" as both a practice and as a stance she takes towards her work, embodies a style of leadership which places authentic connections front and centre.

This balance between leadership and humility extends to the creative process itself. As Gillian explains:

> Sometimes a participant might say, "Oh, I've got a new idea. I actually want to change it." But I will suggest, "Maybe that's a different song. Maybe this one can be finished and go in the book, and that's a new song idea we can work on next."

While part of leadership is helping guide such decisions, Gillian reflects that cultural humility means "not making any assumptions until you understand the lay of the land a little bit more. That just takes a lot of time and exposure—a lot of opportunity to be sitting in this space and not just thinking about it theoretically."

Cultural humility and culturally responsive leadership as exemplified in Gillian's work align with the leadership approaches discussed throughout this book. All approaches require an understanding and awareness of context, and a constant navigation by music leaders between the interests of the part and the whole, the individual and the collective, the group and society more broadly—even, as IPNB and Camlin (2023) both argue, between our species and the planet we inhabit.

Bringing the leadership frameworks together

This chapter has discussed the interpersonal neurobiology framework, with its emphasis on fostering integration through differentiation and linkage, and PART to foster a strong sense of connection between the music leader and group members. You may be wondering how IPNB and PART relate to the other frameworks for leading others presented earlier. Table 8.1 shows how the relational integration of IPNB and PART aligns with the leadership strategies of positively energising leadership (Chapter 5) and identity leadership (Chapter 6).

At the heart of all the frameworks in this book is the idea that leadership is about building connection and creating the conditions for people to thrive and

Table 8.1 Relationship between PART in IPNB, positively energising leadership and identity leadership.

PART element	Positively energising leadership	Identity leadership
Presence	Creates positive climate through full awareness and receptivity to "what is"; fosters environment where positive emotions can flourish	Supports identity entrepreneurship by helping leaders authentically craft a "sense of us" through genuine presence with the group
Attunement	Enables positive communication by helping leaders tune into others' inner states and respond with empathy and understanding	Enhances prototypicality by helping leaders better understand and embody group values and norms
Resonance	Builds positive relationships by allowing leaders to understand and connect with others' feelings without becoming overwhelmed	Strengthens identity advancement by helping leaders better sense and champion group interests and needs
Trust	Underpins all aspects of positive leadership, particularly fostering virtuous behaviours like compassion, gratitude, and authenticity	Essential for identity impresarioship—creating and maintaining activities that build group identity requires deep mutual trust

flourish. Leadership in this sense is no longer about persuading followers to do the leader's bidding. Positive music leadership is about fostering social connection through participatory music making in community settings. Building connection in this way has incredible ripple effects: when we feel more connected and that we belong, we have better social health, which in turn means better physical and mental health, and overall improved wellbeing.

Refrain

This chapter has introduced interpersonal neurobiology as a powerful framework for understanding and working with the complexity inherent in positive music leadership. We've seen how IPNB's elegant equation for wellbeing—integration through differentiation plus linkage—manifests in participatory music making when skilled leaders honour both individual expressions and foster intra-group connections. The PART framework (presence, attunement, resonance, trust) offers practical strategies for fostering integration, creating environments where participants can truly "feel felt" and experience meaningful connection. Beyond these tools, we've explored how cultural humility and culturally responsive leadership extend and deepen our practice, acknowledging that working with human diversity requires a commitment to lifelong learning, critical self-reflection, and constant attention to power dynamics. For positive music leaders, the frameworks of positively energising leadership, identity leadership, and interpersonal neurobiology offer complementary paths to creating transformative musical experiences that support connection and social health. By embracing complexity rather than trying to reduce it, maintaining presence while staying humble, and balancing individual dignity with collective belonging, we can create spaces where genuine connection flourishes.

As we move into the final chapter, we'll explore some final frameworks which will help us understand the value of this work, and how to champion positive music leadership as an important public health resource.

Call and response

1   Consider IPNB's "equation": integration = differentiation + linkage. How do you currently balance honouring individual differences while fostering connection in your music groups? What might you do differently with this understanding?
2   Reflect on how you typically approach challenges in your music leadership. Do you tend towards reductionist thinking (breaking things into parts and looking for "silver bullet" solutions) or holistic thinking (seeing interconnections)? How might developing both approaches serve you better?
3   How might the PART framework (presence, attunement, resonance, trust) enhance your current leadership practice? Choose one element you'd like to develop further and think of specific ways you could strengthen it.

4   Think about diversity within your music groups. How does understanding complexity help you approach cultural differences more sensitively? What aspects of cultural humility or culturally responsive leadership could you develop further in your practice?

For practical reasons, this chapter has merely introduced complex topics rather than explored them in depth. Many books have been written on interpersonal neurobiology, some of which are referenced below. Interested readers are encouraged to explore the suggested readings to gain a deeper appreciation of the ideas introduced in this chapter.

Suggested readings

The following references from the list below provide further information and advice about the issues discussed in this chapter: Siegel (2012, 2022) and Siegel and Drulis (2023).

References

Allen, K.-A. (2021). *The psychology of belonging*. Routledge.

Camlin, D. A. (2023). *Music making and civic imagination*. Intellect Books.

Camlin, D. A., Daffern, H., & Zeserson, K. (2020). Group singing as a resource for the development of a healthy public: A study of adult group singing. *Humanities and Social Sciences Communications, 7*(1), article 1.

CMA Assembly. (2020). Deanna Yerichuk—Reciprocity in community music: Practicing cultural humility [Video]. YouTube. https://youtu.be/QAS2Esggz8k?si=wjiTflxB-_kKfINt.

Fisher-Borne, M., Cain, J. M., & Martin, S. L. (2015). From mastery to accountability: Cultural humility as an alternative to cultural competence. *Social Work Education, 34*(2), 165–181. doi:10.1080/02615479.2014.977244.

Hicks, D. (2021). *Dignity: Its essential role in resolving conflict* (10th anniversary edition). Yale University Press.

Higgins, L., & Willingham, L. (2017). *Engaging in community music: An introduction*. Routledge.

Howell, G., Higgins, L., & Bartleet, B.-L. (2017). Community music practice: Intervention through facilitation. In R. Mantie & G. D. Smith (eds), *The Oxford handbook of music making and leisure* (pp. 601–618). Oxford University Press.

McGilchrist, I. (2009). *The master and his emissary: The divided brain and the making of the Western world*. Yale University Press.

McGilchrist, I. (2021). *The matter with things: Our brains, our delusions, and the unmaking of the world*. Perspectiva Press.

Siegel, D. J. (2012). *Pocket guide to interpersonal neurobiology: An integrative handbook of the mind*. Norton.

Siegel, D. J. (2022). *Intraconnected: MWE (me + we) as the integration of self, identity, and belonging*. Norton.

Siegel, D. J., & Drulis, C. (2023). An interpersonal neurobiology perspective on the mind and mental health: Personal, public, and planetary well-being. *Annals of General Psychiatry, 22*(1), 5.

Tervalon, M., & Murray-García, J. (1998). Cultural humility versus cultural competence: A critical distinction in defining physician training outcomes in multicultural education. *Journal of Health Care for the Poor and Underserved, 9*(2), 117–125.

9 Championing positive music leadership

Introduction

When we consider the broader context of positive music leadership, many music leaders work in relative isolation within their communities. They may be disconnected from professional networks and largely unaware of the growing research base that demonstrates the value of participatory music making for social connection. This isolation can make it challenging to articulate and advocate for the importance of their work to stakeholders, funders, and even potential participants.

While music leaders intuitively understand the transformative power of their work, they may struggle to translate this understanding into language that resonates with those outside their immediate sphere. Singing leader Jane York identifies this critical barrier: "Anyone who's not already involved in community music has no idea what we're doing!"

This lack of understanding of the power of participatory music making *as a process* can be a major stumbling block for music leaders seeking support for community activities. As Jane explains:

> Funders want outputs. They want a performance output. Not everyone [in a community music group] has the capacity to do that. I've been working with some of the groups from Neighbourhood Houses [a body that runs community centres across Victoria, Australia] and most of these groups don't have the capacity to perform. Some of them do but most of them just don't, and it's not why they're there and it's actually not the function of that group.

Jane observes that funding bodies may not have a nuanced understanding of the function and diverse possible outcomes of participatory music making, like marriage proposals and respite from grief (as we will see in examples below). As Jane puts it, these outcomes may not be immediately visible to those "outside the tent".

The challenges Jane identifies lead to a range of questions: What do positive music leaders seek to achieve? How? How do they know they have achieved it? And if they have achieved it, how is this best communicated? How do we honour the rich complexity of our work while making its value clear and accessible to others?

DOI: 10.4324/9781003426509-13

This chapter takes a systems approach and suggests multiple interconnected ways to address these questions. As we saw in Chapter 7, positive music leaders operate within complex systems in which multiple elements interact in ways that create unpredictable but meaningful patterns over time (Meadows, 2008). The third area of a leader's triple focus—contextual awareness—requires thinking in systems to effectively communicate the impact of positive music leadership with diverse stakeholders.

Thinking in systems requires us to move dynamically between understanding the parts, the relationships between parts, and how these parts interact create the "emergent property" of a system. While it is tempting to see the outcome of participatory music making as "magic" (and indeed that word has been used a lot so far in this book!), Bartleet (2023, p. 32) argues that "relying uncritically on the miraculous" is fraught and unadvisable.

This chapter—and indeed this book—therefore advocates for striking a balance between rigorous frameworks and robust evidence on one hand, and intuitive practice and appreciating the "magic" of music making on the other. This approach is in line with Iain McGilchrist's (2009, 2021) arguments about knowing and experience explored in earlier chapters: our brain's left-hemisphere analytical bent must work in service to the right hemisphere, the true master, with its ability to appreciate the unity and, ultimately, the mystery of our existence.

From this vantage point, the frameworks covered in this chapter operate within this balance—they help us to appreciate and acknowledge complexity, but also seek to identify the many parts which create the experience of music making's manifold benefits. These frameworks provide a starting point for articulating the value and impact of positive music leadership across multiple contexts and audiences. Whether advocating with healthcare providers, funding bodies, community partners, or participants themselves, music leaders need various ways to frame their work that honour its complexity while remaining clear and compelling.

Before we look at these frameworks, let's consider some more time-honoured ways of communicating value and impact: firsthand or embodied experience, and storytelling.

The power of embodied experience

Singing leader Jane York explains the power of singing together in this short anecdote:

> Here's one of my favourite things … I have people who I've sung with for years every week, and felt incredibly connected to, and didn't know their surname and didn't know what they did for a job. Literally three years and just so, oh my God we'd go out and sing together, and maybe occasionally get a beer afterwards. We'd feel so intimate and close, and I love it, I couldn't tell you some basic info about their life, but I stood next to you and we sung together.

Jane describes here the incredible "ice-breaker" and bonding effects of singing together, a feeling of intimacy, without knowing much about your fellow singers—you may not even know their last name!

Embodied experience can play an important role in educating people unfamiliar with participatory music practices, including health practitioners. A recent scoping review found that experiential learning is valuable in communicating to aspiring health professionals about the value of engaging in the arts for health. However, only 10% of the studies identified in the review reported educational programs that provided students firsthand experience of creative health interventions or introduced them to arts-based therapies (Howlin et al., 2025). In a recent study involving Masters-level clinical psychology students, a community musician and music therapist led group singing and music listening activities to explore students' attitudes to music as an adjunct to therapy (Forbes et al., 2025). Results indicated that even a brief three-hour experiential learning session produced significant improvements in students' knowledge, confidence, and willingness to use music as an adjunct to psychological therapy.

The value of embodied experience is supported by arts and health researcher and practitioner, Naomi Sunderland, who has extensive experience in translating the value of this work to different audiences. Naomi says that for people not already inside the tent,

> they really do need an embodied experience of the practice. It needs to be incredibly welcoming and accepting of everyone who walks into that space and very deliberately and consciously held so that it can be a welcoming space for most if not all people.

Naomi cautions that "arts and health and creative practice are not going to be at the centre of a lot of mainstream—'whitestream'—discussions in society" so firsthand experience can play an important role in raising awareness of the value of these practices.

If you don't have the opportunity to deliver an experiential activity for stakeholders, singing for health practitioner–researcher Emily Foulkes has another suggestion:

> My go-to pitch is starting with, everybody's musical. I ask them to just forget their profession, forget their role, and think back to singing or moving or dancing or rhythm. I've walked into a room full of health professionals and they've gone, you're the musician, you're the music person. I say, well, actually, we all are. We all are. We're all musical. If we drill down to the cellular level, did you know that all your cells are dancing? They're all vibrating. Every cell in your body is making music. We are a walking symphony. I start from there, and trying to encourage people to tap into their own sense of musicality, their own sense of, yes, this means something to me as a human. I get people reflecting on themselves as musical beings and then I talk about the research.

Emily's strategy is to remind those she is pitching to for support that we are all musical, right down to our biology!

You may have noticed that in recounting their experiences, the music leaders featured in this book have relied heavily on storytelling to convey the impact of their work. Let's take a closer look at storytelling to communicate impact and promote change.

The power of a good story

Within the field of leadership, storytelling has emerged as a powerful tool for creating meaning, inspiring action, and driving change. Stories engage the listener in ways that data alone cannot—they help others visualise possibilities, build emotional connections, and, like a good metaphor, make the abstract concrete. Emily's metaphors above—our cells are "dancing" and we are a "walking symphony"—are evocative examples of imagery that communicates a fundamental truth about all people: we are musical beings. When leaders share stories and images effectively, they create shared understanding, build trust, and help others see themselves in the narrative of change. This is particularly relevant for positive music leaders who need to communicate the value of their work to diverse stakeholders.

Take this example from musician and community choir leader Emma Dean:

> We've had marriage proposals in our choir! But beyond these grand moments, it's the unexpected connections that move me most. There's this wonderful woman in her mid-70s—bright pink hair, hardcore environmentalist, lives off the grid—who has found her tribe among a group of 21-year-olds in the choir. She said to me, "I can't believe I found my people and they're 21 and I'm 76!" She tells me about how one young woman in the choir, despite her usual discomfort with physical affection, always insists on giving her a hug when they meet. These people would never have met, never in a million years, and now they're really good mates. That makes me so happy.

While this "micro-story" was told "off the cuff" during my interview with Emma, it still captures something that metrics alone can't, namely the unexpected moment when music breaks down social barriers and creates genuine human connection. Even though modern-day neo-liberal societies may be under the spell of "what can't be measured doesn't exist", do not underestimate the power of a good story to sway hearts and minds.

There are many simple storytelling templates available for you to experiment with. Think of an impactful example from your practice, and then consider crafting a short leadership impact story around this example. One simple template is a story of change or transformation. Solomon (2023) outlines a four-step template for telling your leadership impact story:

1 Start: What was the problem, issue, challenge? What did you not know when you started?
2 Decide: What action did you take?

3   Learn: What mistakes did you make? What did you learn?
4   Transform: How were you or your participant/s transformed?

Another framework is from Paul Smith's *Lead With a Story* (2012). Smith's template follows the dramatic arc and rising tension and resolution of a typical narrative: hook, context, challenge, conflict, resolution, lesson, action/implications. Here's a story I crafted for a public presentation about group singing for people with Parkinson's disease using Smith's template …

Singing for people with Parkinson's: "We're pushing back!"

[HOOK] Chances are, someone in this room will be impacted by Parkinson's disease, either directly or indirectly. Parkinson's is now the fastest-growing neurological disorder in the world, with experts warning we face a looming pandemic. The condition is debilitating, progressive, and incurable, affecting not just movement but causing pain, sensory changes, depression, cognitive difficulties and voice problems. Perhaps most devastatingly, its impact extends far beyond the person diagnosed, profoundly affecting spouses, family members, and caregivers.

[CONTEXT] This is the story of Edward and Cathy, whose experience powerfully illustrates how music making through group singing can create spaces of dignity and connection even in the face of profound challenges.

[CHALLENGE] Edward, a gentle man in his seventies with a soft voice partially due to hearing impairment, has been married to Cathy since 1967. When Cathy was diagnosed with Parkinson's disease fifteen years ago, their world began to contract.

[CONFLICT] The simple pleasures many take for granted like going to movies, dancing, or enjoying a restaurant meal became nearly impossible for Edward and Cathy. Like many carers, Edward faced increasing social isolation and disrupted routines, with no prospect of respite from the disease's inevitable progression.

[RESOLUTION] Yet since 2017, Edward and Cathy have regularly found refuge in the Park 'n Songs singing group for people with Parkinson's and their carers. Here, medical appointments and daily struggles momentarily fade as they stretch, vocalise, and sing together. Sometimes it's silly action songs, sometimes it's beautiful ballads. The transformation is profound. As Edward explains: "Life can be fairly empty … you can get sidelined and become insular. [The singing] has meant that the gravity or drift into that has not been as strong. And that we're pushing back against those things, and re-engaging with people, and relationships in a situation which was otherwise just closing in, diminishing."

[LESSONS] Edward and Cathy's story illustrates that while Parkinson's disease only takes away, group singing gives. It offers precious gifts—moments of escape from illness, shared joy between couples, belonging within a supportive community, and a sense of dignity and accomplishment. The group is led by a merry band of community musicians whose positive leadership enables participants to transcend their circumstances, if only temporarily, and connect with something larger than themselves.

[ACTION/IMPLICATIONS] By creating opportunities for meaningful connection through music, leaders like those facilitating Park 'n Songs help combat social isolation and enhance quality of life for vulnerable community members.

Good storytelling is just as important for researchers as it is for practitioners. The book *Story, Not Study* by health researchers Lingard and Watling (2021) is an accessible resource for researchers who want to produce engaging and memorable scholarly publications.

And of course, as creative practitioners, we also have the ability and the option to use other forms of creative media to tell our stories, including song writing. Naomi Sunderland weaves her creative practice into her research. Naomi says she uses group songwriting to give back to communities who are participating in research, or as a way of co-creating data and stories for the research projects she leads. Naomi adds that songwriting "can also be a way of sense making from data as a way of sharing knowledge, stories, wisdom, learnings from masses of qualitative data".

Understanding how to frame and communicate impact—and to use a medium appropriate for the audience you are pitching to—is a crucial leadership skill because it demonstrates contextual awareness, the over-arching area of the leader's "triple focus". While compelling stories can powerfully illustrate the value of our work, many stakeholders, particularly funders and policy makers, also need evidence of impact presented in more structured ways. This is where monitoring and evaluation comes in. By combining the art of storytelling with systematic approaches to measuring and documenting impact, positive music leaders can expand their reach and influence in their communities.

Monitoring and evaluation

Monitoring and evaluation of social programs like community music groups for social connection is increasingly required, especially where programs are publicly or philanthropically funded (Dunphy, 2017; Fancourt, 2017; Howell & Bartleet, 2022; Warran et al., 2023). While detailed coverage of this topic is beyond the scope of this book, it's important for positive music leaders to understand that funders and organisations often require robust, evidence-based evaluation of program outcomes.

At its core, monitoring and evaluation involves the continuous gathering of data (monitoring) to support a later evaluation of a social program (sometimes at an interim point in delivery, other times at the end of delivery). To ensure robust and credible monitoring and evaluation, delivery of these programs needs to be based on a "theory of change" and/or "program logic" which sets out what the program seeks to achieve, how it will be achieved, and the markers or key performance indicators of achievement (Markiewicz & Patrick, 2016).

While a theory of change is a "conceptual model that underpins the planning and design of your evaluation" (Warran et al., 2023, p. 17), a "program logic" or "logic model" is usually a graphic representation of program inputs, outputs, short-, medium- and long-term outcomes (depending on how long the program has been running) and program impacts, or may be framed as "interventions, components, responses, and outcomes" (Frechtling quoted in Fancourt & Warran, 2020, p. 18). While logic models can help "identify causal relationships in complex systems", they are still only representations of reality and not exhaustive, nor are they a strict recipe that guarantees a certain result (Fancourt & Warran, 2020). In this sense, logic models might be considered more of a map than the terrain, and as a starting point rather than a destination.

While monitoring and evaluation may sound similar to research (and in many ways it is), the main difference is that research seeks to produce new knowledge, where evaluation seeks to assess whether a social program has achieved its aims and objectives (Warran et al., 2023; see also Fancourt, 2017). In short, evaluation makes a value judgement or assessment about the success or otherwise of a program of work.

An illustrative example of rigorous evaluation comes from the Queensland Music Festival's "Absolutely Everybody" vocal ensemble project (Bartleet & Walton, 2021). This massed choir event, held online and via a day of recording in May 2021 at a public space in Brisbane, Australia demonstrates how evaluation can capture the multi-layered impact of community music initiatives.

The evaluation used "mixed methods" for data collection combining "an online survey, focus groups, interviews, and non-participant observations" producing both quantitative and qualitative data (Bartleet & Walton, 2021, p. 8). The published report uses data visualisation, narrative, photos, and diagrams to present its findings in an easy-to-digest format. Indicators reported on included the quality of the production, access and inclusion, community and connection, and benefits for participants (Bartleet & Walton, 2021). This example shows how systematic evaluation can complement the stories we tell about our work, providing stakeholders with concrete evidence while honouring the complexity of community music experiences.

Beyond this brief discussion, there are many free resources available to assist practitioners who find themselves in the position of not only having to deliver programs but monitor and evaluate them and produce evidence of their efficacy. Daisy Fancourt's book, *Arts in Health: Designing and Researching Interventions* (2017) is a comprehensive resource on arts and health evaluation and research. Fancourt's Social Biobehavioural Research Group at University College London has also produced a fantastic guide to arts and health evaluation (Warran et al., 2023). This guide provides an excellent overview of arts and health evaluation practice, and includes arts and health-specific approaches, frameworks, toolkits, and tools. These resources and others are listed at the end of this chapter.

It is vitally important that music leaders are aware of this landscape of accountability, and that they develop fundamental language and tools to "talk the talk" of program evaluation, should they be required to do so.

The following section provides an overview of some key frameworks for understanding impact developed by leading researchers in the fields of community music for social impact, and the broader field of arts and health. These frameworks can be drawn on to inform "theories of change" and "program logics" for monitoring and evaluating programs, and less formally, can help build positive music leaders' understanding of how and why their practice produces certain outcomes.

Frameworks for articulating the value of positive music leadership

> Effective implementation, inescapably, is a systems issue!
>
> (Goleman & Senge, 2014)

For positive music leaders seeking to demonstrate their impact, frameworks offer valuable tools for understanding and communicating the multi-layered value of their work. While frameworks might seem overly academic or constraining at first glance, they can actually help us appreciate the rich complexity of music making while providing practical ways to articulate its benefits to diverse stakeholders.

The following frameworks have been carefully selected because they explicitly acknowledge complexity (see Chapter 7). Rather than reducing music's impact to simple cause-and-effect relationships, these frameworks recognise that arts engagement operates within complex systems where multiple components interact in dynamic ways:

1   Bartleet's (2023) multi-dimensional framework provides the foundation, helping music leaders understand and articulate how their work creates change across individual, relational, community and societal levels. This framework speaks directly to the heart of positive music leadership's mission to foster social connection through participatory music making.
2   The INNATE framework (Warran et al., 2022) offers practical tools for program design, implementation and evaluation by identifying the essential "active ingredients" that make arts activities effective. For music leaders, it provides a structured way to plan, implement, and assess their work while maintaining flexibility to adapt to local needs.
3   The RADIANCE framework (Fancourt & Warran, 2024) completes the picture by illuminating the complex web of factors that either enable or prevent arts participation. Understanding these systemic barriers and enablers helps music leaders extend their reach and create more inclusive, accessible programs.

Together, these frameworks create a comprehensive toolkit for positive music leaders. They help us navigate from big-picture impact (Bartleet) to practical implementation (INNATE) to addressing barriers to participation (RADIANCE). Importantly, none of these frameworks view leadership in isolation. Rather, they recognise leadership as one vital element within the complex ecosystem of participatory music making.

Bartleet's multi-dimensional framework

For positive music leaders, one of the most relevant and comprehensive frameworks comes from leading community music researcher Brydie-Leigh Bartleet. Her multidimensional framework for understanding and articulating community music's social impact (Figure 9.1; Bartleet, 2023) is particularly valuable because it emerges from deep engagement with community music practice, acknowledging both its complexity and its profound impacts on individuals and communities.

Bartleet understands the tension many music leaders face: while their work happens in specific local contexts with unique participants, they often need to communicate its broader value to influence policy and secure resources. This supports Jane York's observations at the start of this chapter that "Anyone who's not already involved in community music has no idea what we're doing!" Bartleet challenges practitioners to engage in cross-sectoral conversations with health, justice, and other domains without losing the essence of what makes community music magical (Community Music Learning, 2023).

This multi-dimensional framework therefore strikes a balance between acknowledging the intrinsic value of music participation (how it makes people feel) and its instrumental benefits (social outcomes). Beyond the immediate benefits to individuals, we need to consider how impacts might flow "upstream" to influence larger social structures, policies, and the root causes of social issues. Bartleet emphasises the importance of understanding community music within its wider context of social forces and place-based initiatives. Rather than operating in isolation, she argues that community music should be viewed as one piece of a larger social puzzle, working alongside other sectors and fields to address complex social issues. This broader perspective positions community music work within larger cross-sector efforts for social change, and encourages practitioners to be more measured and realistic about the claims they make regarding small-scale, localised projects (Bartleet, 2023).

The framework explores community music's social impact across four dimensions—individual, micro, meso, and macro. Rather than presenting these dimensions as separate domains, Bartleet (2023) emphasises their interconnectedness through bidirectional arrows, showing how music can generate simultaneous impacts across personal, relational, community and structural dimensions. This "porous" approach invites us to explore how change at one level might influence or enable change at other levels, providing a nuanced and precise way to conceptualise and investigate community music practices such as positive music leadership. The "stages of impact" continuum encourages reflection about the time-bound implications of the work and prompts us to ask perhaps difficult questions about whether our work has any lasting benefits. Finally, the "degrees of change" continuum poses another challenge to those in the field, namely, to consider whether their work may have negative as well as positive outcomes.

To understand how Bartleet's framework can illuminate the multi-layered impact of positive music leadership, let's examine a case study of the Whoopee-Do Crew, a socially inclusive community music group in Brisbane, Australia.

Dimensions of Social Outcomes in Community Music

Individual	Micro	Meso	Macro
Personal Transformations Aesthetic pleasure Creative stimulation Creative expression Cultural connection Emotional wellbeing Identity affirmation Personal mindsets Physical safety Self confidence Self awareness	**Relational Transformations** Dialogic interactions Friendships developed Intergenerational connections Recognition from others Relational habits Respect for diversity Social integration Social networks Social participation	**Community Transformations** Collective identity Shared culture Equality of opportunity Sense of belonging Shared understanding Social capital – bonding *(within community)* Social capital – bridging *(with other communities)* Social and cultural enterprises	**Structural Transformations** Economic orders and investment flows Historical conditions Human rights Ideologies (e.g. racism, sexism, social justice) Political orders Public policies

Stages of Impact

Immediate	Intermediate	Long-term impact

Degrees of Change

Stasis	Small	Significant

Preconditions for change		
Negative		

Figure 9.1 Conceptual framework for researching the social impact of community music.
Source: Bartlect (2023)

RESONANCE—The Whoopee-Do Crew case study in social impact (Heard & Bartleet, 2024)

In an inner-city Brisbane park in Queensland, Australia, a diverse group of musicians and community members gather weekly to create music together. This grassroots initiative, known as the Whoopee-Do Crew, operates on principles of radical inclusion. Under the guidance of a First Nations facilitator, the group combines original songwriting with cultural elements, including the use of Indigenous language in opening and closing rituals.

A research project (Heard & Bartleet, 2024) analysed the group's impact using Bartleet's (2023) framework, revealing how seemingly simple music activities can generate ripple effects across multiple social dimensions.

- At the individual/personal level, members experienced personal growth through creative expression and skill development. The joy of making music together provided therapeutic benefits, while mastering new abilities boosted their self-confidence.
- At the micro/relational level, the group bridged social divides, creating meaningful relationships between people who would rarely interact in daily life. These connections evolved into support networks extending beyond music making.
- At the meso/community level, regular performances in public spaces transformed the park's atmosphere and fostered neighbourhood connections. The initiative became woven into the local identity, creating informal opportunities for diverse community members to interact.
- At the macro/structural level, the program created pathways for marginalised voices to be heard and understood. Through music, participants could share their stories and perspectives, contributing to broader conversations about social justice and cultural understanding.

The analysis demonstrates how community music programs can create "ripple effects" far beyond individual participants, supporting Bartleet's (2023) argument that community music should be viewed as one piece of a larger social change puzzle.

As this case study demonstrates, conceptually robust frameworks help us understand impact beyond immediate, individual benefits to reveal deeper, more nuanced layers of change. This broader perspective is particularly valuable for positive music leaders seeking to articulate the full value of their work.

Research by van Zijl and De bisschop (2023) reinforces this multi-layered view. Their study found that music leaders see social impact as both inherent in the activities themselves and extending beyond them and as a dynamic, ongoing process rather than just an end result. This aligns with Bartleet's

(2023) framework, which recognises that impact occurs across multiple stages, from pre-conditions for change, through immediate effects during sessions, to intermediate and long-term outcomes.

RESONANCE—Applying the multi-dimensional social impact framework to positive leaders' work

The multi-level impacts articulated in Bartleet's (2023) framework come alive through stories from positive music leaders. Their experiences show how impact ripples from individual transformations to broader social change.

Musician and community choir leader Emma Dean recalls a powerful example of how group singing can provide emotional sanctuary:

> One of our founding choir members joined shortly after losing her brother to suicide. She would cry the entire drive to rehearsal, but during our two hours together, she'd find herself completely present and joyful—in a state of flow. Then she'd cry all the way home. This pattern demonstrated the remarkable power of those two hours of communal singing to provide respite from grief. Along with other stories of members finding lifelines through choir during depression or experiencing dramatic growth in confidence, it shows how personally transformative group singing can be.

Viewed through Bartleet's (2023) framework, this is an example of impact at the individual level. The participant experienced emotional wellbeing during the singing sessions—respite from grief, as Emma puts it. The impact is immediate for the participant, and perhaps significant during the session, but seemingly could not be sustained afterwards. Viewing this experience through the multi-levelled framework provides some nuance to the experience and the stages and degrees of impact.

Musical inclusion advocate Graham Sattler illustrates transformation at both individual and community levels:

> I've witnessed remarkable identity transformations when people who have been traditionally excluded from music are finally included. A particularly striking example involved a senior psychologist in our remote health workers' virtual choir. Despite his professional success, he was convinced he couldn't sing in tune—a belief stemming from childhood when he was sent outside to prune roses during choir practice. After six months of work together, he discovered he could indeed sing, challenging a lifelong belief that his voice wasn't worth being heard. This transformation went beyond music, speaking to deeper issues of identity and self-worth.

Applying Bartleet's framework to these examples can help us understand and articulate the layered impacts of positive music leadership on individuals—for example, providing immediate emotional relief, fostering unlikely friendships—to challenging systemic exclusion from music participation.

INNATE framework

When Emma Dean first started her community choir, she was figuring everything out on the fly. Emma recalls that she "really didn't know much about being in a choir at all". The INNATE framework (Warran et al., 2022) offers positive music leaders a practical tool for the design, implementation, and evaluation of participatory music making activities for social connection. By breaking down activities into three key categories—project, people, and contexts—it provides a structured way to set up, think about, and communicate the various ingredients that go into effective participatory music programs for social connection while also acknowledging the complexity of these activities.

For example, the framework and accompanying worksheet (available for download) can be used to design a new program, a logic model, and later a program evaluation. The framework could be used to establish a shared language to discuss the nature of the program with stakeholders and potential funders, or it may guide music leaders' critical reflection on practice. In addition to the very helpful worksheet, a full list of the active ingredients (that is, the mechanisms which "activate" to improve health and wellbeing through arts engagement) is also available for download online. Just follow the links to the supplementary materials which accompany the published framework.

Let's say you are a music leader who wishes to start a social choir for newly arrived migrants in your community to help build their social connections. You could use the INNATE framework as follows.

As Table 9.1 illustrates, there is a lot to consider when designing community music activities and programs, and this example only scratches the surface! The INNATE framework's structured yet flexible approach helps ensure you've considered all key elements while allowing for adaptation to your specific community's needs and resources.

The framework is particularly valuable for evaluation, helping music leaders systematically document what works. For instance, in the above example you might track how different ingredients like having bilingual volunteers or including non-musical sharing time contribute to participants' sense of belonging.

The phrase "active ingredients of arts engagement" used in the INNATE framework might seem to imply there is a formula for successful community arts programs but, as we've seen, these activities are complex systems. While no framework can capture every nuance of engaging in arts activities for health and wellbeing, INNATE provides music leaders and other arts practitioners with comprehensive practical tools for planning, implementing and evaluating their work without losing sight of music making's transformative power.

Table 9.1 Example of using the INNATE framework to design a community choir program for recent migrants.

INNATE framework category	Key considerations for migrant community choir	Specific examples
PROJECT	Format and structure	Weekly 2-hour sessions incorporating formal singing time and informal social interaction
	Resources and content	Multilingual materials, culturally diverse repertoire, practice recordings
	Planning and documentation	Clear session structures, attendance tracking, progress monitoring
PEOPLE	Participant characteristics	Cultural protocols, cultural backgrounds, language abilities, prior musical experience
	Leadership requirements	Cultural humility, trauma-informed practice, strong musical skills
	Support roles and interactions	Cultural liaisons, interpreters, opportunities for cultural exchange
CONTEXTS	Physical environment	Accessible venue, adequate space, good acoustics, proximity to transport
	Partnerships and pathways	Links with migrant services, referral processes, support networks
	Organisational elements	Management structure, funding sources, communication channels

By providing a common language and structured approach to program design and evaluation, the INNATE framework helps music leaders transform intuitive understanding into clear, compelling evidence of impact. This is increasingly crucial as we seek to demonstrate the value of community music making for social health.

RADIANCE framework

When we think about barriers to arts participation, what first comes to mind are often obstacles for individuals. "I can't sing" or "I'm not musical" are common self-limiting beliefs that prevent people from engaging in group music making. While these barriers for individuals are real and significant, the RADIANCE framework (Fancourt & Warran, 2024) reveals that the factors that enable or prevent arts engagement can be far more complex. Drawing on ecological systems theory, ecosocial theory, and complex adaptive systems science, RADIANCE maps the different factors that influence arts participation across individual, community and societal levels. The framework shows how seemingly personal barriers like "I can't sing" operate within broader social, cultural and systemic forces.

For positive music leaders, RADIANCE offers a powerful tool for understanding and addressing barriers to participation in their communities. Rather than focusing solely on individual factors like skills or confidence, it encourages consideration of the broader ecosystem in which community music making takes place.

The RADIANCE framework identifies 35 different factors that can act as determinants (either barriers or enablers) of arts engagement across five levels of influence. These determinants are broadly categorised as:

- **Social factors**—where the primary feature is human interaction.
- **Tangible factors**—involving physical assets or resources.
- **Intangible factors**—which have a virtual or imaginary basis rather than physical form.

At the *micro* (individual) level, arts engagement is directly influenced by our perceived capabilities (mental and physical capacities), motivations (automatic and reflective habits and beliefs), individual characteristics (observable traits, personality and genetic factors) and individual capital (economic, symbolic or cultural resources).

Moving outward to the *meso* level, we encounter the opportunities we are presented with (both social and physical) and our social networks (the ties between people and the networks those ties create).

At the *exo* level, we find factors like our built environment (human-made structures and spaces), natural environment (living spaces and organisms), social environment (demographic composition, civic participation, discrimination), and virtual environment (infrastructure for online interaction).

At the *macro* level, broader cultural and social structures come into play, including patterns of social stratification, social inequality, and social cohesion.

Finally, the *chrono* level encompasses developments across lifetimes including social histories, cultural heritage and patterns of social change. Table 9.2, adapted from the original paper presenting the RADIANCE framework by Fancourt and Warran (2024) provides an overview of how the elements of the framework relate to each other.

While the RADIANCE framework reveals the complex web of factors influencing arts participation, positive music leaders may feel overwhelmed by the many determinants beyond their direct influence. Indeed, individual practitioners cannot be expected to transform major societal structures or economic systems. However, understanding these broader determinants serves several important purposes.

First, it helps explain why simple "downstream" solutions instigated at the community level focused solely on individual barriers often fail to increase participation. Second, this awareness can inform more strategic program design that works within or around existing constraints. Third, understanding these determinants helps music leaders articulate to stakeholders why certain barriers exist and what broader changes might be needed to address them.

Most importantly, this systems view reinforces that when participation barriers arise, they rarely reflect individual deficits but rather complex societal factors. Armed with this understanding, positive music leaders can focus on creating welcoming, inclusive spaces that help people overcome internalised barriers while advocating where possible for broader systemic changes that would enable greater participation.

The RADIANCE framework thus complements both Bartleet's (2023) social impact framework and the INNATE framework (Warran et al., 2022) by illuminating the complex context in which community music making takes place. Together, these frameworks help music leaders understand, articulate, design, implement, evaluate and enhance their vital work of fostering social connection through participatory music making.

Table 9.2 Overview of RADIANCE framework with examples of barriers and enablers to arts engagement.

Level	Social determinants	Tangible determinants	Intangible determinants	Example barriers & enablers
Micro (individual)	Social networks, interpersonal relationships	Individual capabilities (physical), financial resources	Motivations, beliefs, cultural capital	Barrier: Belief "I can't sing" prevents participation Enabler: Previous positive choir experience motivates joining new group
Meso (system of microsystems)	Social opportunities, group interactions	Physical opportunities, access to resources	Group norms, shared values	Barrier: Lack of transport to rehearsal venue Enabler: Friend attends group and provides encouragement/carpooling
Exo (connected microsystems)	Social environment, civic participation, discrimination	Built environment, public services, arts organisations	Virtual environment, online platforms	Barrier: No suitable venues in local area Enabler: Active community centre network promotes activities
Macro (culture and social structures)	Social cohesion, social movements, national identity	Creative industries, economic systems	Cultural norms, values, politics	Barrier: Limited public funding for community arts Enabler: Strong cultural policy supporting participatory arts
Chrono (time-based developments)	Social histories, patterns of change over time	Environmental change	Cultural heritage, evolving traditions	Barrier: COVID-19 restrictions on group gatherings Enabler: Growing public understanding of arts' role in social wellbeing

Final thoughts

For music leaders and community arts practitioners, "proving" the value of the work can seem like a daunting and never-ending task, with little assurance that any evidence offered will be taken seriously. With this in mind, there is another option here which was raised by arts and health researcher and community music practitioner Naomi Sunderland—the option to push back on proving anything! Naomi says:

> When I get sassy, I say, "I don't need to reduce myself to your para-digms." I think that's the benefit of being a creative practice practitioner and researcher in an arts health space but also an Indigenous woman in the world. You just have to walk through the fire and get to that point and maybe it's every woman at a certain age who just goes, "This is how it is". There is a point where I think we just have to say, "The party is over here and we're doing this and we love it, and if you want to join in, come." And make sure we offer regular opportunities for people to join the party.

The party metaphor captures the joyful, invitational essence of positive music lea-dership. Naomi credits this metaphor to Marianne Wobcke—Indigenous artist, curator, story-teller, midwife and nurse—who advocates for the self-assurance that arts-health and Indigenous knowledges need no validation: we know what works, and we can proceed with confidence.

Naomi makes another important observation:

> I notice in a lot of Indigenous contexts and projects we often end up at this point of, how do you explain something as interwoven and rich and wholistic and multigenerational and spiritual as this? So, often, especially in arts health contexts and mental health, there's this kind of subtle, some-times strong taboo around discussing spirituality or intuition, but in a lot of Indigenous contexts, it's going to be there whether you're talking about it or not.

While evaluation and conceptual frameworks may make room for topics like "spirituality" can (should?) the spiritual experience of music making ever be codi-fied? As we heard Naomi ask in Chapter 7, "How do you describe the ocean?"

The spiritual (or magical) dimension of making music with others is one which must be experienced to be truly understood. As Iain McGilchrist writes:

> What makes life worth living is what can only be called resonance: the encounter with other living beings, with the natural world, and with the greatest products of the human soul—some would say, with the cosmos at large, or with God. Only in encountering the uncontrollable do we experience the world in its depth and complexity and come fully alive.
>
> (McGilchrist, 2024, n.p.)

Such experiences, often created by positive music leaders, arguably defy quantifi-cation and categorisation. To borrow a phrase from the legal realm, *res ipsa loquitur*—the experience speaks for itself.

Refrain

Effectively communicating the value of positive music leadership requires a delicate balance between rigorous evaluation and compelling storytelling. The frameworks presented in this chapter provide structured ways to understand and articulate impact across multiple dimensions, from individual transformation to systemic change. Even so, these tools are meant to illuminate rather than gloss over the "magic" that happens when people make music together. By combining clear evidence of impact with authentic and creatively told stories of connection and change, positive music leaders can build broader understanding and support for their vital work in enhancing social health through participatory music making. The challenge now is to use these tools thoughtfully while staying true to the deeper purpose that draws us to this work—creating spaces where people can connect, belong, and thrive through participatory music making.

Call and response

1　How might these frameworks help you articulate the value of your work to different stakeholders?
2　What barriers to participation have you observed in your community? Use the RADIANCE framework as a thinking tool.
3　How could systematic monitoring and evaluation enhance rather than detract from the "magic" of music making?
4　A final provocation: Do music leaders need to provide evidence from randomised controlled trials to "prove" the value their work? What are the consequences of saying to those outside the tent, "The party is over here. Come join us if you want!"?

Suggested readings

The following references from the list below provide further information and advice about the issues discussed in this chapter: Creative & Credible (2015), Culture, Health & Wellbeing Alliance (2023), De Cotta et al. (2024), Dunphy et al. (2020), Golden et al. (2024), and Measure Wellbeing (n.d.).

References

Bartleet, B.-L. (2023). A conceptual framework for understanding and articulating the social impact of community music. *International Journal of Community Music, 16*(1), 31–49. doi:10.1386/ijcm_00074_1.
Bartleet, B.-L., & Walton, J. (2021). *QMF's Absolutely Everybody vocal ensemble project: Evaluation report* [Report]. Creative Arts Research Institute, Griffith University. https://research-repository.griffith.edu.au/handle/10072/410895.
Community Music Learning. (2023). Social impact of community music by Brydie Bartleet [Video]. YouTube. www.youtube.com/watch?v=-Lf6WX32vk8&ab_channel=communitymusiclearning.

Creative & Credible. (2015). Creative & credible: How to evaluate arts and health projects. https://creativeandcredible.co.uk.

Culture, Health & Wellbeing Alliance. (2023). Creative health quality framework. www.culturehealthandwellbeing.org.uk/resources/creative-health-quality-framework.

De Cotta, T., Verhagen, J., Farmer, J., Karg, A., Sivasubramaniam, D., Savic, M., & Rowe, C. (2024). Social connection program evaluation toolkit. https://social-connection.au/practice-toolkits-database/social-connection-program-evaluation-toolkit.

Dunphy, K. (2017). Theorizing arts participation as a social change mechanism. In B.-L. Bartleet & L. Higgins (eds), *The Oxford handbook of community music* (pp. 301–321). Oxford University Press.

Dunphy, K., Smithies, J., Uppal, S., Schauble, H., & Stevenson, A. (2020). Positing a schema of measurable outcomes of cultural engagement. *Evaluation, 26*(4), 474–498. doi:10.1177/1356389020952460

Fancourt, D. (2017). *Arts in health: Designing and researching interventions.* Oxford University Press.

Fancourt, D., Aughterson, H., Finn, S., Walker, E., & Steptoe, A. (2021). How leisure activities affect health: A narrative review and multi-level theoretical framework of mechanisms of action. *The Lancet Psychiatry, 8*(4), 329–339. doi:10.1016/S2215-0366(20)30384-9.

Fancourt, D., & Warran, K. (2020). A logic model for the effects of singing on health: Introduction to Part I. In R. Heydon, D. Fancourt, & A. J. Cohen (eds), *The Routledge companion to interdisciplinary studies in singing* (pp. 17–29). Routledge.

Fancourt, D., & Warran, K. (2024). A fRAmework of the DetermInants of Arts aNd Cultural Engagement (RADIANCE): Integrated insights from ecological, behavioural and complex adaptive systems theories. *Wellcome Open Research, 9*, 356. https://wellcomeopenresearch.org/articles/9-356/v1.

Forbes, M., Kennelly, J., Ireland, R., Brown, S., & Richardson, M. (2025). *Interprofessional musical care education: Expanding clinical psychology trainees' therapeutic repertoire.* Manuscript submitted for publication.

Golden, T. L., Sonke, J., & Rodriguez, A. K. (2024). An evidence-based framework for the use of arts and culture in public health. *Health Promotion Practice, 26*(3). doi:10.1177/15248399241228831

Goleman, D. (2013). *What makes a leader a leader: Why emotional intelligence matters.* More Than Sound.

Goleman, D., & Senge, P. (2014). *The triple focus: A new approach to education.* More Than Sound.

Heard, E., & Bartleet, B.-L. (2024). How can community music shape individual and collective well-being? A case study of a place-based initiative. *Health Promotion Journal of Australia, 36*(2), article e921. doi:10.1002/hpja.921.

Howell, G., & Bartleet, B.-L. (2022). A capability approach to evaluating the social impact of music residencies and touring in remote Australia. *Community Development Journal, 57*(4), 673–694. doi:10.1093/cdj/bsab022.

Howlin, C., Trupp, M., Sin, J., Mehkri, S., Chatterjee, H., & Dhital, R. (2025). Visual arts, performing arts and creative writing in health professional education: A scoping review. OSF. doi:10.31234/osf.io/ac97t_v1.

Lingard, L., & Watling, C. (2021). *Story, not study: 30 brief lessons to inspire health researchers as writers* (vol. 19). Springer International Publishing.

Markiewicz, A., & Patrick, I. (2016). *Developing monitoring and evaluation frameworks.* Sage.

McGilchrist, I. (2009). *The master and his emissary: The divided brain and the making of the Western world*. Yale University Press.

McGilchrist, I. (2021). *The matter with things: Our brains, our delusions, and the unmaking of the world*. Perspectiva Press.

McGilchrist, I. (2024). Resist the machine apocalypse. 1 March. www.firstthings.com/article/2024/03/resist-the-machine-apocalypse.

Meadows, D. (2008). *Thinking in systems: A primer* (illustrated edition). Chelsea Green Publishing Co.

Measure Wellbeing. (n.d.). Evaluating wellbeing—Better evaluations for social change. https://measure-wellbeing.org.

Smith, Paul. (2012). *Lead with story*. HarperCollins.

Solomon, K. (2023). How to tell impact stories: A simple formula. www.kishasolomon.com/stories/a-formula-for-telling-impact-stories.

Warran, K., Burton, A., & Fancourt, D. (2022). What are the active ingredients of "arts in health" activities? Development of the INgredients iN ArTs in hEalth (INNATE) Framework. *Wellcome Open Research*, 7, 10. doi:10.12688/wellcomeopenres.17414.2.

Warran, K., Daykin, N., Pilecka, A., & Fancourt, D. (2023). *Arts and health evaluation: Navigating the landscape*. Social Biobehavioural Research Group, University College London.

van Zijl, A. G. W., & De bisschop, A. (2023). Layers and dynamics of social impact: Musicians' perspectives on participatory music activities. *Musicae Scientiae*, 28(2), 348–364. doi:10.1177/10298649231205553.

10 Finale
The future of positive music leadership

Looking back

The following rousing words from my interview with Nsamu Moonga are a fitting way to draw this book to a close. They capture a spirit of rebellion and resistance that I didn't know this book had until Nsamu articulated it:

> I feel in my body, the only way forward, is for those of us that have to resist, have to continue resisting, and for those of us that have to believe in a different future, must continue to believe in a different future that is informed by other values like reciprocity, collective accountability, respect. All those values for me that are informed by Indigenous sensibility that do not see an "other". We see everything as sharing in our equal dignity, whether it's a wallaby, or a kangaroo, or koala bear, they're all intricately connected with our existence. We are not free until everything else is free. So, my success should therefore not be measured by the extent to which I amass whatever resources at the cost of other existences, other beings. We exist not just as individual humans, and we do exist in these relational spaces.

The vision laid out by Nsamu—one of collective accountability and respect for all living things as the one true pathway to freedom—resonates with the vision of positive music leadership, a style of leadership that takes a stand against the callousness, indifference, and extractivist mentality of modern capitalist societies (thanks to Gillian Howell for introducing me to the concept of extractivism!). Being a musician is no longer about only what you can get—fame, fortune, reputation—but what you can give; it is about taking responsibility for your own talents and using them in service of a greater good—one much bigger than yourself.

At the start of this book, I drew your attention to an urgent challenge: the growing crisis of social disconnection affecting communities worldwide. I've argued that positive music leadership—combining musical expertise with strengths-based leadership approaches that foster social connection—offers a powerful response to this crisis. Drawing on positive psychology's focus on human flourishing, we've explored how music leaders can harness both their own strengths and those of their participants to create spaces of authentic connection and belonging, leading to better social health.

DOI: 10.4324/9781003426509-14

Our journey through the book's three parts—Solo, Ensemble, and Tutti—followed Goleman's "triple focus" for effective leadership, with positive psychology's strengths-based orientation providing the theoretical foundation throughout. In Part I, we explored how self-leadership provides the foundation for positive music leadership. Through developing self-awareness and understanding our aspirations, character strengths, and values, while maintaining our own wellbeing through positive psychology interventions, we create the stable base from which we can lead others.

Part II revealed how positive music leaders create energising relationships and build strong social identities within their groups. By combining positively energising leadership—which emphasises virtuous behaviours and positive relationships—with identity leadership approaches that foster belonging through shared social identity, music leaders create transformative spaces where participants experience genuine connection.

In Part III, we widened our lens to examine the broader context in which positive music leaders work. Interpersonal neurobiology (IPNB) emerged as a powerful framework for understanding the complexity of human connection, offering practical strategies like presence, attunement, resonance, and trust (PART) to help music leaders foster integration and wellbeing. We then explored frameworks for articulating impact while honouring music's magical, transformative power.

Throughout, we've heard from music leaders working in diverse settings—from community choirs to health programs and remote communities—whose experiences bring these concepts to life. Emma Dean discovered unexpected joy in leading a community choir on her friend's verandah after burning out as a solo performer, demonstrating how aligning work with personal values generates a sense of fulfilment. Kym Dillon showed how highly trained musicians use their skills to create inclusive spaces where "every voice contributes to creating this larger sound". Allison Girvan revealed how viewing leadership as conducting energy creates profound opportunities for connection, even among very diverse groups. These stories, and the other leaders featured throughout, show how positive music leadership creates ripple effects far beyond individual participants.

What emerges is a picture of music leadership that transcends traditional notions of performing, conducting, or teaching. When skilled musicians combine their artistic expertise with strengths-based approaches drawn from positive psychology, leadership theory, and interpersonal neurobiology, they become agents of social health in their communities. This expanded vision of musicianship responds directly to contemporary challenges while offering deeply rewarding work for the musicians themselves (Forbes & Bartlett, 2020).

This integration of multiple theoretical perspectives—positive psychology and its focus on strengths and flourishing, leadership theory that emphasises positive relationships and shared identity, and interpersonal neurobiology's insights into human connection—provides music leaders with robust tools for fostering social health through participatory music making. As we look to the future, these complementary approaches offer both conceptual frameworks and practical strategies for expanding the impact of positive music leadership.

The way forward: Capacity building

For positive music leadership to reach its full potential as a public health resource, we must develop robust training, mentoring, and professional development pathways. As musical inclusion advocate Graham Sattler argues, "If we have the opportunity to develop skills that create such positive outcomes, we should pursue it." Graham suggests that educational institutions, with their existing resources and potential partnerships with performing organisations, are uniquely positioned to provide this training in practical and cost-effective ways.

However, this training must be grounded in realistic expectations for graduates. As Graham notes, it would be irresponsible to suggest that community music leadership alone will lead to significant financial rewards—just as the unspoken promise of financial success through traditional performance training can create unrealistic expectations. Instead, training should focus on developing the diverse skill set needed for impactful community work while preparing musicians for the realities of portfolio/protean/precarious careers.

Professional networks play a crucial role in supporting emerging and established music leaders (Creative Australia, 2023). Jane York's experience with Community Music Victoria in Australia exemplifies how these networks can nurture leadership development: "Community Music Victoria has a whole culture … the conversations around leadership, leading groups, facilitating—there's some fantastic mentoring around that sort of stuff, it's really valuable." Such networks provide practical support and a sense of belonging for leaders, who may often, ironically, be working in isolation.

As we've learned, several key elements emerge as priorities for building capacity:

1   Formal education, especially at the university or college level, might consider integrating the development of positive music leadership into existing music programs. Some institutions already do this. Alternatively, micro-credentials, undergraduate majors, and postgraduate qualifications are ways to build capacity (Sattler, 2023). These formal learning opportunities should balance the development of musical and leadership skills, and include practical placements (Sattler, 2023).
2   Professional networks provide much-needed peer support and mentoring, shared resources, and knowledge exchange. They can also act as a catalyst for collective advocacy to advance the field, secure funding, and provide regular opportunities for professional development.
3   Cross-sector partnerships are becoming more common between community arts organisations, healthcare providers and social services, educational and research institutions, funding bodies, and policy makers. The opportunities for cross-disciplinary capacity building are significant (Spiro & Sanfilippo, 2022).

While this book has focused on music making for social health in community contexts, the breadth of applications for positive music leadership skills extends beyond these settings. As Graham Sattler points out, many schoolteachers lack confidence in delivering even basic music curriculum—a reality that provides another compelling reason for expanded training opportunities in music leadership. By developing more comprehensive approaches to music leadership education, we can better serve dedicated community practitioners as well as those who might incorporate these skills into other roles in education and performance.

Building capacity requires investment of time, resources, and institutional support. As the evidence base for music's impact on social health strengthens, such investment becomes increasingly justified. Through thoughtful development of training pathways, support networks, and professional development opportunities, we can ensure positive music leadership continues evolving as a vital social health force.

Meeting challenges, seizing opportunities

While positive music leadership offers powerful ways to support social health, practitioners face significant operational, contextual, and structural challenges regarding the sustainability of their work. Understanding these challenges and how leaders are addressing them is crucial for the field's development.

At the most fundamental level, the field faces significant structural barriers. As Jane York observes, "The work is not valued as something that should be paid correctly as a job or career." Many music leaders either work part-time across multiple roles or supplement their community work with other income streams. Cultural expectations that such work should be voluntary or low-paid create additional barriers to fair compensation. Funding models often fail to support ongoing programs. Jane notes that "funding is not designed to deliver broader community music programs, but instead is tailored to specific one-off events, workshops series or special holidays. Ongoing support for a community group to run year-round is rare."

Despite this challenge, or perhaps because of it, music leaders are finding creative ways to build sustainable practices. James Sills has crafted a diverse portfolio career that combines online and in-person choirs, corporate workshops and writing projects. By strategically grouping similar activities—in-person choirs one day, online work another—he maintains both impact and sustainability. Similarly, Emma Dean's experience shows how finding the right balance of activities can create stable income while maintaining joy in the work. The reality is that music leadership will not pay the bills in and of itself, and so music leaders will need to supplement any income they receive through the building of a portfolio career.

Beyond financial challenges, music leaders often struggle with the sheer breadth of responsibilities required. As Jane explains, "We often need to be a program designer, producer, marketing professional, social media strategist, graphic designer, admin, musical director, risk assessor, and only then a singing leader." Emma Dean agrees: "There's a lot of work that goes into [music making] because I'm also writing all of the arrangements for the choir. All of the songs we sing I arrange and then record for them". Jane also emphasises another point:

People think community music magically happens with little or no effort, when in fact, there is a lot behind the scenes to get anything happening. It is reliant on a large skill set unrelated to music by the leader and/or a group of unpaid volunteers at a time when volunteerism is in steep decline.

Where music leaders are also juggling other full-time or part-time roles to earn income, the onus of running community music programs can drain time and energy. At the broader societal level, Jane York points out that the COVID-19 pandemic has changed how community music groups operate. These changes include new or ongoing considerations for vulnerable participants, adaptation to hybrid delivery models, and the need for flexible programming. As Jane astutely observes, these post-pandemic shifts will continue to reverberate through community music ecosystems in concrete ways: "Declining health in older generations who make up the majority of choir attendees" will create a shrinking participant base. At the same time, the "inability to deliver performances and workshops as reliably [as before] due to sudden and severe illness" will threaten the very stability and continuity that these groups depend on. The fallout from the pandemic will be felt within the community music sector for years to come.

Looking ahead, several opportunities are emerging that could help address these challenges.

Structurally, social prescribing initiatives are gaining traction globally, which promises new opportunities for community music programs. However, social prescribing funding models must extend to resourcing the community services that ultimately deliver the social prescription (Dayson, 2017; Oster & Bogomolova, 2024). Social prescribing provides the opportunity for cross-sector partnerships, particularly in health and education, and will, if adequately funded, lead to more sustainable program delivery (Corbin et al., 2021; Golden et al., 2024).

We urgently need more equitable funding models that both recognise the public health value of this work and find ways to balance administrative and other demands with core musical activities (which is inevitably tied to funding and resources). Moreover, we must ensure community programs remain accessible while at the same time compensating leaders for their work. Arts and culture are increasingly recognised as central features of alternative economic models that challenge mainstream ideas of growth for its own sake. For example, a "wellbeing economy" serves "people and the planet, not the other way around" (see https://weall.org). A "foundational economy" views the arts as foundational to a well-functioning society, just like education, health, and infrastructure (Barnett, 2024; see also https://foundationaleconomy.com). Transitioning to such models could lead to more stable support for community-based creative work.

To address practitioner isolation, professional networks and mentoring programs are growing in number. Organisations like Community Music Victoria and the Singing for Health Network (UK) provide crucial support for practitioners, as well as guidance on evidence-based practice, and high-quality professional development opportunities. We must develop stronger networks for mutual support and advocacy—an imperative that has been identified in Australia as a priority area for development, especially for arts workers in mental health settings (Creative Australia, 2023). Importantly, we also need to develop clear pathways for training and professional development, including critically examining the role that higher music education might play in preparing graduates for socially engaged work (Gaunt et al., 2021; Sattler, 2023).

The challenges for participatory arts and music making are significant but so are the opportunities. By working collectively to advocate for the value of positive music leadership while building more sustainable models of practice, we can create the conditions for this vital work to flourish.

Positive music leadership as a public health resource

Throughout this book, we've explored how positive music leadership can revitalise social connections in an increasingly fragmented world. When skilled music leaders create safe spaces for participatory music making using positive, strengths-based approaches, they foster belonging, build health-enhancing social identities, and boost the social health of their participants. As we face what the World Health Organization (2023) has termed a global crisis of social disconnection, such work becomes not just valuable but vital.

Positive music leadership stands as a powerful public health resource precisely because, as Heard and Bartleet (2024, p. 13) argue, "addressing health inequity requires working with communities in strengths-based ways to bolster capacity for individuals and communities to both define and achieve health and well-being". This strengths-based approach aligns perfectly with the fundamental aims of public health—disease prevention, life extension, and health promotion (Griffiths et al., 2005)—but accomplishes these goals through creative, participatory processes that empower communities rather than treating them as passive recipients of services.

The Ottawa Charter for Health Promotion, a foundational document in public health, identifies five core action areas that, when mapped onto the music-making context, reveal how well positioned positive music leaders are to advance health promotion objectives:

1   Strengthening community action: through participatory music making, positive music leaders create spaces where people connect, support each other, and build collective resilience.
2   Developing personal skills: beyond musical abilities, participants develop social capabilities, emotional intelligence, and the confidence to engage with others.
3   Creating supportive environments: music groups become micro-communities of belonging where members feel valued, heard, and understood.
4   Reorienting health services: by focusing on prevention through social connection rather than just treating the symptoms of social isolation, positive music leadership offers a proactive approach to public health.
5   Building healthy public policy: as evidence of music's impact on social health accumulates, policy makers have new opportunities to invest in community wellbeing through support of the participatory arts.

As Corbin et al. (2021, p. 5) confirm, "These action areas require concentrated and intentional efforts, and the arts can be easily adapted in many ways to work toward achieving change in each of them" (see also Golden et al., 2024). Heard and Bartleet (2024, p. 13) also reiterate that "identifying and reinforcing community resources is a key starting point for good health promotion practice".

Positive music leadership is one such resource. The time has come to move beyond seeing community music programs as "nice-to-have" additions to social services. Instead, they should be recognised and funded as essential public health initiatives. The positive music leaders interviewed for this book demonstrate how skilled leadership of participatory music making can transform lives by creating spaces where people experience true connection and belonging.

At the time of writing the final pages of this book, the UK government has just released a report that monetises the impact of culture and heritage on health and wellbeing (Frontier Economics, 2024). Just in case the stories, experiences, and research evidence presented in this book still aren't enough to convince you of the value of participatory music making, perhaps putting this value in monetary terms will be more persuasive. The report's findings are quite extraordinary: the per-person annual benefits range from £68 to £1,310 depending on the type and frequency of engagement, while society-wide benefits range from £18.5 million to £8 billion annually! Benefits include improved quality of life for individuals, health and social care cost savings, and societal impacts like improved productivity. This report positions cultural participation, including music, alongside other recognised public health resources such as nature-based activities.

In Australia, Community Music Victoria (CMVic) has also just made a submission to the state government's inquiry into the cultural and creative industries. CMVic argued that "a targeted increase in support for independent artists who create participatory music experiences would not only improve individual mental health and public health outcomes for participants but also return at least $2 for each $1 invested to the Victorian Economy" (Community Music Victoria, 2025). The submission relied on evidence compiled in a white paper by Ending Loneliness Together (2022), which demonstrates the significant return on investment for programs that address loneliness, as well as the costs to society for failing to address the loneliness epidemic.

With mounting evidence of the social and economic value of participatory arts, the time for action is now. The research evidence, theoretical frameworks, and practical strategies presented in this book provide tools for this vital work.

But ultimately, this work is up to you: what transforms communities is combining your musical skills with the courage to embrace leadership, a commitment to lifelong learning, and an unwavering belief in music's power to mend our social fabric.

As we conclude our exploration of positive music leadership, let's return to our central premise: music matters most deeply when it nourishes both the musician and their community. The positive music leaders we've met throughout this book reveal that career fulfilment and social impact can be complementary pursuits. By embracing positive music leadership, you can create music that reverberates beyond performance, transforming lives, healing social disconnection, and leaving an enduring musical legacy that truly matters—to you, your groups, and the communities you serve.

References

Barnett, T. (2024). The arts are being sidelined in the cost of living crisis. It's time we stopped framing them as a luxury. *The Conversation*, 4 June. http://theconversation. com/the-arts-are-being-sidelined-in-the-cost-of-living-crisis-its-time-we-stopped-fram ing-them-as-a-luxury-228902.

Community Music Victoria. (2025). Making the case for funding participatory music. https://cmvicblog.wordpress.com/2025/02/05/making-the-case-for-funding-parti cipatory-music/.

Corbin, J. H., Sanmartino, M., Hennessy, E. A., & Urke, H. B. (eds). (2021). *Arts and health promotion: Tools and bridges for practice, research, and social transformation.* Springer Nature. doi:10.1007/978-3-030-56417-9.

Creative Australia. (2023). Creative solutions: Training and sustaining the arts for mental health workforce. https://creative.gov.au/advocacy-and-research/creative-solutions-tra ining-and-sustaining-the-arts-for-mental-health-workforce/.

Dayson, C. (2017). Social prescribing "plus": A model of asset-based collaborative inno- vation? *People, Place and Policy, 11*(2), article 2. doi:10.3351/ppp.2017.4839587343.

Ending Loneliness Together. (2022). Strengthening social connection to accelerate social recovery: A white paper. https://endingloneliness.com.au/wp-content/uploads/2022/ 08/ELT_Whitepaper_July2022-1.pdf.

Forbes, M., & Bartlett, I. (2020). "This circle of joy": Meaningful musicians' work and the benefits of facilitating singing groups. *Music Education Research, 22*(5), 555–568.

Frontier Economics. (2024). *Culture and heritage capital: Monetising the impact of culture and heritage on health and wellbeing.* Department for Culture, Media and Sport, UK Government. https://assets.publishing.service.gov.uk/media/675b166a348e10a16975a 41a/rpt_-_Frontier_Health_and_Wellbeing_Final_Report_09_12_24_accessible_final.pdf.

Gardner, H., Csikszentmihalyi, M., & Damon, W. (2001). *Good work: When excellence and ethics meet.* Basic Books.

Gaunt, H., Duffy, C., Coric, A., González Delgado, I. R., Messas, L., Pryimenko, O., & Sveidahl, H. (2021). Musicians as "makers in society": A conceptual foundation for contemporary professional higher music education. *Frontiers in Psychology, 12.* doi:10.3389/fpsyg.2021.713648.

Golden, T. L., Sonke, J., & Rodriguez, A. K. (2024). An evidence-based framework for the use of arts and culture in public health. *Health Promotion Practice, 26*(3). doi:10.1177/ 15248399241228831.

Griffiths, S., Jewell, T., & Donnelly, P. (2005). Public health in practice: The three domains of public health. *Public Health, 119*(10), 907–913. doi:10.1016/j.puhe.2005.01.010.

Heard, E., & Bartleet, B.-L. (2024). How can community music shape individual and collective well-being? A case study of a place-based initiative. *Health Promotion Journal of Australia, 36*(2), article e921. doi:10.1002/hpja.921.

Oster, C., & Bogomolova, S. (2024). Potential lateral and upstream consequences in the development and implementation of social prescribing in Australia. *Australian and New*

Zealand Journal of Public Health, *48*(1), article 100121. doi:10.1016/j. anzjph.2023.100121.

Sattler, G. (2023). Community music and facilitative leadership: Relationship, relevance and respect. www.churchilltrust.com.au/project/to-evaluate-international-best-pra ctice-musical-inclusion-models-for-application-in-australia/.

Spiro, N., & Sanfilippo, K. R. (eds). (2022). *Collaborative insights: Interdisciplinary perspectives on musical care throughout the life course*. Oxford University Press.

World Health Organization. (2023). WHO commission on social connection. www.who. int/groups/commission-on-social-connection.

Appendix 1: Methodology

Human ethics

The University of Southern Queensland Human Research Ethics Committee approved the research for this book (ETH2024–0465). Each interview participant provided informed consent, including consent to be identified in the book.

Interviewee recruitment

Some interviewees were drawn from the author's professional networks and others through referral or based on their public profile. Participation was entirely voluntary. Where there was an existing personal relationship in addition to a professional connection between the author and participant, the participant was recruited via an independent third party.

Interviewees were considered exemplars of best practice and field leaders, with a strong record of leading participatory music making activities. The final pool of interviewees represented music leaders from four continents who engage in a range of community music practices with diverse communities. However, the leaders interviewed are not necessarily representative of the full range of leader backgrounds and styles or community music practices.

Semi-structured interviews

All interviews were conducted online via Zoom. The prompts and questions below guided the interviews with music leaders; however, because the interviews were semi-structured, the conversations were allowed to flow freely.

Interview protocol

- Tell me about your practice as a musician.
- How aware are you of people seeking connection? Is this what drives your participants?
- What values and core beliefs do you have as a musician and person? Do these values inform your work?

- To what extent do you feel your work aligns with your strengths and values?
- What is your identity as a musician? How prominent is this within your overall identity?
- What do you hope to achieve as a musician? What does success as a musician look like?
- What does the word "leadership" mean to you as a musician?
- What is your stance/your philosophy/your orientation towards each person in your group/s?
- Tell me about the practical ways you cultivate a sense of belonging for people in your group/s.
- How aware are you of the individual personalities in your group/s, honouring them, and helping them to connect?
- What role does the music play in connection?
- What role does cultural competency play in your work? What are some of the ethical issues you encounter? How do you navigate these?
- Have you ever received feedback from a participant which really touched you? What was it? What role do you think your leadership played?
- How do you communicate the value of your work? Or advocate for it?
- Do you feel your work is valued by society? By government? What would it take for this work to be better understood/supported?
- What are the greatest challenges you face in your work?
- Is there anything else you would like to share with me on this topic?
- If you had to choose one word to describe your work, what would it be?
- Is there anyone else you think would be great for me to talk to?

Data analysis

Audio files from the Zoom meeting were transcribed by a professional transcription service. Analysis of interview data was mostly deductive in that the chosen theoretical frameworks drove the analysis from a top-down perspective. Deductive reasoning tests theories or generalisations by applying them to specific cases (Hyde, 2000). Each transcript was read and coded for specific instances of theoretical concepts from the various frameworks presented in the book. These instances were then used in the writing process to support and provide contextual specificity for theoretical concepts via in-text quotation and RESONANCE case examples.

The findings presented throughout the book are not intended to prove or even suggest that there is or should be a universal approach to music leadership in participatory contexts. Rather, the links between theory and practice are presented to promote discussion about the theoretical underpinnings of music leadership and the ways in which this knowledge can inform more intentional practice and future training.

References

Hyde, K. F. (2000). Recognising deductive processes in qualitative research. *Qualitative Market Research: An International Journal, 3*(2), 82–90. doi:10.1108/13522750010322089.

Appendix 2: Key Terms

Community music

Bartleet (2023, p. 36) defines *community music* as "participatory music-making by, for and/or with a community". Bartleet explains that rather than being defined by musical genres or styles, community music is characterised by its inclusive, locally based, and community-driven approach to musical engagement. The practice is inherently shaped by and responsive to its cultural context and the participants involved. While community music initiatives may not always explicitly state these aims, they typically embody "values of inclusivity, access, equity, justice and self-determination" (Bartleet, 2023, p. 37).

Facilitator

The term *facilitator* is commonly used to describe a person who leads a community music group (Howell et al., 2017). The process of facilitation is designed to make an activity easy for participants (Howell et al., 2017). The term facilitator has been used to distinguish musicians' role in community musical activities from the more traditional roles of conducting or teaching (Forbes & Bartlett, 2020). Although community groups may still value musical accomplishment (Lamont et al., 2018), their primary focus is on ensuring that participants feel supported, engaged, cared for, and empowered through the act of making music together. In other words, participants' engagement needs to be made as easy as possible.

While the arguments in favour of the term "facilitator" help differentiate community music work from other activities (and indeed, I have used the term "facilitator" in some of my previous research), in this book I favour the term "leader" to highlight the skilful invocation of personal and musical skill to positively impact group participants. I have come to the position that "facilitation" underplays the skill involved in positively influencing the behaviour, thoughts, and feelings of other people in a way that "positive music leadership" captures more accurately.

Leader and leadership

There is a long history of theorising and philosophising about leadership and leaders which other books have covered in great depth (see Haslam et al., 2020 for an overview of this literature). However, for the purposes of defining leadership at the broadest level for this book, I will keep it brief and simple. Here, "leader" does not refer to a designated role in an organisational hierarchy—anyone can build their capacity to be a leader. When we lead effectively and positively, we bring out the best in ourselves and in each other (Cameron, 2018, 2021; Lucey & Burke, 2022). This can occur whether or not a leader is formally designated as such.

The term leader is contested terrain in community music with some musicians eschewing the term because of the implied hierarchies of authority which are at odds with much of community music's activist roots (Mullen, 2008 discussed in Howell et al., 2017). Some forms of leadership involve exerting *power over* others to achieve the leader's desired ends. This is not how leadership is presented in this book. This book explores *positive* and *social* orientations of leadership which are primarily concerned with how leaders use their own strengths generously and virtuously to bring out the best in others to promote social health and wellbeing.

Some would argue that you can't discuss leadership without followership. After all, isn't leadership concerned with getting people to follow the leader? Again, this isn't how leadership is presented in this book. Throughout, I refer to music leaders *working with* participants, or with their groups, rather than *leading followers*. This is a deliberate choice. The aim of positive music leadership is not to have people "follow the leader". Rather, it is for the leader to work alongside their groups to positively influence and support participants' wellbeing and build social connection. This certainly requires some "buy-in" on the part of participants, however, it is not a matter of group members blindly following the leader. Positive music leadership is far more collaborative and democratic than traditional notions of leading and following; it is non-hierarchical, relational, and strengths-based, and recognises the unique value and inherent dignity of each person.

Participatory music

Participatory music or participatory music making is considered one of the key characteristics of community music (Bartleet, 2023). Participatory activities are led by musicians who balance two core objectives: achieving musical growth through active engagement with music making, while also pursuing broader social aims such as fostering dialogue between cultures, strengthening community bonds, and supporting marginalised populations (van Zijl & De bisschop, 2023). The practice is distinguished by its collaborative educational approach, where leaders embrace group input to guide creative processes. Participatory music often engages diverse participants, particularly those facing social challenges or disadvantages, though this is not a defining requirement of the practice (van Zijl & De bisschop, 2023).

According to Camlin (2022, 2023), in the aesthetic tradition of music (primarily associated with conservatoire training) the focus is on performing musical "works" with an emphasis on technical perfection and artistic beauty. In contrast, participatory music emphasises the performance of "relationships" through collective musical engagement. Here, the focus shifts to creating social connections and fostering human relations, where musical quality is intrinsically linked to the social context of participation. Camlin draws on Small's (1998) concept of "musicking" that argues music's primary meanings are inherently social rather than individual and emphasises that when we examine the full scope of musical performance, we must consider the entire set of relationships it creates. This understanding underpins participatory music, where the social connections and collective engagement are as crucial as the musical output itself.

Positive psychology and wellbeing

This book takes a positive psychology orientation to leadership development for musicians to lead community activities that support social health.

Positive psychology explores "what works, what is right, and what can be nurtured" (Rashid et al., 2024, p. 1056). The field emerged in the late 1990s, marking a paradigm shift in psychological research and practice. Rather than focusing solely on treating mental illness, the positive approach cultivates human flourishing and wellbeing (Rashid et al., 2024; Seligman, 2002, 2011). Positive psychology transcends traditional disciplinary boundaries, offering a comprehensive framework for understanding what constitutes a life well-lived (Nakamura & Csikszentmihalyi, 2009). At its core, this field seeks to identify and explore those aspects of life that we inherently value and pursue for their own sake (Seligman, 2011).

A focus of positive psychology is identifying and leveraging our character strengths. Examples of these strengths are love of learning, bravery, curiosity, creativity, and social intelligence. There are 24 character strengths classified according to six virtues: courage, temperance, wisdom, transcendence, humanity, and justice. The character strengths were devised and researched by Christopher Peterson and Martin Seligman, foundational figures in the field of positive psychology (Peterson & Seligman, 2004). There is now a large body of research on character strengths, and evidence that using our strengths contributes to our wellbeing.

Seligman's (2011) wellbeing theory views wellbeing as a multifaceted construct, composed of distinct yet interconnected elements. The theory identifies five key elements, conveniently summarised by the acronym PERMA:

- Positive emotions (P);
- Engagement (E);
- Relationships; (R);
- Meaning (M);
- Accomplishment (A).

Public health and health promotion

Public health is concerned with collective, societal level efforts to prevent disease, prolong life and promote, protect, and improve health (Winslow quoted in Griffiths et al., 2005). The Ottawa Charter for Health Promotion (World Health

Organization, 1986) outlines the core principles of health promotion, emphasising the importance of engaging all sectors of society to enhance health and wellbeing. The charter identifies five key action areas: strengthening community action, developing personal skills, creating supportive environments, reorienting health services, and building healthy public policy (discussed in Corbin et al., 2021). According to the charter, health promotion should empower people to take control of and enhance their health. Much has been written about the important role of the arts in health promotion (see e.g. Corbin et al., 2021; Fancourt, 2017). This book adds a very specific thread to this conversation, namely, how we can harness the power of positive music leadership to promote, protect, and improve health, especially social health.

Social connection and belonging

These terms are often used interchangeably but there are subtle differences. *Belonging* is a subjective experience of the unconditional positive regard of others (Allen, 2021). When we feel we belong, we feel valued, accepted, and integrated within a social group or groups. Belonging has an evolutionary basis (Baumeister & Leary, 1995). To satisfy Baumeister and Leary's (1995) "belongingness hypothesis" we need to have regular, positive interactions with the same individuals over time, and those interactions need to occur within a framework of mutual care and concern. Within interpersonal neurobiology, belonging is "the experience of being a part of something, to be accepted for one's unique features while also being a member of something larger than the individual alone" (Siegel & Drulis, 2023, p. 4).

Social connection or *social connectedness* is a quality or feeling within a person that represents their lasting sense of being close and connected with people and society (Lee et al., 2001). When we are socially connected, we feel consistently and meaningfully linked to others and to society more broadly.

Social health

In *The art and science of connection: Why social health is the missing key to living longer, healthier, and happier*, social health is defined as follows:

> Social health is the aspect of overall health and wellbeing that comes from connection—and it is vastly underappreciated. Whereas physical health is about your body and mental health is about your mind, social health is about your relationships. Being socially healthy requires cultivating bonds with family, friends and the people around you, belonging to communities, and feeling supported, valued, and loved, in the amounts and ways that feel nourishing to you.
>
> (Killam, 2024, p. 8)

Social health is just as fundamental to our survival and flourishing as other necessities of life.

Social isolation and loneliness

The flipside of social connection and belonging is *social isolation* and *loneliness*. Social isolation means being cut off from relationships with other people, organisations, or the wider community, and is characterised by a lack of regular social contact (Pantell et al., 2013; see Seeman, 1996). Loneliness has been referred to as painful isolation (Cacioppo & Patrick, 2008). People experience loneliness when their fundamental need for belonging is not being met (Baumeister & Leary, 1995). Loneliness is our perception that our social relationships are deficient, either in number or in quality (Russell et al., 1984, p. 1313).

References

Allen, K.-A. (2021). *The psychology of belonging*. Routledge.

Bartleet, B.-L. (2023). A conceptual framework for understanding and articulating the social impact of community music. *International Journal of Community Music, 16*(1), 31–49. doi:10.1386/ijcm_00074_1.

Baumeister, R. F., & Leary, M. R. (1995). The need to belong: Desire for interpersonal attachments as a fundamental human motivation. *Psychological Bulletin, 117*(3), 497–529.

Cacioppo, J. T., & Patrick, W. (2008). *Loneliness: Human nature and the need for social connection*. W. W. Norton & Co.

Cameron, K. S. (2018). *Positive leadership: Strategies for extraordinary performance* (2nd ed.). Berrett-Koehler.

Cameron, K. S. (2021). *Positively energizing leadership: Virtuous actions and relationships that create high performance* (1st ed.). Berrett-Koehler Publishers.

Camlin, D. A. (2022). Encounters with participatory music. In M. Doğantan-Dack (ed.), *The chamber musician in the twenty-first century* (pp. 43–71). MDPI. doi:10.3390/books978-3-03897-563-2.

Camlin, D. A. (2023). *Music making and civic imagination*. Intellect Books.

Corbin, J. H., Sanmartino, M., Hennessy, E. A., & Urke, H. B. (eds). (2021). *Arts and health promotion: Tools and bridges for practice, research, and social transformation*. Springer Nature.

Fancourt, D. (2017). *Arts in health: Designing and researching interventions*. Oxford University Press.

Forbes, M., & Bartlett, I. (2020). "This circle of joy": Meaningful musicians' work and the benefits of facilitating singing groups. *Music Education Research, 22*(5), 555–568.

Griffiths, S., Jewell, T., & Donnelly, P. (2005). Public health in practice: The three domains of public health. *Public Health, 119*(10), 907–913.

Haslam, S. A., Reicher, S., & Platow, M. J. (2020). *The new psychology of leadership: Identity, influence and power*. Routledge.

Howell, G., Higgins, L., & Bartleet, B.-L. (2017). Community music practice: Intervention through facilitation. In R. Mantie & G. D. Smith (eds), *The Oxford handbook of music making and leisure* (pp. 601–618). Oxford University Press.

Killam, K. (2024). *The art and science of connection: Why social health is the missing key to living longer, healthier, and happier*. Piatkus.

Lamont, A., Murray, M., Hale, R., & Wright-Bevans, K. (2018). Singing in later life: The anatomy of a community choir. *Psychology of Music, 46*(3), 424–439. doi:10.1177/0305735617715514.

Lee, R. M., Draper, M., & Lee, S. (2001). Social connectedness, dysfunctional interpersonal behaviors, and psychological distress: Testing a mediator model. *Journal of Counselling Psychology, 48*(3), 310–318.

Lucey, C., & Burke, J. (2022). *Positive leadership in practice: A model for our future.* Routledge.

Mullen, P. (2008). Issues in leadership for community music workers. In D. Coffman (ed.), *CMA XI: Projects, perspectives, and conversations; Proceedings from the International Society for Music Education (ISME) 2008 Seminar of the Commission for Community Music Activity* (pp. 249–258). ISME. www.isme.org/sites/default/files/documents/2008%2BCMA%2BProceedings%20%281%29.pdf.

Nakamura, J., & Csikszentmihalyi, M. (2009). Flow theory and research. In S. J. Lopez & C. R. Snyder (eds), *Oxford handbook of positive psychology* (pp. 195–206). Oxford University Press.

Pantell, M., Rehkopf, D., Jutte, D., Syme, S. L., Balmes, J., & Adler, N. (2013). Social isolation: A predictor of mortality comparable to traditional clinical risk factors. *American Journal of Public Health, 103*(11), 2056–2062.

Peterson, C., & Seligman, M. E. P. (2004). *Character strengths and virtues: A handbook and classification.* American Psychological Association.

Rashid, T., Summers, R. F., & Seligman, M. E. P. (2024). Positive psychology model of mental function and behavior. In A. Tasman et al. (eds), *Tasman's psychiatry* (pp. 1055–1078). Springer.

Russell, D., Cutrona, C. E., Rose, J., & Yurko, K. (1984). Social and emotional loneliness: An examination of Weiss's typology of loneliness. *Journal of Personality and Social Psychology, 46*(6), 1313–1321.

Seeman, T. E. (1996). Social ties and health: The benefits of social integration. *Annals of Epidemiology, 6*(5), 442–451.

Seligman, M. E. P. (2002). *Authentic happiness: Using the new positive psychology to realize your potential for lasting fulfillment.* Free Press.

Seligman, M. E. P. (2011). *Flourish: A visionary new understanding of happiness and well-being.* Simon & Schuster.

Siegel, D. J., & Drulis, C. (2023). An interpersonal neurobiology perspective on the mind and mental health: Personal, public, and planetary well-being. *Annals of General Psychiatry, 22*(1), 5.

Small, C. (1998). *Musicking: The meanings of performing and listening.* Wesleyan University Press.

van Zijl, A. G. W., & De bisschop, A. (2023). Layers and dynamics of social impact: Musicians' perspectives on participatory music activities. *Musicae Scientiae, 28*(2), 348–364. doi:10.1177/10298649231205553.

World Health Organization. (1986). The Ottawa Charter for health promotion. www.who.int/healthpromotion/conferences/previous/ottawa/en.

Index